Primitive
Passions

—————

FILM AND CULTURE SERIES

John Belton, General Editor

Film and Culture

A series of Columbia University Press

Edited by John Belton

Primitive
Passions

Visuality, Sexuality,

Ethnography,

and Contemporary

Chinese Cinema

Rey Chow

COLUMBIA UNIVERSITY PRESS

New York

Columbia University Press
New York   Chichester, West Sussex
Copyright © 1995 Columbia University Press

Library of Congress Cataloging-in-Publication Data

Chow, Rey.
Primitive passions : visuality, sexuality, ethnography, and
contemporary Chinese cinema / Rey Chow.
p.   cm.—(Film and culture series)
Includes bibliographic references and index.
ISBN 0–231–07682–7
ISBN 0–231–07683–5 (pbk.)
1. Motion pictures—China.   2. Motion pictures—Social aspects—
China.   I. Title   II. Series.
PN1993.5.C4C465   1995
791.43'0951—dc20   94–27796
                                                             CIP

Casebound editions of Columbia University Press books are printed on
permanent and durable acid-free paper.
Printed in the United States of America
C 10 9 8 7 6 5 4 3 2 1
P 10 9 8 7 6 5

To my father, Chow Chak-hung,
and to the memory of
my mother, Tuet Wai-ching

———

Contents

——

Contents

Preface

When I wrote my first essay on Chinese film, I had little idea that I was going to write a book on the subject. It was the eventful summer of 1989, when authorities in Beijing used tanks to crush civilians demonstrating for democracy, but my motives for writing were far more modest and largely personal. I had lost my mother to cancer and, in mourning, had gone to see again a film that she had liked very much, *Yellow Earth*. The film so overwhelmed me that, although I had not written about Chinese film before, I had to write about it. Several months later I lost another person who was very dear to me, and the attempt to cope with that loss led me to write on the film *King of the Children*. In both cases, film provided me with a discursive framework in which the articulation of otherwise entirely subjective sensations became possible. Even though the book as it now stands is rather different from the perspectives I had on contemporary Chinese cinema at the time when these pieces were first written, it remains, I believe, marked by an emotional intensity that I have felt toward this subject since I began writing and that I hope will come across to my readers.

Each section of the book contributes to my general reading of con-

temporary Chinese cinema by way of what I call "primitive passions,"
and each can also be read as an independent discussion. In the process
of writing I have visually structured the events of the book as follows:

	TYPE OF EVENT	FORM OF PASSION
Part 1	The emergence of technologized visuality	Modernity
Part 2	1. The tribal ritual	Reverence for the dead
	2. The young woman's song	Melancholy
	3. The philosophical lesson	Narcissism
	4. The new ethnographic picture	Defiance
Part 3	Translation between cultures	Fidelity

Because these sections were written at different stages, my emphases,
while related, are not always continuous, and there are, from time to
time, repetitions of minor points and references. Where tensions exist
between different arguments, I have refrained from deliberately elimi-
nating them, in the belief that certain competing modes of thought,
because they are equally valid, should best be left in their irreconcil-
ability with one another.

To be specific, part 1 is an attempt to produce a cultural history and
anthropology of modern China through the technologized visual image;
part 2 offers a set of close readings of major contemporary Chinese
films; part 3 is a theoretical discussion of Chinese film as "ethnography"
and as a kind of translation between cultures. Unlike the first two parts,
part 3 met with considerable resistance from otherwise enthusiastic and
supportive readers during the manuscript review process. The basic
question raised by these readers is a simple and understandable one:
why conclude a book about film with a discussion about translation, in
which most of the texts examined are not about film but about language, anthropology, and ethnography?

In anticipation of similar questions upon this book's publication, I ask
that my general readers think of what I am offering as not simply a project on film alone. Instead, what I am attempting is a theory of film as a
transcription between media, between cultures, and between disciplines—a transcription that should, I think, force us to rethink not only

currently predominant notions of ethnography and translation on the one hand but also of film on the other. Throughout the book there is a double movement: first, a movement from "history" and "literature" to film, from experience that is considered "primary" and "original" to experience that is considered secondary, derivative, and thus insignificant; second, a movement, corresponding and responding to the first, that illustrates how film has always been there, making itself felt in the most "historical" and "literary" spaces even when it is dismissed as a mere image. This double movement registers the contradictions inherent to the transformation—in what is commonly called modernity—of "national culture" and "ethnic identity" in and into the newly developed mass media. Part 3 brings this double movement to a crux by explicitly articulating the contradictions involved in terms of ethnography and translation, highlighting through a discussion of various translation theories our conventional biases for the so-called original and the implications of such biases for cultural translation. My ultimate argument is that contemporary Chinese cinema, as a kind of postmodern *self*-writing or *auto*ethnography, is nonetheless also a form of *intercultural* translation in the postcolonial age. If, by allowing part 3 to stand as it is, I go against the advice of my reviewers, I do so with the full understanding of the risks I am taking—risks that perhaps characterize all interdisciplinary work in one form or another.[1] In addition to film specialists, I hope that my general readers will include literary and cultural theorists, scholars of gender politics, and those who are concerned with the cultural "exchanges" between the "first" and "third" worlds.

As an academic project, this book has been blessed with tremendous goodwill from many different groups of people, who must be put on the record as having contributed to its possibility, progress, and completion. I thank first of all Roswitha Mueller, Patrice Petro, Sharon Willis, and Kathleen Woodward, who made possible the timely publication of my first two essays on contemporary Chinese cinema. John Belton gave me the idea of writing this book, and Jennifer Crewe helped make it an institutional reality. I cannot sufficiently express my gratitude to Nancy Armstrong, Harry Harootunian, Patricia Mellencamp, Gabriele Schwab, and Ellen Widmer, who tirelessly and enthusiastically recommended me whenever I applied for funding. A talk given by Nancy Armstrong for the Critical Theory Institute of the University of California at Irvine in January 1993 inspired the final form of the book title.

Many organizations assisted with financing the project at various stages, and I will remain grateful to the selection committees who considered my work to be worthy of support. These include the McKnight-Land Grant Professorship, the China Center, the Office of International Education, and the Graduate School Grant-in-Aid Program, all of the University of Minnesota, where the project began. A summer stipend from the National Endowment for the Humanities and a grant-in-aid award from the American Council of Learned Societies made it possible for me to travel in the summer of 1992. A generous fellowship from the John Simon Guggenheim Memorial Foundation enabled me to devote 1992–93 to writing. I thank also the School of Humanities of the University of California at Irvine, which granted me a leave of absence during my first year of employment there and thus allowed me to complete the book before I returned to teaching.

During 1990–93, small portions of the book were presented in lectures and conferences at Harvard University, the University of Valencia (Spain), the University of Chicago, the University of Wisconsin at Milwaukee, the University of Colorado at Boulder, and Stanford University. I thank my hosts and audiences for giving me opportunities to test my ideas and for some very encouraging feedback.

Since film is a topic on which information comes not only from books and journals but also from such diverse sources as newspaper feature articles and interviews, little-known trade publications, nonacademic magazines, film festival program notes, and so forth, I am very grateful to those friends and colleagues who took the trouble to share with me whatever bits of information they happened to come across: Yu-shih Chen, Chris Connery, Jennifer Jay, Kwai-cheung Lo, Tonglin Lu, Livia Monnet, Leonard Tennenhouse, and Ming-bao Yue. Marie-Claire Huot and the dynamic collective of organizers at the annual Montréal International Chinese Film Festival have been invaluable sources of assistance and stimulation. William Tay, whose knowledge of Chinese as well as Western literary culture is encyclopedic, has been a most faithful contributor of useful materials even when he was out of the country. Chris Berry and Ping-kwan Leung, who know much more about Chinese film than I, have generously shared their own writings, published and unpublished, for my reference.

Austin Meredith helped with editing innumerable drafts of the various chapters as well as with effectively locating appropriate source materials. His elaborate and sophisticated computer backup system, which is entirely beyond my comprehension, enabled me to write, edit, and make mistakes with relative ease. Like the magnanimous companion that he always is, he sat with good humor through many viewings of Chinese films on poorly reproduced videotapes, often without English subtitles. Pearl Chow, Enn Chow Wahab, and Abu Bakar bin Wahab provided wonderful camaraderie during the viewings of many films and videos in Canada and Hong Kong.

In those attempts to imagine that are typical of our need to reconstruct the past, I have always associated my interest in film and mass culture with my mother, who was by her mid-twenties an accomplished broadcaster, scriptwriter, and radio program producer. As a child, I knew my mother much less as a domestic presence than as the familiar voice on the radio, the surprising image on the screen, the storyteller in radio and film scripts, and the name on the cover of popular novels. Was it this peculiar mix of mediatized experience and primary intimacy that led me in my later years to the study of mass cultural forms such as film? The answer to this question must remain speculative, but of something else I am much more certain: it was my mother's career, together with the circles of people it brought into our lives, that made me realize from an early age the inevitable commodification of creative writing in modernity, the competition writing faced in the new media culture dominated by film and television, and most of all—since we were living in Hong Kong—the socially inferior status that was given to creative writers who happened to be writing in the language of the colonized, Chinese. Even though "literature" is the basis of my own profession, then, I tend to distrust the kind of academic romanticism that holds modern/modernist literature to be at once "revolutionary" (or "subversive") and hierarchically superior to mass cultural forms such as the visual image, which I examine in this book. It is to the memory of my mother and to my father, who collaborated with her in many writing, broadcasting, film, and television projects, that this book is dedicated, in filial piety.

Previously Published Versions

An early and shorter version of part 2, chapter 1, can be found in Spanish in *Feminismo y theoría filmica*, ed. Giulia Colaizzi (Madrid: Cátedra, forthcoming). An early version of part 2, chapter 2, was published in

Discourse (Spring–Summer 1990): 82–109; this version has also been anthologized in *Film/Theatre: Doubling the Discourse of Performance*, ed. Timothy Murray (Baltimore: Johns Hopkins University Press, forthcoming). Early and shorter versions of part 2, chapter 3, were published in *camera obscura* 25–26 (1991): 9–40; in *Male Trouble*, ed. Constance Penley and Sharon Willis (Minneapolis: University of Minnesota Press, 1993), pp. 87–118; and in *From May Fourth to June Fourth: Fiction and Film in Twentieth-Century China*, ed. Ellen Widmer and David Der-wei Wang (Cambridge, Mass.: Harvard University Press, 1993), pp. 327–59. An early version of the same chapter has been translated into Chinese (by Kwai-cheung Lo and Kwun-man Kwok) for the journal *Nüxing ren* 6 (forthcoming) and anthologized in *Wenhua piping yu huayu dianying*, ed. William Tay (Taipei: Ryefield Publishing, 1995); it has also been abridged and translated into French (by Bérénice Reynaud) for *20 ans de théories feministes sur le cinéma*, a special issue (no. 67, 2e trimestre, 1993) of the journal *CinémAction*, ed. Ginette Vincendeau and Bérénice Reynaud, pp. 85–91.

Note on Romanization

All transcriptions of Chinese are in pinyin, except for cases in which a different system, usually the Wade-Giles, was used originally in a quoted text. Translations of Chinese titles that do not exist in English are given in square brackets rather than parentheses. Except when specifically indicated, all translations are mine.

Primitive
Passions

———

Visuality, Modernity, and Primitive Passions

The meaning of any linguistic sign is its translation into some further, alternative sign.

Roman Jakobson, "On Linguistic Aspects of Translation"

Is the passing from literary writing to cinema a manifestation of extreme modernity, or of regression?

Pier Paolo Pasolini, "Quips on the Cinema"

"One Newsreel Helped to Change Modern Chinese History": An Old Tale Retold

Among stories told by modern writers about themselves,[1] Lu Xun's account of how he decided to engage in literature is perhaps one of the best known but least understood. During 1904–6, Lu Xun, a poor student from China, was studying medicine at the Sendai Medical School in Japan. He had high hopes that upon graduation he would return home to assist his countrymen with the urgent task of national reform. Lu Xun's plans were drastically changed one day, when he was confronted with a spectacle. This is the way this well-known episode of conversion is described in his writings:

I do not know what advanced methods are now used to teach microbiology, but at that time lantern slides were used to show the microbes; and if the lecture ended early, the instructor might show slides of natural scenery or news to fill up the time. This was during the Russo-Japanese War, so there were many war films, and I had to join in the clapping and cheering in the lecture hall along with the other students. It was a long time since I had seen any compatriots, but one day I saw a film showing some Chinese, one of whom was bound, while many others stood around him. They were all strong fellows but appeared completely apathetic. According to the commentary, the one with his hands bound was a spy working for the Russians, who was to have his head cut off by the Japanese military as a *public demonstration*, while the Chinese beside him had come to *appreciate this spectacular event*.

Before the term was over I had left for Tokyo, because after this film I felt that medical science was not so important after all. The people of a weak and backward country, however strong and healthy they may be, can only serve to be made *materials or onlookers of such meaningless public exposures*; and it doesn't really matter how many of them die of illness. The most important thing, therefore, was to change their spirit, and since at that time I felt that lit-

Visuality, Modernity, and Primitive Passions

erature was the best means to this end, I determined to promote a literary movement. . . . I was fortunate enough to find some kindred spirits. . . . Our first step, of course, was to publish a magazine, the title of which denoted that this was a new birth. As we were then classically inclined, we called it *Xin Sheng* [New life].[2]

Occurring merely a decade after films were first introduced into China—in 1896, by agents of the Lumière Brothers[3]—and at roughly the same time when Chinese people began making films,[4] Lu Xun's story is not simply part of a famous writer's autobiography about his writing career but a story about the beginning of a new kind of discourse in the postcolonial "third world." This is the discourse of technologized visuality. I have made modifications in the standard translation (indicated by italics in the preceding passages) in order to highlight the language of visuality that is in the original Chinese,[5] somewhat at the expense of the idiomatic smoothness of the English. As we can see, this account is about an experience of the power of a spectacle transmitted by the film medium. The lantern slide captures in a vivid manner the horrifying process of a countryman about to be executed by foreign aggressors. But what exactly is horrifying? As is the case of many of Lu Xun's texts, there is a gap between seemingly continuous events, leaving it to the reader to look for connections between what are, upon close reading, discursive fragments.

This episode of an emerging "modernity" that is specifically grounded in visuality would find many parallels elsewhere in the world. Lu Xun's experience anticipated the ways European intellectuals such as Martin Heidegger and Walter Benjamin were to write about modernity. Both Heidegger and Benjamin would associate modernity with the changing conceptualizations of art. In the essay "The Origin of the Work of Art," Heidegger would compare the effect of a work of art on the observer to a thrust or a blow; Benjamin, specifically discussing film in his essay "The Work of Art in the Age of Mechanical Reproduction," would describe it in terms of shock. According to Gianni Vattimo, who alerts us to the fact that these two otherwise very different essays were both published in 1936, Heidegger's and Benjamin's conceptions have at least one feature in common—"their insistence on disorientation." Vattimo goes on to define this disorientation, which for many European

intellectuals is characteristic of the creativity of art in the age of generalized communication, as "fundamentally . . . nothing but metropolitan
man's nervous and intellectual inconstancy and hypersensitivity."[6]

Once outside the European metropolis, however, disorientation
would take on a very different set of connotations. The surprise, shock,
and oscillation described by Heidegger, Benjamin, and Vattimo were no
doubt experienced by Lu Xun at the projectile of the images unexpectedly launched at him in his unassuming perceptual security. And yet this
disorientation is not only about the meaning of art and creativity; nor is
it only about the gratuitousness of human existence as has been generalized about the modern European metropolis. For the young Lu Xun,
what are shocking and disorienting are the destruction that descends
upon the victim, the apathy and powerlessness of the onlookers, and the
meaning of these for China as a modern nation—this, indeed, is the
rational explanation Lu Xun himself offers; it is also the explanation that
most readers and critics of modern Chinese literature have accepted.
Seldom is it mentioned that what is shocking and disorienting is also the
process of magnification and amplification that is made possible by the
film medium, which, as it were, makes the spectacle spectacular, the
demonstration monstrous, and thus underscores the significance of a
technologized visuality. Lu Xun's reaction, we might say, is not simply
focused on the victim about to be executed or simply on the passive
observers; more important, it is an index to the relationship between
visuality and power, a relationship that is critical in the postcolonial non-
West and that is made unavoidable by the new medium of film.

Once introduced, visuality enables us to notice that Lu Xun himself
is in the position of a spectator and observer.[7] Further, it enables us to
see how this well-known episode could be rewritten in terms of the
complex relationships among different groups of spectators—the
observers who are there to "appreciate" the execution;[8] Lu Xun and his
classmates, who watch the event of murder and spectatorship on cellu-
loid; Lu Xun the writer watching himself and others watching, and so
forth.

In spite of the prominence of visuality and spectatorship in Lu Xun's
story, however, critics have always interpreted it from a strictly literary
perspective, making it part of the founding narrative of modern Chinese
literary history—of how a major writer began writing.[9] Even when it is
recognized that, in the 1920s and 1930s, one alternative adopted by

writers to the increasingly denigrated status of literature was "a redefinition of writing that reorients it as a part of, rather than differentiated from, activity in the socio-material world,"[10] the connection between such "activity in the socio-material world" and visuality is usually not made. The habitual privileging of the literary on the part of scholars (even when dealing with an age in which the literary is in demise) means that the mutual reciprocities between literary and visual modes of representation, together with the questions of power those reciprocities entail, are bypassed if not altogether suppressed. Thinking only in terms of literature, critics uniformly move their attention from Lu Xun's story to the implications it has for literary history alone, leaving unasked questions that are crucial to the interpretation of what in this case is first and foremost a visual encounter. For instance, how does Lu Xun, looking at the screen, know that the Chinese observers *are* apathetic? How do we know that the looks on their faces mean that they are apathetic? (For what we know about the practice of executions around the world, the observers could well have been part of a deliberate setup by the executors to warn the public.) By uncritically accepting Lu Xun's own explanation of his reaction to the lantern slide, literary scholars forget that visual images, because they do not have possibilities of interiorization and abstraction that are typical of the written word, operate differently as a mode of signification. What fails to be considered in the exclusively literary approach is the fact that Lu Xun's explanation is already a retroactive attempt to verbalize and narrativize a mute visual event.

My point in retelling this old story is not to suggest that Lu Xun's account was a fabrication.[11] What makes his story interesting is not whether it "really happened" but that it is a filmic experience he uses to explain why he started writing. The story points to the ambiguities involved in the activity of watching, especially as watching is so deeply inscribed in the events of modernity and national strengthening for a "third world" culture.

If this visual encounter caused a major change in Lu Xun, what is clear is the visual encounter and the change, but not *how* the visual encounter caused the change. The central question in all visual encounters boils down to this simple *how*. Because the visual image itself is silent, how do we go about explaining the changes it causes in us? This central question of a silence-to-be-interpreted structures both the "form" and the "content" of Lu Xun's narrative: just as it is impossible to know for sure what the spectacle did to the observers, it is equally impossible to know exactly how the spectacle of the execution as watched by the observers affected Lu Xun and his subsequent construction of the event. The various rounds of spectatorship involved point up the same problem with regard to visual experience—the need for interpretation, the need to make up for the lack/silence in the visual image with an act of nonvisual filling. And yet, this problem cannot be solved simply through a resort to literary writing.

Let us return now to the happening of the visual encounter. What exactly is it that Lu Xun *sees*? How does he see it? If we say that he sees the horror of an execution, we must also say that he sees the horror of the activity of watching. This horror of watching is not, as most interpretations of this story (including his own) go, due simply to the apathy on the part of the observers. Would the observers watching the execution have had the same effect on Lu Xun if he himself was not watching them on the screen? This question is, by and large, what is missing from most interpretations of this story. From the viewpoint of Lu Xun himself as a film spectator, we may say that what he "sees" and "discovers" is not only the cruelty of the execution or only the apparent cruelty of the observers but the direct, cruel, and *crude* power of the film medium itself. In its projectional thrust, film intensifies the shock inherent to cruelty in the form of an attack: similar to the beheading about to be experienced by the victim, the effect of the film images on Lu Xun was that of a blow. What confront Lu Xun, *through his own act of watching*, are thus: first, the transparent effect of a new medium that seemingly communicates without mediation; second, the affinity between the power of this new medium and the violence of the execution itself.

Further, if the implication of the affinity between film and execution is ultimately—as we learn from the history of the twentieth century subsequent to Lu Xun's visual encounter in the 1900s—fascism, then part of the shock for Lu Xun is that the reaction of the Chinese bystanders on the screen is part of this fascism also. The way *their* fascism comes across is not simply a matter of apathy but rather immobility vis-à-vis a spectacle of inhuman horror: faced with the monstrous vision of the execution, these other men act as if what is in front of them is some *final* meaning that requires absolute submission. It is as if these men have, in the course of watching, become themselves a spectacle and a film. It is *this* spectacle, this image of a passive collective mesmerized in spectatorship, that projects itself on the spectator Lu Xun with the effect of shock.

In its quiet, unassuming voice, then, Lu Xun's little account is already marked by the media-bound disorientation that other theorists are to define as the characteristic of modernity. Clearly, vision and visuality bear for Lu Xun the implications of a *menace*.[12] This menace, a great force imposing upon him a heavy task against his own will, would henceforth constitute the "beginning" of his writing career, which can be reinterpreted as an attempt to deal with the filmic spectacle and with his own implication as a spectator. Even though Lu Xun's "solution" is to take up writing, the menacing effects of visuality would always be there to haunt him. The ingredients of his encounter with the unexpected slide show would become the chief concerns of his writings as well as the writings of his fellow intellectuals in the years to come. These concerns would express themselves as a combination of two things: on the one hand, the pathetic contents or "materials" of China's backwardness, poverty, powerlessness, and general apathy; on the other, the formal demand for an effective "language" of communication that would enable China to catch up with the rest of the modern world.

Retelling Lu Xun's story as a story about modernist shock is, among other things, a good way of showing how "self-consciousness" is produced in the postcolonial "third world." This self-consciousness is inextricably linked to the position of being a spectator. To put it simply, Lu Xun discovers what it means to "be Chinese" in the modern world by watching film. Because it is grounded in an apprehension of the aggressiveness of the technological medium of visuality, self-consciousness henceforth could not be separated from a certain violence that splits the self, in the very moment it becomes "conscious," into seeing and the seen. "Being Chinese" would henceforth carry in it the imagistic memory—the memorable image—of this violence. National self-consciousness is thus not only a matter of watching "China" being represented on the screen; it is, more precisely, watching oneself—as a film, as a spectacle, as something always already watched.

As in the case of all conversion narratives, Lu Xun's story is marked by suppressed ambivalence. Ostensibly, we remember, this story is about Lu Xun's change from being a medical student to being a writer, with the message that the urgent task of national reform lies in changing people's attitudes and habits of thinking rather than in simply improving their physical health. But what kind of *professional* realization precedes this turn to literature? With the shock of self-consciousness comes the realization that the visual medium is an extremely efficient mode of communication. Here we arrive at *the second major meaning of the menace of vision and visuality*: if the first feeling of shock for Lu Xun is national consciousness—that is, the realization of his and his country-men's existence as a spectacle in the eyes of the world—the second feel-ing of shock has, I think, to do with his realization that he is in the pres-ence of a powerful medium that, in due course, might usurp and sup-plant the role traditionally enjoyed by literature and writing.[13] At the same time that the spectacle of the execution makes Lu Xun realize the plight of China in the era of transnational imperialism, it also shows him the *enviable* effects of a clear, direct, and seemingly transparent new "lan-guage" that is, precisely, the representational goal toward which the gen-eration of modern Chinese writers in the 1920s and 1930s aspired.

The aggressivity of the film medium signifies the immediacy and effi-cacy of a form of communication that is beyond words and beyond the linearity of verbal writing. Lu Xun's story, placed at the crossroads of an ancient, word-centered culture's entry into the twentieth century, thus carries with it the foreboding of the soon-to-be-realized, all-encom-passing force of the visual image in modern and postmodern culture, when entire nations, histories, and peoples are to be exposed, revealed, captured on the screen, made visible as images; when visuality is to become the law of knowledge and the universal form of epistemologi-cal coercion.

The second meaning of *menace* here is therefore not national con-sciousness through spectatorship as such but intellectual consciousness in an age when intellectuals are about to lose their traditional hold on culture through their mastery of the written word. Revealingly, Lu Xun's subsequent response to this menace is not an explicit rejection of the visual but a return, via the predicament of visuality, to literature. If this story is indeed the foundational story about the "origins" of modern Chinese literature—about how the "father of modern Chinese litera-ture" began writing—then these origins are illuminatingly self-contra-dictory. Like the intellectual narrator in his story "Zhufu" ("The New Year's Sacrifice"), who, greatly disturbed by his encounter with a beggar woman, withdraws into the study,[14] Lu Xun's resolve to heal China's "mind" rather than "body" through writing is, we might say, a kind of

Visuality, Modernity, and Primitive Passions

withdrawal as well. Literary critics, for their part, have only perpetuated the belief that this resolve, even though it does not save China, is nonetheless salutarily radical. And when they do point to the traditional nature of Lu Xun's actions, they tend to fail to point out the way this traditionalism takes the form of a privileging of the written word over other types of representation.[15] What they repress in their literary readings is that Lu Xun's "radical" move is the *neurotic* attempt to resurrect as "new life" a traditional practice that has, by the very event that prompted it, been shattered in its foundations.[16] The consistent literary-historical misreading of Lu Xun's story attests to the kind of critical blindness described in this manner by Paul de Man:

> In the history as well as in the historiography of literature, this blindness can take on the form of a recurrently aberrant pattern of interpretation with regard to a particular writer. . . . The more ambivalent the original utterance, the more uniform and universal the pattern of consistent error in the followers and commentators. Despite the apparent alacrity with which one is willing to assent in principle to the notion that all literary and some philosophical language is essentially ambivalent, the implied function of most critical commentaries and some literary influences is still to do away at all costs with these ambivalences; by reducing them to contradictions, blotting out the disturbing parts of the work or, more subtly, by manipulating the systems of valorization that are operating within the texts.[17]

In Lu Xun's case, this "blindness" is doubly ironic because what the critics fail to see is the image itself: instead of registering the manner in which literary writing is permanently disturbed and disabled by the filmic image, they seek tirelessly to unsee this image *as image* by rewriting it into *literary* history. Only by invoking film could Lu Xun talk about the "origins" of his literary writing: literary writing's self-sufficiency and effectiveness are thus denied by the very gesture that inaugurates it in modernity—this is the basic ambivalence of Lu Xun's story, an ambivalence that is inscribed in the historical changes in mediatized representation. But literary critics would continue to read it as merely a personal account of motivation, as autobiographical detail.[18]

Decentering the Sign of Literature

In an essay called "The Scopic Regimes of Modernity," Martin Jay writes: "We confront again and again the ubiquity of vision as the master sense of the modern era," but "what precisely constitutes the visual culture of this era is not so readily apparent."[19] In the contemporary studies of the non-West that derive their ethical impetus from Edward Said's *Orientalism*, the visual culture of postcoloniality is usually associated with European cultural hegemony—a hegemony, moreover, that is defined as Europe's dominating, exploitative *gaze*.[20] In his work on Egypt, for instance, Timothy Mitchell writes that the West is characterized since the nineteenth century by an "ordering up of the world itself as an endless exhibition": "Everything seemed to be set up as though it were the model or the picture of something, arranged before an observing subject into a system of signification, declaring itself to be a mere object, a mere 'signifier' of something further."[21]

In arguments that recall the definition of modernity made by Heidegger in pieces such as "The Turning" and "The Age of the World Picture"[22] as well as "The Origin of the Work of Art," critics who share Mitchell's view mobilize criticism of the West's scopophilia and of the passive, objectified, fetishized status in which non-Western peoples and cultures have been cast. The assumption about visuality here is usually a simple one. For the European photographer or writer, it is thought, the problem was "to create a distance between oneself and the world, and thus to constitute it as something picture-like—as an object of exhibit."[23] Because it clearly establishes seeing as a form of power and being-seen as a form of powerlessness, this view of visuality, even though it is greatly reductive, has become the basis for much antiorientalist criticism. Ironically, however, such a view of visuality also leads antiorientalist critics to focus their attention excessively on the details of the European "gaze"—a gaze exemplified by film, ethnography, and tourism alike[24]—and thus unwittingly to help further knowledge about *Europe* rather than the non-West, in a manner that is quite opposite to their moral intentions.

Although they undoubtedly expose the fine turns of the European "gaze," the arguments that set up "West" and "East" in terms of spectator and exhibit inevitably dwarf the fact that "the East," too, is a spectator who is equally caught up in the dialectic of seeing. As we read in the works of media theoreticians such as Guy Debord, Friedrich Kittler, Paul Virilio, Gianni Vattimo, and others, visuality is part of the speed technology that is rapidly homogenizing the world toward a state of transparency.[25] Though "the West" might have been the "origin" of such technology, the materiality as well as the politics of spectatorship are equally crucial to the non-West. When critics concentrate their analyses overwhelmingly on the complexities of the "dominant" Western gaze in the process of deconstructing it, what they in effect accomplish is a superimposition upon "West" and "East" the great divide between seer and seen, active eyes and passive spectacle—a great divide that can as easily perpetuate as disable orientalism.

What is needed, after the ethical polemic of Said's *Orientalism* is understood, is the much more difficult task of investigating how visuality operates in the postcolonial politics of non-Western cultures besides the subjection to passive spectacle that critics of orientalism argue. How do we deal with the fact that non-Westerners also gaze, are voyeurs and spectators? What does it mean for non-Western intellectuals to live as "subjects" and "agents" in the age of "the world as exhibition"? After demonstrating the bloodiness of the Western instruments of vision and visuality, how do we discuss what happens when "the East" uses these instruments to fantasize itself and the world?

The first step toward answering such questions, it seems to me, is by showing that the contempt for visuality, a contempt that leads to the repudiation of visual objects as examples of mere subjugation and passivity in contemporary antiorientalist discourses, is fully shared by non-Western modern intellectuals. In a discussion of Chinese films from the 1920s, 1930s, and 1980s, Paul G. Pickowicz refers to this contempt for visuality in the following manner: "Most May Fourth literary intellectuals simply refused to take the film medium seriously. In spite of their professed interest in bringing about a democratization of culture, a modern culture for the masses, they expressed nothing but contempt for the cinema and made no effort whatsoever in the teens and early twenties to 'bring' the May Fourth movement to the film studios of Shanghai."[26]

If modern self-consciousness in China as well as elsewhere in the "third world" cannot be severed from ethnicity ("being Chinese" and its equivalent) and a sense of collective victimization ("the Chinese have been trampled upon" and its equivalent), the "solution" of the literary turn that Lu Xun adopts is, as already noted, a continual privileging of the age-old signification of *words. In a way that reminds us of much of our contemporary antiorientalist criticism*, in Lu Xun's response to his shock at being forced to sit and watch the slide show, the image is regarded as a graphic record of violence in such a way as to associate being-seen with passivity; whereas the written word is reinvested with the meaning of an active agent that can mobilize cultural transformation. If the image is linked with victimization, the written word is imagined to be a form of empowerment. Besides the radical conversion from medicine to litera-ture, therefore, the *other* conversion in Lu Xun's story is a reconversion to tradition, a reaffirmation of culture as literary culture, which is to be centered in writing and reading, in opposition to the technology that includes film as well as medicine.

This return, however, would henceforth never be free from anxiety, guilt, and an increasing sense of impotence. If the lantern slide con-vinced Lu Xun of the need to revitalize national culture through writ-ing, this return to writing—the "original" practice of the Chinese tradi-tion—would henceforth be haunted by the implications of an erasure. What is erased is precisely the violence experienced through the tech-nologized decentering of "China" into a screen image. The written text, in which the erudite male intellectual seeks refuge, thus becomes a cover-up that veils the vulgar and brutal exhibition of Chinese men being slaughtered in the midst of transnational imperialism, an exhibi-tion that, unlike cultivated writing, comes across without subtlety or reserve. Lu Xun himself is not unlike the mythic hero Yi he satirizes in the story "Ben yue" ("The Flight to the Moon"). In this "old tale retold," Yi, once the hero who shot down nine of ten suns in order to protect the earth, is reduced to the unglamorous chore of shooting for daily food. As Yi keeps bringing home nothing but old black crows for their meals, his wife Chang E escapes to the moon.[27] Just as Yi's big arrows now serve only to remind him of his impotence, so the pen, which Lu Xun picks up in order to save China, is now but a symbol of the contrast between its past glory and its present futility.

Meanwhile, if literature is a way to evade the shock of the visual, that shock would come to inhabit and transform literature by other means. Aside from a recognizable sensitivity to eyes and gazes[28] and a percep-tive use of cinematic techniques in his fiction,[29] the most interesting

Visuality, Modernity, and Primitive Passions

aspects of Lu Xun are that he became a writer primarily of short literary forms such as short stories and essays, and that his writings are strongly ironic. Unlike the traditional chatty novel of the previous dynasties, short literary forms are verbal texts that deliver *condensed, pointed* messages. If the classical Chinese novel is like a scroll painting that unrolls in leisure, the short story is like a snapshot, a quick capturing of life with minimal background detail within a frozen span of time. In Lu Xun's fiction, the effectiveness of such snapshots is further enhanced by irony, which resembles the camera eye in that it simply displays and juxtaposes without comment.[30]

In other words, visuality would be repressed only to return to change the conception of writing and reading from within, even though, in modern Chinese literary history, such changes are often mechanistically attributed to outside forces such as "influences" of the Western short story or of the terse *wenyan* style of classical Chinese prose.[31] Short, ironic forms are, we might say, a way to write and read visually, a way to write and read an earlier medium (the verbal text) with the technology of later ones (photography and film), thus making it clear that literature, in becoming modern, is itself inextricably bound to the perceptual changes brought by visuality. It is less a matter of the picture becoming text (as is often assumed nowadays in poststructuralist readings of visuality) than one of the verbal text becoming a picture. Long before the study of visual forms was institutionalized and thus textualized, the visual image was already inscribed in the modernist reorganization of literary writing itself.

Apart from Lu Xun, there exist many other examples of modern Chinese literature that, even if they do not seem to have anything to do with film and photography, are clearly embedded in the larger epistemological problems of technologized visuality. One can point, for instance, to the abrupt sentences and compressed descriptions in the writings of Xiao Hong; the experiments with objective-observation-as-social-analysis in the panoramic narratives of Mao Dun; the close-up penetration of characters' inner emotions in the essays and novels of Ba Jin; the voyeuristic, confessional tales of Yu Dafu; or the documentary details of local color in the travelogues of Shen Congwen. Be these new literary attempts autobiographical, feminine, or centering on the lower classes or minority groups, they all bear within them traces of filmic visuality in terms of the technologies of abbreviation, cutting, and focalization. Chief of all, writers such as Ding Ling, Bing Xin, LuYin, Ling Shuhua, Xu Zhimo, and others seem to have discovered a primal inwardness that propels writing in a new direction. These writers' explorations of what can be called subjective vision, together with their new narrative techniques for sustaining and managing the attention created by such vision, constitute a new intellectual discipline. The close affinity between modern Chinese literature and film is what leads Jay Leyda to describe authors such as Lu Xun, Xiao Hong, and Shen Congwen as offering lessons, through their writing, to a "word-bound cinema."[32]

At this point, it is possible to reverse the conventional way of thinking about the "evolution" of cultural production—the thinking that would insist, for instance, that literature exists "prior" to film. Preoccupied with chronological continuity, this way of thinking usually considers it acceptable to use an earlier mode of discourse as the criterion for judging a later one but not vice versa.[33] Instead, I would suggest, in the twentieth century it is the power of visuality brought along by new media such as photography and film that transforms the ways writers think of literature itself. Whether conscious or unconscious, the new literary forms are, arguably, thoroughly mediatized, containing within them a response to technologized visuality. Like other traditional modes of discourses, including visual ones such as painting and architecture, literature must devise ways of dealing with the emerging predominance of visuality as a general technology of communication.

But the impact of visuality on writing goes far beyond the effects of pointedness, brevity, immediacy, and focalization. As I already mentioned, part of the shock implied in Lu Xun's account has to do with how overwhelmingly effective the visual mode of communication is. It must therefore be added that, as the visual medium insinuates itself in the new literary forms, its capacity for transmitting messages with transparency also leads to what must in retrospect be seen, as I stated, as a neurotic view of language and literature. On the one hand, as all those who are familiar with modern Chinese literature and, for that matter, any literature of the "third world" know, there is the moral imperative, imposed by the oppressive circumstances of postcolonial poverty and degeneration, that literature should realistically contain and convey the dense and heavy subject matter of history. (For instance, literature must reveal the sufferings of the downtrodden classes and the injustice of society.[34]) On the other hand, as the passionate instigators of the new language and literature in the 1910s and 1920s such as Hu Shi proclaim, language and literature must also be cleansed of the burdens of the past. Language and literature must, it is said, resemble the people's vernacular and communicate their messages simply and directly.[35] Put the historical nation-saving agenda side by side with the agenda for changing the forms of language and literature, and you have the impossible task of transmitting the messy burden of history via an up-to-date medium that is clean, fast, and weightless—of being truthful to the impoverished conditions of China's masses while subjecting them to a brand-new, efficient language that would put China on a par with the rest of the industrially successful world.[36]

Instead of being simply a "culturally specific" instance of modernity, therefore, Lu Xun's story in fact illustrates a global movement in media technology that is, as Michel Foucault describes in *Discipline and Punish*, intimately tied to the evolving conceptions of social education and control. In the kinds of physical torture practiced by premodern societies, Foucault writes, "the example was based on terror: physical fear, collective horror, images that must be engraved of the memories of the spectators."[37] While the execution of the Chinese "spy" could be described in these premodern terms, the fact that for Lu Xun, it came as a film—as a projection with an invitation for introjection—indicates the significant change that conceptions of discipline and punishment go through in modern times. Discipline and punishment are now internalized phenomena, and the social effects they have on individuals are effects of *subject-ion*—to a gaze that can only be felt but not clearly seen. The crucial thing about such subjection, as Foucault's argument also shows, is that it does not work by physical force; rather it relies on civil and gentle coercion: "The example is now based on the lesson, the discourse, the decipherable sign, the representation of public morality."[38] Rather than punish the body, such subjection specializes in reforming the heart and the mind. In Lu Xun's case, therefore, the means of confronting the modern social gaze—of dealing with it—was literature and writing.

There is, furthermore, a double movement involved in the modern Chinese intellectual's "conversion." First, it is a movement in which an elite class tries, in the emergence of technologized visuality, to return to literary culture as the way of salvation. Second, it is a movement in which an elite class *of a "third world" nation*, in response to the pressure of modernity and imperialism, converts an older, premodern notion of discipline and punishment by physical torture and visual spectacle to a "progressive," because more efficient, notion of discipline and punishment by education. In both movements the (re)introduction of literature and writing has to do with a kind of circumvention of visuality—in the first case, by suppression and rejection of visuality as "modern," foreign, and thus vulgar; in the second case, by an incorporation, in the very return to literature and writing, of visuality as efficiency, progress, rapid communication, collective penalization—in short, as a new form of social discipline and control. In both cases, "Chinese modernity" can be seen to involve movements between sign systems, between the competing politics of old and new semiological subject formations.

It should be emphasized once again, however, that although the search by modern Chinese writers for an effective language has been discussed with great sensitivity in linguistic and literary terms, scholars tend to restrict their focus entirely to the literary realm and do not connect the implications of this search to the development of a new medium such as film. What is significantly missing is a consideration of the mutual implications between literature and film as different kinds of social discourses participating in that condition that is generally recognized as Chinese modernity. For Chinese intellectuals in the early twentieth century, the entry of film represents a moment of an epochal dislocation of the linguistic and literary sign. This dislocation has been more than a straightforward movement from verbal language to visual medium. As we realize through Lu Xun's story, even when visuality is not discussed or responded to explicitly as such, its impact as new technology, as transformative agent, is inevitably present. In fact, it is precisely when visuality is not focused on as such, when we seem to be reading the story of how "the father of modern Chinese literature" began his career as a writer, that its indomitable effects, amplified by film, can be most clearly, if paradoxically, felt. And finally, unlike the case of photography and painting, in film what is visible also moves in time. This narrative-in-motion that is the hallmark of film means that film can, in a way unmatched by other modes of visuality, compete fully with that traditional holder of the monopoly to narrative, the verbal text.

The Emergence of Primitive Passions

The dislocation of the literary sign is also the point where history enters. As Chinese literary production can no longer merely "be itself"—that is, can no longer pretend it is the only kind of signification that matters—literature is inevitably historicized. The dislocation of the linguistic and literary sign leads to a new way of looking at China by Chinese intellectuals themselves *as if it were a foreign culture peopled with unfamiliar others*. This look would involve the systematic reexamination of China's literary past, as for instance Lu Xun's *Zhongguo xiaoshuo shi lüe* (*A Brief History of Chinese Fiction*).[39] Increasingly also, the old literary culture would be decentered by a new focus on anthropological and sociological issues. To paraphrase Roman Jakobson, the meaning of the sign "Chinese" is, as modern Chinese intellectuals discover, its translation into some further, alternative sign.[40] If one side of this translation has to do with the appearance of the technologized visual image in and outside the traditional verbal text, the other has to do with the increasing prominence, in representation, of "the people."

Indeed, "modernity" arrives with this fundamental question: how to deal with "the people"? If the centrality of the literary sign is (re)moved by the increasing omnipresence of the visual sign, and reading and writing decentered by the coming of the film medium, the literary sign is also (re)moved democratically, from being the agent of record of life among the elite classes to being the agent of record of life among the masses.[41] Reflection on "China" would increasingly mean coming to terms with China's people, in particular the oppressed classes. As we will see, this process of democratization—both in the sense of an emancipation from literary language and in the sense of the introduction of the masses into literature—is structured by what I will term "primitive passions."

In the liberal West, it is well known that what is now termed "high" modernist art, such as is associated with the painters Picasso, Cézanne, Gauguin, Matisse, Modigliani, and so forth, is inseparable from a certain fascination with the primitive. Scholars such as Sally Price, Marianna Turgovnick, and the contributors to anthologies such as *Modernist Anthropology* have demonstrated how the artistic aspirations of modernism and the disciplinary underpinnings of anthropology reinforce each other, and how the global renown enjoyed by Western modernists is the result of a massive appropriation of the works of peoples in the non-West, who remain unrecognized and nameless. Most important, these scholars argue, the formal innovations of Western modernism, when read historically, are simply the other side of a continual *primitivization* of non-Western lands and peoples.[42] In what is perhaps the most obvious example in Anglo-American literature, consider the liberation and sanctification of sexuality that takes place in the famous works of high modernist "rebels" such as James Joyce, D. H. Lawrence, and Henry Miller. Following the norm of high modernist thinking, these works are often taught in schools and universities as creative attempts to debunk the pretentiousness of Western bourgeois society and to return humanity to its basic instincts. As such, the languages of creative writing, by giving "frank" and "honest" portrayals of sexual practices that are, in turn, suggestively associated with "exotic" cultures, constitute part of the process in which Western signification systems become modernized and high-tech'd by primitivizing others.[43]

In the relations between the West and China in modern times, similar processes of primitivizing "China" can be traced not only in art and literature but also in politics, and in the deliberate fabrications of such primitivism for diplomatic ends. In his book *Dragon Lady*, for instance, Sterling Seagrave demonstrates with remarkable evidence the fantastical constructions of the Manchurian empress Cixi that were circulated around the world at the turn of the twentieth century as part of the steamy "reality" about late imperial China. Western discourses, including those of journalism, personal diaries, correspondence, and diplomacy, as well as scholarly investigations under the rubric of sinology, were more than happy to collaborate in the creation, in Cixi, of a horrific female figure with insatiable sexual appetite, hunger for power, and capacity for murder. For British sinologists such as Sir Edmund Backhouse, Cixi, who was already a "barbarian" in Han Chinese eyes, became the consummate primitive who served as a means to denigrate female sexuality and oriental civilization at once. Even though Backhouse's descriptions were based on Victorian pornography about male homosexual activity, his lies about Cixi continue to be repeated by China scholars—Chinese and non-Chinese—whenever they refer to the empress.[44]

For me, the lesson from such eye-opening works on the question of primitivism in East-West relations is not only the exploitation of the non-

West by the West but how this dialectic between formal innovation and primitivism characterizes the hierarchical relations of cultural production *in the "third world" as well*. In the "third world," there is a similar movement to primitivize: the primitive materials that are seized upon here are the socially oppressed classes—women, in particular—who then become the predominant components of a new literature.[45] It would not be far-fetched to say that modern Chinese literature turns "modern" precisely by seizing upon the primitive that is the subaltern, the woman, and the child. We would therefore need, once again, to reverse the conventional way literary history is written: not that modern Chinese intellectuals become "enlightened" and choose to revolutionize their writing by turning their attention to the oppressed classes; rather, like elite, cultured intellectuals everywhere in the world, they find in the underprivileged a source of fascination that helps to renew, rejuvenate, and "modernize" their own cultural production in terms both of subject matter and of form.

This turn to the "primitive" must be seen in conjunction with the changes in the technologies of "writing" and "communication," with the democratization of the media, and with the emergence of a predominant form of visuality such as film. This is most obvious in the wide-ranging interests in women's issues at the turn of the twentieth century. Women's issues occupy an attention-catching place in the cultural production of modern China because they are, in many respects, *obscene*. The lurid sentimentality of the Mandarin Duck and Butterfly literature of the 1910s and 1920s, for instance, provided a kind of material that was readily comprehensible and thus suitable for mass consumption. The sensationalism, superficiality, indeed repeatable because hackneyed qualities of Butterfly novels, judged not against the old literature but against the new medium of film, would suggest that Butterfly novels were themselves already visual, filmic events. Similarly, when May Fourth writers needed to rejuvenate literature, they turned to the miseries and frustrations of the lower classes for their inspiration. Just as the high modernist novelists and painters used pornographic explorations of "primitive" sexuality to articulate what they believed to be the basic humanity in us all, so modern Chinese writers, Butterfly or May Fourth, would write about women and subalterns in such a manner as to primitivize them. This "primitivism" then becomes a way to point the moral of the humanity that is consciously ethnicized and nationalized, the humanity that is "Chinese."

In the medium of film, Chinese intellectuals find a wonderful means of elaborating these dialectical meanings of primitivism. This is in part because, just as the problematic of "the primitive" seems inexhaustible in its relation to modernity, the filmic image in its crude, silent modes, in its allegorical appearance of lack (requiring interpretation) and fullness (having a meaning all its own) at once, allows the paradoxes of origin and primitivism that are such a fundamental obsession of modernity to play out much more pertinently than words. The peculiar affinity between film and primitivism is, I think, one reason why Chinese cinema, together with Indian and Japanese cinemas, has been perceived as a major place for the negotiation of cultural identity.[46]

Before I elaborate further upon this affinity between film and primitivism, I would like to formulate in more precise terms what I am calling "primitive passions."[47] The following points seem to me to be essential:

1. The interest in the primitive emerges at a moment of *cultural crisis*—at a time when, to use the terms of this discussion, the predominant sign of traditional culture, such as the written word, is being dislocated amid vast changes in technologies of signification.

2. As the predominant sign of traditional culture can no longer monopolize signification—that is, as democratization is forced upon it—fantasies of an origin arise. These fantasies are played out through a *generic* realm of associations, typically having to do with the animal, the savage, the countryside, the indigenous, the people, and so forth, which *stand in* for that "original" something that has been lost.

3. This origin is now "democratically" (re)constructed as a common place and a commonplace, a point of common knowledge and reference that was there prior to our present existence. The primitive, as the figure for this irretrievable *common/place*, is thus always an invention after the fact—a fabrication of a *pre* that occurs in the time of the *post*.

4. The primitive defined in these terms provides a way for thinking about the *unthinkable*—as that which is at once basic, universal, and transparent to us all, *and* that which is outside time and language.

5. Because it is only in this imaginary space that the primitive is located, the primitive is phantasmagoric and, literally, ex-otic.

Visuality, Modernity, and Primitive Passions

This *exoticizing* of what is at the same time thought to be generic and commonplace characterizes the writing of history *within a culture* as much as the writing between cultures such as the practices of orientalism.

6. In a culture caught between the forces of "first world" imperialism and "third world" nationalism, such as that of twentieth-century China, the primitive is the precise *paradox*, the amalgamation of the two modes of signification known as "culture" and "nature." If Chinese culture is "primitive" in the pejorative sense of being "backward" (being stuck in an earlier stage of "culture" and thus closer to "nature") when compared to the West, it is also "primitive" in the meliorative sense of being an ancient culture (it was there first, before many Western nations). A strong sense of primordial, rural rootedness thus goes hand in hand with an equally compelling conviction of China's primariness, of China's potential primacy as a modern nation with a glorious civilization. This paradox of *a primitivism that sees China as simultaneously victim and empire* is what leads modern Chinese intellectuals to their so-called obsession with China.[48]

7. Although there may be nothing new about reinterpreting the past as a way to conceive of the present and the future—and this is definitely one possible way of understanding primitivism—my proposal is that this "structure of feeling"[49] finds its most appropriate material expression in film.

In the following sections, I continue my discussion by focusing on various moments of filmic visuality in twentieth-century China. I will begin with an early example of Chinese film, in order to show how the multiple strands of primitive passions are brought together in the representation of that predominant primitive in modern Chinese culture, woman.

Goddess

Goddess (Lianhua Film Company, 1934) is a silent film directed by Wu Yonggang (1907–82). The title is a Chinese euphemism, *shennü*, for a prostitute. As Paul Clark writes, this film "was perhaps the first in world cinema to examine prostitution directly and without moralistic overtones as an occupation in which women tried to make a living."[50] The story of *Goddess* is a simple one. A young woman, played by the glamorous actress Ruan Lingyu (who was to commit suicide in 1935),[51] tries to provide for her illegitimate son's education by becoming a prostitute. A scoundrel becomes her pimp after forcing sex on her, and keeps extorting money from her. Despite several attempts, she is not able to rid herself of this persecutor. She tries to pin her hopes on her son, and yet, because of her profession, his school dismisses him. As she tries to take the boy and move somewhere else, she discovers that her secret savings have been stolen by her persecutor. By accident she kills him during a quarrel, and she is sentenced to twelve years in prison.

This film explores the "primitive" not in the rural countryside but in a metropolis, Shanghai. With this location, Wu intensifies our awareness of how primitivism, as the imaginary foundation of industrialized modernity, is crucial to cultural production regardless of the geographical setting. The prostitute is a *fetish* in both Marx's and Freud's senses.[52] In Marx's sense, she is a laborer whose work (performing sex) is appropriated from her while she is denounced by the same society that thrives by commodifying her services. The life of this prostitute is thus an emblem of the alienation of labor in a modern society; her human form personifies the process of commodification that must conceal its origins. Meanwhile, in the manner of Freud's theory, the prostitute's body functions as a fetish for the sexuality that a "civilized" society represses. Before the camera eye, the different parts of her body, such as a smile, a leg, an arm, a coiffure, or a beautiful dress, serve as the loci of society's displaced desire. And, even though she is a mother, the prostitute's access to her own feminine sexuality is continually obstructed, policed, and punished by society's patriarchal codes of female chastity.

The Marxian and Freudian meanings of the fetish unite to produce what I have been discussing as the dislocation of the literary sign, the sign of traditional culture. Instead of someone from an upper-class background, representation now focuses on a lower-class woman whose life reveals the reality of social injustice. But what makes Wu's film truly outstanding is not simply his use of a prostitute (other films of the 1930s also feature lower-class characters and women[53]); rather it is the making of a new language that welds together the historical content of social oppression and the innovative formal elements that are specific to the film medium.

Unlike numerous other silent films, many scenes of *Goddess* go without verbal explanation. Words, whenever they are used, are used very sparingly, so that the audience must learn to see the film through the visual composites that we conventionally call images.[54] Clearly subordinate to visuality, the verbal text no longer exclusively possesses the expressive function of narrative. This expressive function is now taken up by things and objects, which, as Pier Paolo Pasolini writes in his classic essay "The Cinema of Poetry," "appear charged with multiple meanings and thus 'speak' brutally with their very presence."[55] The city lights of Shanghai at night, the human face with its many emotions (happiness, worry, viciousness, sorrow, and fear), the bodily gestures of sympathy and indignation, the simple belongings of the prostitute such as a table, chairs, and clothes hanging against the wall—these images together make up the rich significations of time, place, gender and class identity, and human social interactions. The movie screen becomes an inventory of concrete and oneiric signs that make up a "history" of China of the time.

The sparse and direct film language also transforms the economics of the use of characters and dramatic details: the prostitute, her son, the pimp, the headmaster, and a few other characters play out a compelling story in a few bare scenes and simple locations, such as the prostitute's rented rooms, the street, the school, the gambling house, and finally the prison. Because space, place, time, and characterization are so minimally deployed, what comes across is a striking portrayal of an immense social problem with archetypal effects. *Goddess* crystallizes the issues central to twentieth-century Chinese cultural production at the crossroads of the decentered, democratized sign. These are the issues of the fatherless child, the loving but powerless mother, the vicious exploiter of the powerless, the commodification of sex and the disciplining of the female body, female sacrifice, and, finally, the hope arising from such sacrifice. (The last scene shows the prostitute, now in prison, at the lower left corner of the screen: she is looking up over her shoulder and imagining her son's happily smiling face, which appears in the upper right corner.)

Goddess is exemplary of the affinity between the innovativeness of film and primitive passions. Not only does it turn its gaze to the "primitive" that is the socially oppressed woman; it also articulates this epochal fascination with the primitive in ways that are possible only with the new technology of visuality. The film's careful visual structure signals the successful dismantling of the older sign, the verbal text, and its translation into the filmic image. This translation is at the same time, even in its revolutionary mode, a culture-collecting, whereby the repressions and brutalities of society are consciously ethnographized. The prostitute, a mother, a commodity, a sex laborer, becomes literally the divine: she is the source of fetishizing that connects the superstitious practices of "primitive" cultures with the harsh social realities of modernized metropolises like Shanghai.

The movie screen here is not simply the philosopher's mind as was, perhaps, the literary text; nor is it simply the window, frame, or mirror as theorized by Western film critics.[56] It is a scene of crime with the woman's body as evidence and witness, a new type of ethnographic picture, and, as we will see later on in this book, a "front" and an arcade in the international culture marketplace.

Chinese Film in the Age of "Interdisciplinarity"

In the 1980s, the same kind of astute use of film—based on an awareness that film is, first and foremost, a visual medium—reemerged in the People's Republic of China after more than three decades of propaganda-filled media. The complex history of Chinese film from the 1890s to the 1980s has been well documented, and many essays discussing thematic trends, conditions of production and reception, and individual films of the 1980s continue to be written.[57] Instead of simply duplicating these efforts, which I cite throughout this book, what I would like to do is plot another kind of cultural history—what in due course may be called a cultural anthropology. My interest in Chinese film does not exist because it is yet another type of art or discourse that arrives "after," say, literature; nor does it exist because I think film is a medium that needs to be idealized and defended. Rather, my interest is in arguing how film, particularly Chinese film and more particularly contemporary Chinese film, makes it impossible to ignore the general worldwide orientation toward the sense of sight. Film is, in brief, an opportunity to rethink other modes of discourse in the twentieth century.

The cross-cultural implications of the general orientation toward sight are vast. From the perspective of the world at large, film shares with other institutions such as museums and art galleries the important function of exhibiting ethnic cultures. But while museums and art galleries are still bound to specific locales, film is not. Film therefore serves as a major instrument for making the visuality of exotic cultures part of our everyday mediatized experience around the globe. Because of this, film belongs as much with disciplines such as anthropology and ethnography as it does with literature, women's studies, sociology, and media studies.

The present institutional boundaries of cultural studies, however, have yet to form that connection between film and ethnography. Currently, many scholars of anthropology are borrowing from poststructuralist theory in order to show the figurative, metaphoric, and literary implications of anthropological endeavors;[58] and most writings on cinema are informed by considerations of "film as social practice."[59] And yet these "new" undertakings, far from bridging the disciplinary chasm that gapes between film and ethnography, may in due course simply reinforce the conventional disciplinary boundaries of literature (anthropology is now a kind of writing), sociology and psychoanalysis (film is about social and psychic life), and the nation-state (the study of film is equated with the study of national culture, especially in the non-West). To see this, we need only to contrast titles of studies of "first-world" film with titles of studies of non–"first-world" film. While the former typically adopt generic theoretical markers such as "the imaginary signifier," "the cinematic apparatus," "feminism," "gender," "desire," "psychoanalysis," "semiotics," "narrative," "discourse," "text," "subjectivity," and "film theory," the latter usually must identify their topics by the names of ethnic groups or nation-states, such as "black cinema," "Latin-American cinema," "Israeli cinema," "Brazilian cinema," "Japanese cinema," "Indian cinema," "Spanish cinema," "Chinese cinema," "Hong Kong cinema," and so forth. To the same extent, it has been possible for Western film critics to produce studies of films from cultures whose languages they do not know, whereas it is inconceivable for non-Western critics to study the French, German, Italian, and Anglo-American cinemas without knowing their respective languages.[60]

What this means is that even though anthropology and film studies are undoubtedly being "revolutionized" through some kinds of interdisciplinary work, interdisciplinarity itself is no guarantee against the active imposition on the relations between West and non-West of an old epistemological hierarchy that continues to divide them into "general theory" and "specific culture." In other words, we have still to bring together the implications of the figurative revaluations of anthropology *and* the sociological import of film in such a manner as to make the disciplines of anthropology and film reformulate their respective disciplinarity from within—so that anthropology would include within its definition of ethnographic practice the culture-collecting capacities, accomplishments, and complicities of film, and so that film study would step beyond its currently fashionable national, intracultural, and "sociological" parameters to consider the cross-cultural, anthropological, and ethnographic implications of filmmaking and film watching.

This interdisciplinary dialogue between anthropology and film should not see film simply as a tool. Instead of arguing how sophisticated a tool film is for purposes of ethnography, what I am saying is that film—especially film from and about a "third world" culture— changes the traditional divide between observer and observed, analysis and phenomena, master discourse and native informant, and hence "first world" and "third world," that forms the disciplinary basis of anthropology and ethnography.[61] Meanwhile, since "the other" has always already been classical anthropology's mise-en-scène, this necessary dialogue between anthropology and film cannot simply be sought in the institutionally *othered* space of an "alternative" or "third" cinema that adopts an oppositional stance toward "mainstream" culture.[62] Instead, what needs to be theorized and articulated is the fact that more so than literature and art, film—even mainstream film— because it does not depend on high literacy and aesthetic cultivation for its consumption, contributes ever more urgently to the ongoing processes of "writing culture" that have become such a daily phenomenon in the *shared*, common visual spaces of our postcolonial, postmodern world.

To illustrate this point, I will turn to another moment of visuality, the Chinese Cultural Revolution of the 1960s. Focusing on the Cultural Revolution is necessary because it is *the* event to which the Chinese films of the 1980s and 1990s constantly respond. Moreover, it is also a moment in the relations between China and the West when the conventional epistemological division between "third world" and "first world" breaks down—when the mediatized image of an "other" becomes an index to "primitive passions" not only in the West but in China as well.

Visuality, Modernity, and Primitive Passions

The China Picture of the 1960s

In terms of cultural production, the period of the 1960s in China is commonly dismissed as drab and uninteresting, because writing, film-making, and other artistic activities were overwhelmingly subordinated to the official doctrines of the party. However, as Paul Clark writes, "The comfortable presumption that the Cultural Revolution that Mao launched officially in 1966 was simply a distorted and atypical phase of political extremism and forced mobilization, distinct from the years before and after that unfortunate period, is misleading. The Cultural Revolution is significant as much for its continuities with the rest of Chinese history since 1949 as for its disjunctions with what came before and what followed."[63]

The insight of Clark's passage can be demonstrated in a number of different ways. For my part, I will demonstrate it by invoking a type of image often seen from that period. This image is not taken from the films and writings of the 1960s; rather it is one that characterizes the popular media memory of China in the 1960s—the image, seen around the world, of hundreds of thousands of Chinese people, in particular youths, gathering at Tiananmen and other public places, smiling, waving the "little red book" (a collection of Mao Zedong's writings prepared by Lin Biao), shouting slogans in unison in adoration of Mao.

Despite having left China in the backwaters of technological progress because of ideological struggles and corrupt bureaucracy, communism in China means, among other things, implementing effectively the change from literary to visual culture. This does not, for me, refer simply to what is familiarly known as the demolition of the old literary culture based on Confucianism. The end of literary culture comes, in fact, not so much in the sheer destructive aspects as in the constructive, positive aspects of communist practice. I am thinking of the various means and methods the communist state uses for propaganda. At a time when young people in the liberal West were addicted to the visual culture of cinema, television, pop music, sex, and so forth, young people in the China of the 1960s were partaking of mediatized culture in a different way. This description by Maurice Meisner summarizes the excitement of this other mediatized culture:

In early August of 1966, young students wearing armbands bearing the characters for "Red Guard" appeared on the streets of Peking. Within a few weeks, and with the encouragement of Maoist leaders in the capital, Red Guard groups were organized at virtually every university and middle school in the land. Rallying under the slogans "it is justified to rebel" and "destruction before construction," rebellious youth numbering in the tens of millions soon were marching in the streets of cities and towns throughout the country, conveying the Maoist injunction to destroy all "ghosts and monsters." They flocked to Peking to receive the Chairman's personal blessing, which was bestowed in dramatic fashion on August 18, when a million youths crowded into the square beneath the Gate of Heavenly Peace, the symbolic site of revolutionary upheaval since the May Fourth Incident of 1919. Mao appeared atop the gate at sunrise in a godlike posture and solemnly donned a red armband, thereby becoming the "Supreme Commander" of the Red Guards as well as their "great teacher," "great leader," and "great helmsman."[64]

In the words of Jiang Wen, mainland China's leading contemporary actor, Mao's appeal was that of the rock-and-roll star in an era when Western pop music as such was unheard of: "People in the West forget that that era was a lot of fun. Life was very easy. No one worked; no one studied. If you were a member of the Red Guards, you arrived in villages and everyone came out to greet you and everyone sang revolutionary songs together. The Cultural Revolution was like a big rock-and-roll concert, with Mao as the biggest rocker and every other Chinese person his fan."[65]

On film the images of Mao-worship were recently redocumented in *1966, Wo de hongweibing shidai* (*1966: My Time in the Red Guards*), directed by Wu Wenguang (Walk Company Ltd., Japan, 1992). Wu's film includes many interviews with people who, as youths, wholeheartedly participated in the passion of Mao-worship. Besides interviews, the film features an all-woman rock band, Cobra, rehearsing a new song, "1966, Hongse lieche" ("1966, Red Train"), with the refrain:

1966—

Red train—

Crowded with happy lambs.

Visuality, Modernity, and Primitive Passions

Wu Wenguang describes his motives in making the film this way: "I hope in my efforts to 'rewind' history, a certain period of time will become 'freeze-framed,' so that we can look at the movements of history, and see how people have actually lived."[66] Between the Lu Xun shocked at the spectacle of an apathetic China in the 1900s and the Chinese masses drugged by the spectacle of their national leader at the height of the Cultural Revolution, what kind of "history" can be said to have taken place?

If the May Fourth period was one in which modern Chinese writers began investing in subjective vision, what happened in the subsequent decades with the communist revolution was, one could argue, the repression of such subjective vision as private property. Instead, vision, like property, was to become communal—to be owned, used, and disseminated by the party. The great jubilant moments of 1966 belong, as does Lu Xun's story, to a history of visuality that has yet to be written. What the images of Mao, be they in the form of his real person or of portraits, statues, murals, or sayings, offered the Chinese youths of the time was the direct opposite of what Lu Xun saw on the slides in Japan. These were the feelings of strength, unity, power, and an infinite sense of hope for the future. The same act of beholding a spectacle in collectivity in 1966 constituted the ethnic and nationalistic self-consciousness of "being Chinese" once again—this time, "being Chinese" was a proud, rather than shockingly shameful, experience. Even though Mao the historical person did exist, he was, in the process of this massive worship, already a dead body: he was, for his nation, the most enchanting *film* of the time.[67]

In an essay called "The Stalin Myth in Soviet Cinema," André Bazin provides an interesting analysis of the use of the hero image in the communist state.[68] Writing around 1950, Bazin was amazed by the fact that the mythically positive images of Stalin—as a hyper-Napoleonic military genius, as an omniscient and infallible leader, but also as a friendly, avuncular helper to the common people—were made while the man was still alive. Bazin's point is that only the dead is larger than life: "If Stalin, even while living, could be the main character of a film, it is because he is no longer 'human,' engaging in the transcendence which characterizes living gods and dead heroes." The glorifying films have the effect of mummifying and monumentalizing Stalin, so that it is the Stalin image that becomes the ultimate authority, which even Stalin himself had to follow in order to "be." Thus, according to Bazin, the power of filmic images is that they are *retroactive*, calling for a submission to that which has, in the process of being turned into an image, already become past or dead.[69] The Stalin myth in Soviet cinema commands an absolute surrender—an identification that is possible only with the cessation of history.

The Stalin images as analyzed by Bazin coincide with what Pasolini, discussing filmmaking in general, describes as the crucial relationship between death and cinema:

> Man . . . expresses himself primarily by his action. . . . But this action lacks unity, that is, meaning, *until it has been completed.* . . . In a word, so long as he has a future, that is, an unknown quantity, man is unexpressed.

> It is therefore absolutely necessary to die, *because, so long as we live, we have no meaning.* . . . *Death effects an instantaneous montage of our lives;* that is, it chooses the truly meaningful moments (which are no longer modifiable by other possible contrary or incoherent moments) and puts them in a sequence, transforming an infinite, unstable, and uncertain—and therefore linguistically not describable—present into a clear, stable, certain, and therefore easily describable past. . . . It is only thanks to death that our life serves us to express ourselves.

> Editing therefore performs on the material of the film . . . the operations that death performs on life.[70]

Bazin's and Pasolini's observations offer a good way of understanding how Mao works as an image during the 1960s. Like Stalin in the Soviet films, Mao is already dead because, for the Chinese masses, his meaning is complete. Clear, stable, certain, Mao's fatherly presence is an image of light, not only in the sense that he is bringing salvation and enlightenment to his people but also in the sense that he is himself transparent. This transparency enables a total submission on the part of the masses, whose "subjectivity" is constituted through an identification with the-other-as-spectacle that dissolves the boundary between inside and outside, subject and object, people and leader, and most of all, introjection and projection. The dominating impact of Mao as a mesmerizing film is so thoroughly mediatized that it becomes thoroughly internalized. The love for Mao comes from "deep within" people's "hearts."

Referring to the way crowds in the Europe of the 1930s and 1940s came to internalize fascism not as the ideology of cruelty but as a monstrous, propagandist form, Alice Kaplan writes: "The crowd comes to know itself as film. Subjects knowing themselves as film—that is, internalizing the aesthetic criteria offered in film—have a radically different experience, than if they knew themselves through film. In the film experience the spectators do not merely control a model that remains exterior to their untouched subjectivity; rather, their subjectivity is altered and enlarged by the film."[71]

In other words, what is "internalized" in the age of film is no longer some "ideology" but the very projectional mechanism of filmic projection. If individuals are, to use Louis Althusser's term, "interpellated,"[72] they are interpellated not simply as watchers of film but as film itself. They "know" themselves not only as the subject, the audience, but as the object, the spectacle, the movie.

In a comment that resonates richly with our topic of primitive passions, Bazin writes that the only difference between Tarzan films and the Stalin films is that the former do not pretend to be documentaries.[73] The implications of this observation are far-reaching: Stalin in the former Soviet Union and Mao in China function the same way Tarzan does in the liberal West. Both types of heroes belong to the fantasy of a primal origin, a mythical beginning that is nowhere to be found except in our "minds" and "hearts." Submitting to the power of such heroes produces a gratifying self-image: like readers of Tarzan, youths in the Soviet Union and China *find themselves* in the processes of mass consumption.[74]

For all the customary belief that the China of the 1960s was cut off from the world, therefore, what these images of Mao-worship tell us is that Chinese communism, too, was capitalizing on all crucial aspects of the technology of visuality. Precisely because these aspects manifest themselves more crudely in a "third world" nation, they point out in ever more succinct ways the fundamentally mediatized structure of even the most basic and mundane perceptions in global modernity. Redefined in terms of visuality, the propaganda weapons deployed by the communist state are single-mindedly unified in purpose. Even when they have a literary base, slogans, catchphrases, and revolutionary songs are in fact abbreviated texts, texts in the form of pictures and snapshots, whose meanings are clear at one glance and whose force comes from their detachability and infinite repeatability.

Similarly, big-character posters (*dazibao*), loudspeakers, pompously stylized acting in drama and film, and the high-pitched, theatrical voices of radio announcers accompanied by bombastic revolutionary music—all such "propaganda" make an imprint on people's minds with the intensity of the most advanced scientific weapons, with the speed of electronics. Paul Virilio has linked such phenomena of fascistic manipulation of crowds with the scientific production of light and luminosity in the modern age. Speaking largely of the context of Europe, Virilio's point over and over again is the fatal interdependence of the technologies of warfare and vision, "the conjunction between the power of the modern *war* machine . . . and the new technical performance of the *observation* machine."[75] Hitler and Mussolini, Virilio writes, clearly understood the coterminous nature of perception and destruction, of cinematic vision and war. While Hitler commented in 1938, "The masses need illusion—but not only in theatres or cinemas," Mussolini declared, "Propaganda is my best weapon."[76] Such remarks show us the technologized nature of fascism and totalitarianism, not only in the sense that fascism and totalitarianism deploy technological weapons but also in the sense that the scale of the representational illusion or transparency that is inherent to fascism and totalitarianism is possible only in the age of the projector and the amplifier. The mediatized images and voices of Hitler, Mussolini, Stalin, and Mao are not the results of humans using machines; rather they are machines acting in human form.

The co-dependence of the technologies of vision and the technologies of war leads Virilio to conclude: "If photography, according to its inventor Nicéphore Niepce, was simply a method of engraving with light, where bodies inscribed their traces by virtue of their own luminosity, nuclear weapons inherited both the darkroom of Niepce and Daguerre and the military searchlight."[77] Paraphrasing Virilio, we might add that fascism and totalitarianism are forms of engraving with light on people's "minds": fascist and totalitarian leaders inscribe their traces by virtue of their own luminosity; fascist and totalitarian propaganda inherit both the darkroom of Niepce and Daguerre and the military searchlight.[78]

If Lu Xun's determination to return to writing could be explained in part as an intuitive apprehension of the fascistic power of the technologized spectacle, then it is precisely this kind of power to which the masses in China became "hooked" during the Cultural Revolution. An alertness to the significance of the technologized image would show that even (and especially) in the decades when China was supposedly completely closed off from the rest of the world, happenings in China were fully participating in the global history of modern visuality. Once again, the spectacle contains within it multiple visual encounters: not only were the Chinese masses watching Mao in mesmerization but the world was watching the masses watching Mao—in total fascination. However, unlike Lu Xun the powerless student in a foreign country who was shocked and shamed by the sight of his countrymen watching a fellow countryman being beheaded, the crowds in the West received this other sight—of the Chinese masses mirror-imaging their leader—with awe. The wheel of fortune for modern China had—so it seemed at least in the mid-1960s—come full circle: China as a nation had vindicated itself. The movement of the sign, from tradition to modernity, from verbal text to visual image, seems to have crystallized into the concrete picture of a brand-new, because revolutionized, beginning, with the communist national leader looming as a new type of noble savage.

"Returning to Nature": Visuality in Films of the 1980s and Early 1990s

Since the 1980s, when China became open again after more than three decades of closure, it is to this China picture of the 1960s that Chinese directors have obsessively responded. The new beginning that was spearheaded by Mao is now criticized and deconstructed as a myth that left China in utter poverty and an ideological vacuum. In the mood of a vast cultural devastation, the films of the 1980s and early 1990s actively seek alternative "meanings" by what I will call "returning to nature." The prominent nature images and nature figures in these otherwise diverse films include landscape, rural life, and oppressed women.

Visuality, Modernity, and Primitive Passions

This distinctive return must be seen, first of all, not in terms of contemporary Chinese directors' fondness for nature but in terms of the collage of visual events that make up modern China's history. Among the events to be included in this history would be Lu Xun's story, the many focalizations on women in early twentieth-century Chinese literature, the images of women and working classes in the silent films of the 1920s and 1930s, the pictures of the massive worship of Mao during the Cultural Revolution, and, more recently, the Tiananmen massacre of 1989.

A history of visuality as such would enable us to see the oft-discussed relation between tradition and modernity primarily in terms of the politics of the technologized image. Pre-twentieth-century China could then be understood in terms of an older visuality that is located not only in paintings, calligraphy, and other "visual arts" but also in poetry, fiction, and other discourses that may not immediately be classified as visual. This older visuality continues to fascinate the students and specialists of classical China, and continues to live a life in museums, art galleries, books, and academic teaching, writing, and publishing. It has, in the confrontation between tradition and modernity, become "aestheticized," whereas modern visuality is politicized.

But what exactly does this last statement mean? What does it mean to say that the older visuality has become "aestheticized"? It means, among other things, that the older visuality is increasingly associated with "origins," with notions of the past, the ancient, and the lost. Against the more ardent forms of the modern, be they the urgent writings of the May Fourth period or the efficient propagandist forms of communist state culture, the older visuality with its leisurely modes becomes "primitive art." This is not because this older visuality often contains "contents" of nature but because the modes in which such nature is apprehended, together with everything else, have become coded with connotations of what can no longer be. In the history of visuality, the entire "Chinese culture" of the past, with its elaborate nuances and arcane practices, becomes archaized or antiquated into a kind of "primitivism."

On the other hand, what does it mean to say that modern visuality is politicized? Apart from the obvious sense of the political that we see in, for instance, Lu Xun's story and the mass worship of Mao, the politicization of modern visuality refers to the tendency to see in modernity *the urgency of an inaugural moment, a new beginning*. This politicizing of modern culture, too, is invested in primitivism. In fact, it is precisely when the older culture turns "aesthetic" and "primitive" in the sense of an *other* time, that the flip side of primitive passions, in the form of a concurrent desire to invent origins and primariness, asserts itself. "Primitivism" in politicized modernity signifies not a longing for a past and a culture that can no longer be but the wishful thinking that, somehow, "China" is the first, the prime, the central. The two sides of primitivism go hand in hand: the aestheticizing of old China as "ancient" and "backward" cannot be understood without the images of modern self-strengthening and community building that continue to pervade nationalistic cultural productions with the insistence on the firstness and uniqueness of what is Chinese.[79]

This history of visuality would then enable us to see why it is that the "China picture" of the 1960s represents, in more than one way, the climax of Chinese modernity: it is a spectacle that epitomizes the ingredients structural to the emergence of primitive passions in the modern era by showing them all at once—the complete and successful overthrow of the past; the urgency of a new beginning constructed on a new notion of humanity; the illusion that this new beginning is primary, unique, henceforth invincible; the mobilization of all energy toward the transparency that is embodied in a male fatherly figure.

The coherence and persuasiveness of this picture, together with its underlying brutality and violence, become precisely what needs to be dismantled in the 1980s and 1990s. When China opens its doors after more than thirty years of political repression, the production of culture means, for many intellectuals, a collective deconstruction of the fascistic indoctrination of the Cultural Revolution period. Filmmaking means, once again, decentering the sign. This time decentering the sign means specifically moving it toward the "other" memories, toward the resistances of what I here call "nature," that have survived as a kind of unconscious to the "China picture" of the 1960s.

This post–Cultural Revolution "return to nature" coincides with the increasing trends of postmodern global culture-collecting. Like their counterparts from many areas of the non-Western world, contemporary Chinese films, even though they are always made with the assumption that they represent the ongoing problems within China, become the space where "China" is exhibited in front of audiences overseas.

Visuality, Modernity, and Primitive Passions

These two ongoing motifs—deconstructing the Cultural Revolution and postmodern culture-collecting—find their meeting ground in the images of landscape, rural life, and oppressed women that characterize many films from the 1980s and early 1990s. Regardless of their personal intentions, Chen Kaige, Tian Zhuangzhuang, Zhang Yimou, and their contemporaries become their culture's anthropologists and ethnographers, capturing the remnants of a history that has undergone major disasters while at the same time imparting information about "China" to the rest of the world. In their hands, filmmaking itself becomes a space that is bifurcated between the art museum and the ethnological museum, a space that inevitably fetishizes and commodifies "China" even while it performs the solemn task of establishing records of China's cultural violence.[80] In Mary Louise Pratt's terms, this is the space of "autoethnography," in which "colonized subjects undertake to represent themselves in ways that *engage with* the colonizer's own terms," and that constitutes "a group's point of entry into metropolitan literate culture."[81]

The "return to nature" in part explains why most of the films made in the 1980s and 1990s are meant to be watched on a big screen and why, when viewed on videotape, their filmic effects often diminish. Apart from the astute uses of color and screen design that come across strikingly when these films are watched in the cinema, many of them actually contain explorations of the *bruteness* of unfamiliar landscape, often from western provinces such as Shaanxi and Gansu. This distinctive fascination with stark "nature"—with the awesomeness of nature's mere presence—is a feature that no reviewer of contemporary Chinese cinema has failed to point out. In a perceptive passage that summarizes many critics' views, Geoffrey O'Brien writes that the use of silent nature is actually a way to criticize China's status quo and a form of political resistance:

[The movies of Chen, Tian, and Zhang] were the first to break decisively with the rigid dictates of Maoist "cultural work." Out of imposed muteness came a film language consisting of splendid images seen in isolation—an empty sky, a river basin, a weather-roughened face, a ceremonial procession—hemmed in by a strained terseness suggesting multiple layers of historical, political, and social meaning that could not be directly stated. Nothing, it appeared, could be more challenging in the wake of the Cultural Revolution than sharply defined pictures devoid of any obvious didactic purpose, surrounded by silence and open to multiple interpretations. (An analogous strategy can be observed in the works of contemporary Chinese poets such as Bei Dao and Duo Duo.)[82]

In statements that attach the multiple feelings of history, revolution, and hope to his generation's fondness for nature, Chen Kaige confirms O'Brien's judgment: "In China the east is mountainous, the west is flat; the west is poor, and the east is rich. Chinese history is full of examples of revolutionary movements that spread from west to east. In this spirit, we, recent graduates of the Beijing Film Academy, have chosen this yellow earth—poor, barren, and yet full of possibilities—to begin our artistic careers."[83] For Chen and his contemporaries, who are moved by the sight of monuments of nature such as the Yellow River,[84] filmmaking is a way to *ponder* what had gone wrong with the Cultural Revolution, which was once the pinnacle of hope for Chinese youths of their generation. Nature, especially in the relatively underdeveloped western part of China, suggests that there are ways of reconceptualizing the Chinese culture that are alternative to the manipulative and deceptive "China picture" of the 1960s.

In almost anonymous and generic forms, then, images of the land, the village, the country people, and their seemingly unending sufferings conjure up not only a modern and politicized nation at a specific time and place but also *a timeless collective life* that goes beyond the confines of communist history. The filmic fascination with nature, which is a legacy of the rural imperative of the Cultural Revolution—an imperative that stipulated the exile of intellectuals and educated youth to the countryside[85]—is inseparable from a deep sense of nature's energy and destructiveness, and, with it, the futility of human endeavor. Like the poets and painters of the past who depicted not only nature but more precisely the relationship between human life and nature, the films of the 1980s and 1990s capture nature in such a way as to suggest an awareness of an ecological fate that is beyond the control of human society. This awareness is part of the post–Cultural Revolution knowledge that Mao's peasant campaigns, mobilized in the name of human progress and productionism, were also what caused major ecological disasters in China.[86] What the tranquil, stupendous presence of mountains, valleys, rocks, sand, and water in contemporary Chinese films suggests is thus not exactly the harmony between man and nature but the gigantic capacity of nature for indifference and destructiveness. In spite of the "earth-moving" efforts of human revolutions, these films seem to say, human life, especially in the "backward" rural areas, remains pathetically subjugated to the vast permanence of the land and the stubborn tenacity of its forces.

While directors may consciously express themselves through a premodern visuality that reminds us of the poetry, paintings, and philosophical texts of the past, the images of nature and of rural people indicate a continual politicizing of visuality that is characteristic of modernity. Nature in these films signifies a deliberate *emptying* that, when placed in the context of contemporary events, wrests apparatuses of representation from the kind of rhetorical coercion that typifies communist state discourse. In their cryptic largeness and their stubborn silence, these images are signs of a protest against the unimpeded mediatizing of human sensuous activity toward the concreteness and rigidity of political platitudes and party doctrine. Their elusive quality brings the "China picture" of the Cultural Revolution into crisis.

And yet, if the ecological consciousness of the ancients can be used to criticize the manipulative reasonings of the official media, the burden of the tragedies of contemporary politics also makes suspect the quietistic ambiguity of this ecological consciousness. Precisely because the nature images are filmed as allegorical silences and blank spaces—in opposition to the loud and shrill images of state propaganda—they beg the question as to whether images as such do not become complicitous with the garrulous machines of state power. As Timothy W. Ryback writes in a discussion of the Nazi crimes in Europe, "In the nineteen-sixties, the German cultural critic Theodor Adorno advanced the thesis that after the atrocities of Auschwitz the mere act of writing poetry had become 'barbaric.' The German writer Bertolt Brecht offered a more lyrical rendering of this idea in 1938 when he asked, 'What times are these, when / A conversation about trees is almost a crime / Because it includes a silence about so many horrors?' "[87] Even though this is not the place to compare the European Holocaust of the first half of the twentieth century with the aftermath of the Cultural Revolution in terms of the demands they place on cultural representation, this passage is relevant here because it highlights the difficult question about the relationship between the representation of nature and political totalitarianism. Is that relationship an opposed or a collaborative one? Is the silence of the image of a tree a subversive nonalliance with fascism, or is it, precisely because of its silence, an accomplice?

This question cannot be answered without a consideration of the specific medium in which issues of complicity and/or subversion are said to occur.

Exactly what are the significatory possibilities of the "return to nature" *in film*? If there is nothing unusual about invoking nature (and for that matter any form of the past) as a way to deconstruct the present, what is the peculiarity of such an invocation in film? Why could it be said that it is perhaps only in film that the ambivalence characteristic of modernity—a demand for a brand-new beginning that is at the same time an intense look back to the past—becomes fully materialized?

In order to deal with this cluster of issues, we need to think of the relationship between the filmic image and the notion of time. Both Bazin and Pasolini, by linking the filmic image with death, alert us to the way time works in film. For both theorists, the time of film is the time of *completed* understanding; the visual image, for them, is thus always belated, after the fact. Hence if cinema offers us a kind of decipherability of live events, it is because that decipherability comes with a certain closure, a severance from the time of life.

I suggest supplementing this theory of image as death with another fact about the image, that is, its *life as image*. Once closed off from (the time of) life—that is, once "dead"—the filmic image takes on a secondary life, the life of artificial time, motion, and narrative. As Pasolini himself says:

In cinema time is complete, even if only through a pretense. Therefore one must necessarily accept the story. Time in this context is not that of life when it lives, but of life after death.[88]

Cinema . . . is founded on the abolition of time as continuity, and therefore on its transformation into a meaningful and moral reality, always.

Visuality, Modernity, and Primitive Passions

Cinema, in actuality, is like a life after death.[89]

Because of this "life after death," the form of the film medium is, ultimately, paradoxical: if the visual image is akin to death, it is also akin to life; if its mode of time is belated and retrospective, it is also concurrent and forward-looking.[90]

To return now to the question of images of "nature" in contemporary Chinese films. On the one hand, Chinese directors see in the filmic image what it has in common with all other kinds of human representation—a belated inscription, a means of recording what happened in another time. Hence, in the 1980s, contemporary Chinese film is, first, a means of culture writing, of the ethnography that documents the disasters left behind by the Cultural Revolution. On the other hand, the filmic representation of the past as image has the peculiar effect of being simultaneously past and future, because the past, as that which is completed, is now cast in a different time, the time that unfolds with the process of watching. *The retrospective look back that comes with film-as-document is at the same time a look ahead at images moving spontaneously in front of us.*

The projectional effect of film—throwing images on the screen—means that the time of retrospection is now, paradoxically, also a futuristic casting-in-front. This is why the age-old fact of representation as a belated consciousness, a fact that the filmic image helps confirm, coexists in the film medium with a temporally different consciousness—a dreaming toward, a yearning for the presence that cannot be fulfilled, and a promise for things yet to come. The seemingly impossible amalgamation of two different kinds of time—retrospection and forwardness, nostalgia and idealism—thus finds its most appropriate locus in film images, which act as both a review and a preview, epitomizing the past as much as it imagines the future. If filmic visuality has by the 1980s and 1990s become the most gigantic and spectacular form of "autoethnography" by Chinese intellectuals, it is an ethnography not only of chronological, historical time, but also of dream time, of the time of renewed myths.

Contemporary Chinese directors' fascination with nature therefore allows us to clarify why it is that film provides perhaps the best way of illustrating the "structure of feeling" that I have been calling "primitive passions." We may now reformulate primitive passions further as fol-

Visuality, Modernity, and Primitive Passions

lows: primitive passions emerge not simply because of the love of what is past or old; they are not simply feelings of nostalgia. Rather, they involve a *coeval, co-temporal* structure of representation at moments of cultural crisis. Because, as I explained, the makeup of the filmic image is such that its transcriptive, reflective function is inseparable from its projectional, futuristic technicality, the crisis-laden, ambivalent *time* of primitive passions finds in the filmic image its most pertinent material articulation. If the repeated filmic invocation of nature, together with the many "primitive" customs, rituals, and practices of local regions in Chinese cinema, may be thought of in terms of a "process of formalization and ritualization" that E. J. Hobsbawm calls "the invention of tradition,"[91] then film, too, must be included among the continual attempts to (re)invent "China" in the twentieth century. And to return finally to the question of representational complicity with and/or subversion of totalitarianism: even though filming itself might have begun with the impulses of deconstructing communist history, the repeated quests on the part of contemporary Chinese filmmakers for China's "origins" through "nature" must, I think, be seen ultimately as rejoinders to the aspirations of the communist state, whose acts of violence and brutality are committed in a similar quest.[92]

Ironically, of course, the "return to nature" is always a form of exile. Precisely because these directors are convinced that there is something called the origin of Chinese culture that needs to be known, probed, and affirmed, they bring into the heartland of China the entire machinery of modern filmmaking and information technology that result in the fundamental dissemination of this (myth of an) origin at the center. Making use of the rural imperative and the experience of travel that were imposed upon them during the Cultural Revolution, and taking pains to reveal to themselves and others the "authentic" ways China was and is, these directors explore rural life in ways that, far from consolidating "Chineseness" as some form of essence dwelling in China's center, in effect help to "other" "China" through images of the unfamiliar histories, identities, and livelihoods that persist peripherally in space and time. In spite of these directors' conscious intentions, the quest for the "Chineseness" of their origins becomes, in their works, the necessity to *see China anew*, to see China as an other. Filmmaking captures not China but the unconscious that is lurking beneath Han sinocentrism.[93]

Women's Places

Noting that the Fifth Generation's fondness for the harsh, dry, wild landscape in the northwest is in contrast to the soft, wet, fertile landscape of the south, Clark interprets such fondness to be a message from these directors that China needs to be tough in order to survive.[94] Because this "toughness" is, to borrow from Clark's observation, masculinist,[95] the consideration of contemporary Chinese cinema's "return to nature" will be incomplete without a discussion of issues of gender, in particular of the places occupied by women.

From the perspective of feminism in the 1990s, whose task is not simply that of liberating women but rather one of liberating the human need to control and exploit others the way men have traditionally controlled and exploited women, reading these masculinist films would mean delineating in them the possibilities of emancipation without losing sight of their complicity with patriarchal culture. The places occupied by women in these films are crucial in this consideration. Whether or not they actually appear, women are always the places where primitive passions are cathected. As I indicate in the four chapters comprised by part 2, these cathexes appear in different forms in each film. In *Old Well*, the narrative around well digging is distributed between the domestic woman and the new liberal woman, with the domestic woman being rewarded in the end with a man and social stability. In *Yellow Earth*, the young woman who sings is the occasion for an idealism that necessitates her physical disappearance. In *King of the Children*, the strong woman is depicted in a clownish manner; her healthiness and power seem to have substituted for femininity, a femininity that is placed instead in the man who cannot gratify her sexually. In *Red Sorghum*, *Judou*, and *Raise the Red Lantern*, women occupy the traditional spaces of frustrated, dissatisfied, or tortured young wife, widow, mother, adulteress, and concubine, who despite their strength of character remain always trapped in a hopeless situation.

In sum, "woman" is, in a way that parallels the ambivalence and cotemporal makeup of the visual image, both "nature" and "culture." If she at times occupies a status that has much in common with the landscape, the countryside, and the invested rural origin of "China," she at other times is the embodiment of processes of cultural oppression, exchange, and commodification. As a kind of "goddess"—both in the sense of the divine and in the sense of the prostitute—woman continues to be the paradigmatic "primitive" in the phenomenon of primitive passions.

Chen and Zhang offer interesting points of contrast here. Beginning with *Yellow Earth*, all of Chen's films up to and including *Bian zou bian chang* (*Life on a String*, 1991) can be described as representing serious, thoughtful critiques of the inhuman nature of communist indoctrination and ambitious attempts to rethink Chinese culture at the most funda-mental levels, such as reading and writing. If we take the major elements in Chen's films that are used to indicate a subversiveness vis-à-vis com-munist culture, we realize that the subversive "other" for Chen is always the unfamiliar landscape, simple peasants, mute children, and men who are, by and large, social outcasts or failures. Women seldom appear, and when they do, they are usually sacrificed. What does this mean? What it does *not* mean, I think, is a straightforward disregard of women. Woman is, on the contrary, linked with that which does not exist. In order to understand this, we need to listen for the implications of Chen's words in a recent interview: "If we [the Chinese] still have a philosophy, it would be a philosophy of the practical [*shiyong zhexue*]. We will never identify with what is useless—*what a great tragedy this is for the Chinese people*. As I said in my book, having belief and being able to believe some-thing require innocence [*tianzhen*] and courage. *Especially if it is belief in something that does not really exist.*"[96]

Although I do not necessarily agree with Chen's view, this passage is important in pointing out the clear philosophical and metaphysical basis of his ambition as a filmmaker and intellectual. This ambition has to do with a desire to have faith in that which does not necessarily exist, with the implied admonition that *we should not submit only to that which does*. In the politically repressive context that these remarks address, Chen's view indicates a determination not to give up hope even when every-thing seems hopeless. Its strength notwithstanding, this idealism is, meanwhile, highly ambiguous. Is it a belief in something that does not exist *tout court*, or is it a belief in something that does not *yet* exist— something that has yet to come?

This ambiguity comes across most clearly through the relation Chen constructs between women and visuality. In Chen's first four major fea-ture films, "woman"—whether in the form of a Cuiqiao in *Yellow Earth*, in that of the girls that appear in an adolescent boy's daydreams in *The*

Visuality, Modernity, and Primitive Passions

Big Parade, that of the singer and cook Laidi in *King of the Children*, or that of the mysterious female figures in *Life on a String*—occupies not the place of some original nature but the place that is *beyond this world*. Though it may be possible to attribute this to Chen's simple lack of interest in femininity, it is equally possible to say that for him, woman occupies a place that is more divine than anything else. While "nature" can be shown through images of the most spectacular landscape and sky-line, woman, *like* "China," is that ultimately idealized object, that "something that does not really exist." Woman seems to represent for Chen that ultimate being, that ultimate difference, that can only be evoked but never directly seen or shown. It is as if the entire technology of modern filmmaking must be mobilized in order to approach an Other that, precisely because it is so very precious, must remain occulted.

But precisely because he imagines woman as invisible, Chen allows room for the return of the deepest traditional patriarchal ideology as he does "hope." Precisely because it is so iconoclastic, Chen's idealism, when examined closely, reveals itself to be nothing other than the familiar wish to be completely free of the present—of presence itself—that runs throughout modern Chinese revolutionary thinking from the May Fourth period to Mao. Maurice Meisner describes this type of wish perceptively in a passage about Mao, whose belief in the socialist advantages of culturelessness, backwardness, and poverty continues to inspire other male idealists:

> Mao Tse-tung, by declaring the Chinese people "blank," was driven by a utopian impulse to escape history and by an iconoclastic desire to wipe the historical-cultural slate clean. Having rejected the traditional Chinese cultural heritage, Mao attempted to fill the emotional void by an even more iconoclastic proclamation of the non-existence of the past in the present. A new culture, Mao seemed to believe, could be fashioned *ex nihilo* on a fresh canvas, on a "clean sheet of paper" unmarred by historical blemishes. In his iconoclasm and in his belief in the powers of the human consciousness to mold history, Mao's concept of cultural revolution owed far more to the modern Chinese intellectual tradition of the May Fourth era than to Marxist-Leninist traditions.[97]

Feminism, when confronted with a director like Chen, would have to understand his idealism on its own terms and then decide whether or not it is indeed emancipatory. On its own terms, Chen's idealism is not merely a progress toward some definite site; it is also the "sight" of the visionary, for whom progress forward means exceeding the image—that which can be seen—to become (philosophical) vision. Against the speed and superficial kinetics of modern visuality, Chen insists on the possibility of a contemplative beholder who will discover the mystery of existence and perceive the truth that is unbound by sexual corporeality. Hence visuality in Chen is not only the image of the past or the future; it is also that which is to be transcended; it is the present-and-now in the process of becoming "beyond." The image must deconstruct itself and disappear into (its) nonpresence. As he demonstrates in *Life on a String*, a film he dedicates to the memory of his mother, the wisest man is the blind man, and the ultimate wisdom, despite the effort man spends on procuring it, is a blank piece of paper. Instead of being placed in the social symbolic, women in Chen's films are thus the primitives of utopia, which means, literally, that they are *nowhere*.

If Chen's notion of the primitive is incorporeal—the real primitive is the "goddess" who cannot be seen or represented and who has no place in this world—Zhang Yimou's is, by contrast, a pragmatic one. Zhang's primitive, also woman, is what can be *exhibited*. The woman's body becomes the living ethnographic museum that, while putting "Chinese culture" on display, is at the same time the witness to a different kind of origin. This is the origin of human sexuality, which should be free but is imprisoned in China. Because Zhang's films could be seen as being invested in a kind of "repressive hypothesis" (with which his reviewers, as I indicate in part 2, chapter 4, are readily infected), Zhang's primitive is not veiled in the metaphysical and utopic tones that Chen's is. Instead, she is very visible; she becomes a way to *localize* China's "barbaric" cultural institutions, from which she seeks to be set free.

What is most interesting about Zhang's films, however, is not their tendency to *idealize* some "original" sexual nature. (This is a possible argument, but it is not one that I choose to follow, for reasons that I elaborate in part 2, chapter 4.) Instead of a pure, absolute iconoclasm, Zhang is much more willing to immerse himself in the "dirty" representational conventions that are ridden with the errors of history and redirects "sexuality" and "nature" into the materiality of his filmmaking. The sexual energy (re)discovered and revealed by Zhang's camera— through the "primitive" that is the oppressed woman—is now used pragmatically for a new kind of filmmaking, for filmmaking as ethnography, autoethnography, and cultural translation. In his films, the patriarchal system is demoted from being the ultimate signified to being a signifier,[98] the abundant sensuous presence of which on the screen signals its new status as a mere *movable stage prop*. The primitive is now the site of prostitution—the prostitution of history, of the scars and wounds of history. This primitive is also the "goddess" whose commodified image exudes charm. The co-temporality of the visual image is hence also redefined: instead of a coexistence of retrospection and idealism (as it is arguably in Chen), the past and the future amalgamate in the form of fetish-cum-parody. The "divine" and "primitive," circulating among onlookers in the international film market, is now infinitely reproducible. In a way directly opposed to Chen's semiotics of invisibility and incorporeality, Zhang's "women" draw attention to themselves precisely as spectacular, dramatic *bodies*.

Decentering the Sign "China"

Paul Clark has recently written that Chinese film has moved beyond the Fifth Generation. By this he means that the emotions peculiar to the generation of directors who, as youths, lived through the Cultural Revolution are no longer those that plague the new filmmakers of the 1990s.[99] Recent films that are shown internationally, such as Zhang Yuan's *Mama* (1992; the story about a mother's attempt to cope with her life as a single parent raising a mentally retarded child in present-day Beijing), Li Shaohong's *Bloody Morning* (1992; the story of a murder investigation, adapted from Gabriel García Márquez's *Chronica de una muerte anunciada*), Chen Kaige's *Bawang bieji* (*Farewell My Concubine*, 1992; the story of the secret passion of a Beijing Opera actor from the precommunist days in mainland China to contemporary Hong Kong, adapted from the novel of the same name by Li Bihua), Zhang Yimou's *The Story of Qiuju* (1992; the story of a peasant woman's determined efforts to get justice through the Chinese bureaucratic system), and many others, seem to attest to Clark's view.[100] The rapid changes in Chinese cinema signify how quickly "current" trends become "the past" and how discourses of modernity and primitivism, of new beginnings and old tradition, rapidly reproduce themselves even as we discuss them.

Regardless of whether they really signify an era that has come to an end, the films of the 1980s and early 1990s deserve special attention for several major reasons. First, they represent some courageous efforts in reconceptualizing film culture when making good films is still very difficult in China.[101] Second, they continue to signify a much-needed general resistance toward the domination of media representation by the Chinese government, which since June 4, 1989, has been enthusiastically sponsoring big-budget movies about communist revolutionary history, military achievements, and heroic figures.[102]

Third, and most important, the films of the 1980s and early 1990s are instructive *as ways of deconstructing a cultural centrism of which they, as well as many of their evaluators, are in fact a part.* While I am not reluctant to unite with mainland Chinese intellectuals in mobilizing criticism of the authoritarianism of the communist government,[103] the most important point of what I have hoped to raise with "primitive passions" is that the "primitive" is not only a central part of repressive official discourse but also a prevalent and pervasive obsession that structures the very *"oppositional"critiques* of official discourse we have seen in the majority of Chinese films and film criticism to date. My larger purpose is thus to problematize, through a careful reading of some of the films of the 1980s and early 1990s, Chinese intellectuals' own tendency to see everything in terms of the primitive that is China—to the exclusion of other issues, other peoples, and other struggles elsewhere. This is evident, for instance, in these remarks by Chen Kaige: "Culture has determined that I am Chinese, and all my concerns are about this."[104] The inability to define oneself beyond the "victim and empire" that is China is in part what accounts for the obstinate discourse of nativism that is heard even from a director like Zhang Yimou, whose works demonstrate, in their responsiveness to intercultural politics, the untenability of such a nativism. In spite of his own works, Zhang would, for instance, describe the films of the Fifth Generation directors in terms of "packaging"—meaning *mere* packaging:

Visuality, Modernity, and Primitive Passions

INTERVIEWER: It is almost impossible to understand the Chinese tradition or to understand the miserable, repressed, and twisted lives
of Chinese people through the series of films that began with *Yellow
Earth*.

ZHANG: Correct. Things that have been packaged that way indeed cannot make people understand China . . .[105]

The dismissal of things that are "packaged" here is part of a deeply
ingrained belief in the absolute originality and difference of "China." If
Chinese intellectuals often say that "China" is beyond what "foreigners"
can understand, this saying is, I think, already a figure of speech that
simply makes use of the convenient presence of "foreigners" to gesture
toward something else. What is really meant is not that foreigners cannot understand "China" but that "China" is that ultimate something—
that ultimate essence beyond representation.

In a thought-provoking article, Geremie Barmé refers to the "commonplace that the Chinese intelligentsia has had a more compliant attitude toward totalitarianism than intelligentsia in Eastern Europe."[106]
According to Barmé, this compliant attitude has much to do with a self-
censorship that not only existed in the days of severe political authoritarianism but also exists in the 1980s and 1990s, when a newer, more
progressive government has appeared under Deng Xiaoping. Using the
description of Hungarian dissident poet Miklós Haraszti, Barmé calls
the current situation in the People's Republic of China, in which the
earlier forms of brutal military violence is increasingly replaced by a
repressive, invisible violence partaken of by intellectuals themselves, a
"velvet prison." He describes the "velvet prison" in these terms:

A realm in which the crude and military style of Stalinist (or
Maoist) rule with its attendant purges, denunciations, and struggles has finally given way (or is giving way, as is the case in China)
to a new dawn of "soft," civilian government. Technocrats reformulate the social contract, one in which consensus replaces coercion, and complicity subvents criticism. Censorship is no longer
the job of a ham-fisted *apparat*, but a partnership involving
artists, audiences, and commissars alike. This is "progressive censorship," and it has an aesthetic all of its own. The new dispensa-

tion is described in various ways: the Czech dissident Václav Havel speaks of it as "invisible violence," while Haraszti has dubbed it "the velvet prison." And it is a prison with an aesthetic all of its own; (self-) repression itself has become a form of high art.[107]

Extending Barmé's argument, I would say that this "velvet prison" is the name not only of Chinese intellectuals' complicity, through self-censorship, with the Chinese government's authoritarianism *inside China*; it is also the sign of Chinese intellectuals' indifference toward *China's imperialism* vis-à-vis peoples who are peripheralized, dominated, or colonized by mainland Chinese culture, in places such as Tibet, Taiwan, and Hong Kong. Preoccupied only with China's "victimization" and "marginalization" vis-à-vis *the West*, contemporary Chinese intellectuals, in particular many of those from the People's Republic, specialize in cultivating the form of primitive passion that is sinocentrism or Chinese chauvinism. In spite of their consciously declared rebellious intentions, this primitive passion unites these intellectuals with the ongoing fantasies of their authoritarian government, fantasies that continue to fuel a political and rhetorical orthodoxy, and currently a seemingly unimpeded economic growth, in the name of some original, unique "Chinese" difference.

I write about contemporary mainland Chinese cinema, therefore, ultimately as a foreigner, who, while having been born and raised in the languages and cultures of modern China, will nonetheless always remain a kind of outsider, a barbarian whose interpretations carry within them the risk of illegitimacy and impropriety. As a foreigner from colonial Hong Kong, observing China's encroachment upon other territories and the general apathy and silence on the part of mainland Chinese intellectuals toward Chinese imperialism, I think the problematic of primitivism in contemporary Chinese film has much to tell us about the neurotic symptoms of Chinese modernity and postmodernity. These are the symptoms of an ongoing obsession with progress and innovation—with absolute radicalism and absolute newness—that is the flip side of an inability to let go of the past, which survives in phantasmagoric forms. Instead of simply repeating the theme of China's "victimization" or "marginalization" vis-à-vis the West, my readings of contemporary Chinese cinema are also meant to help deconstruct the "invisible violence" of the viciously circular emotional complex that I have been describing as "primitive passions." If, in addition to being a study of a "third world" cinema, this book succeeds in mobilizing criticism of this invisible violence, it will have accomplished a major task.

Part 2

Some Contemporary

Chinese Films

Digging an Old Well:

The Labor of Social Fantasy

Allegorizing The "Third World": Opposition or Narcissism?

All third-world texts are necessarily . . . to be read as what
I will call national allegories.
Fredric Jameson, "Third-World Literature in the Era of Multinational Capital"

Allegory . . . means precisely the non-existence of
what it presents.
Walter Benjamin, *The Origin of German Tragic Drama*

Perhaps the nearest thing to thought about nationalism
inspired by the Third World—outside the revolutionary left—was
a general scepticism about the universal applicability
of the "national" concept.
E. J. Hobsbawm, *Nations and Nationalism Since 1780: Programme, Myth, Reality*

Some Contemporary Chinese Films

What does the term *third world*[1] conjure up these days? In the academic circles of North America, it often becomes a signifier for opposition, resistance, anti-imperialism, anticolonialism, struggles for national and cultural autonomy, and so on. When we examine "third world" cinema, our expectations also tend to follow these major notions, which operate by identifying Western imperialism of the past few hundred years as the chief enemy. As Ashish Rajadhyaksha writes, "The 'identification' of the enemy, across all historical differences, as something static in space and time, has often been seen as one of the purposes of the Third Cinema, the first step towards liberation."[2]

It follows that arguments for "third world" cinema are always such that the "third world" becomes an extension of the European Marxist avant-garde tradition and that its cultures are loaded, by way of interpretation, with residues of European Enlightenment with an emphasis on cognitive lucidity, on production, on experiment, and on emancipation.[3] What dominates the understanding of the "third world" is thus a masculinist leftism for which "nationalism" becomes the "third world" revenge on "first world" imperialism.[4] The "third world" is attributed an "outside" position from which criticism can be made about the "first world." This outside position is part and parcel of what Gayatri Chakravorty Spivak calls "the continuing subalternization of Third World material"[5] by "first world" critics, who condemn "third world" cultural production in the age of postmodernism to a kind of realism with functions of authenticity, didacticism, and deep meaning.

One question that the inscription of "third world" cultures in opposition does not seem to be able to deal with is what else there is in such cultures besides the struggle against the West.[6] What if the primary interest of a "third world" culture is not that of resistance against Western domination? How are we to read the processes of signification that actually fall outside the currently hegemonic reading of third world cultures, the reading that insists on their *oppositional* alterity to the West only?

The currency of Jameson's notion of "national allegories" is evident in its application by scholars who are otherwise different in their political, national, and gender interests.[7] Instead of simply agreeing or disagreeing with Jameson and his followers, let us first reconsider what Jameson means by "allegory": "The allegorical spirit is profoundly discontinuous, a matter of breaks and heterogeneities, of the multiple polysemia of the dream rather than the homogeneous representation of the symbol."[8]

Although he defines "the allegorical spirit" with care, however, Jameson does not apply it to the word "nation." Using his own definition of allegory, we may ask: why has the notion of "nation" and "the third world nation" not been allegorized and made "discontinuous"? For whom is the nationness of "third world" nations unquestionable in its collectivity? For whom does "third world" collectivity equal the "nation"? Even though "national allegories" might have currently locked the West's others into a particular kind of reading, the notion as such cannot sufficiently account for the "breaks and heterogeneities" and "multiple polysemia" of "third world" texts. Jameson's description of "first world" readers confronted by a "third world" text is actually a good way of describing the feelings of *"third world" readers confronted with "first world" readings of "third world" texts*, readings that, by their emphases on what appeals to "first world" readers, render even familiar "third world" texts "alien": "We sense, between ourselves and this alien text, the presence of another reader, of the Other reader, for whom a narrative, which strikes us as conventional or naive, has a freshness of information and a social interest that we cannot share."[9]

Contemporary Chinese cinema is fascinating because it problematizes the facile notions of oppositional alterity that have for so long dominated our thinking about the "third world." Those readers who have seen something of this cinema would know that the Chinese films that manage to make their way to audiences in the West are usually characterized, first of all, by visual beauty. From Chen Kaige's *Yellow Earth* (1984) to Tian Zhuangzhuang's *Horse Thief* (1986), to Zhang Yimou's *Red Sorghum* (1988), *Judou* (1990), and *Raise the Red Lantern* (1991), we see that contemporary Chinese directors are themselves so fascinated by the possibilities of cinematic experimentation that even when their subject matter is—and it usually is—oppression, contamination, rural backwardness, and the persistence of feudal values, such subject matter is presented with stunning sensuous qualities. One would need to ask whether some of these films are not compelling because of their aesthetic purity and beauty rather than simply because of their content of the "lack of enlightenment." If so, what kinds of issues do they engender for cross-cultural inquiry?

The sharp distinction between the often grave subject matter and the sensuously pleasing "enunciation" of contemporary Chinese film—a distinction we can describe in terms of a conjoined subalternization and commodification, as a subalternized commodification and/or a commodified subalternization—points to the economics that enable the distribution and circulation of these films in the West.

Some may therefore say that contemporary Chinese directors know how to "package" their stories of oppression with fashionable techniques and that were it not for such packaging the films would not sell. The presumption of this kind of argument is that "packaging" is superfluous—something that the films can or should do without. What contemporary Chinese films demonstrate, however, is that packaging is now an inherent part of cultural production. Even the most gruesome story needs to be shot exquisitely, so that it can contend for attention in metropolitan markets. If we follow this understanding of "packaging"—that is, packaging as a kind of production, the production not of deep meanings but of exotic surfaces—we would need to redefine cultural labor and value production as these appear in contemporary "third world" cinema.

To illustrate this point, let us consider briefly a film that attracted quite a bit of attention a few years ago: Zhang Yimou's *Judou*. (I will discuss Zhang's films in greater detail in part 2, chapter 4.) Based on the story "Fuxi Fuxi" by Liu Heng,[10] the film is about the secret relationship between Yang Tianqing, the nephew of Yang Jinshan, and Wang Judou, Yang Jinshan's wife and Yang Tianqing's aunt. In the film, incest and adultery lead to the birth of a son, Tianbai, who officially remains Tianqing's "younger brother" because he is thought to be the offspring of Jinshan and Judou. Tianbai eventually kills both his father-by-name and his biological father.

Rather than simply focus on the sexual content, which caused the film to be banned in China when it was first completed and constituted its main interest for audiences overseas, I want to argue how this film transforms our notions of "third world" cultural production. This can be seen in the changes Zhang Yimou made in the story. Among these changes, the most interesting one is the background of a dye mill, which is not in the original story by Liu Heng.

With the dye mill come the possibilities of experimenting with colors as part of the visual language of the film. However, my reading of the visual here is different from that usually offered by critics who see it in terms of a return to ethnic traditions and a constitution of ethnic identity. Chinese pictorial aesthetics, as is well known, is the favorite choice for such critics in their attempts to establish the "third world difference."[11] An example of this kind of reading goes as follows: "A general criticism leveled at Third World films is that they are too graphic. This spatial factor is part of a general rhythm of pictorial representation in most Third World societies. It is, therefore, precisely because graphic art creates symbols in space that it enables Third World viewers to relate more easily to their films. In the Chinese case, for example . . ."[12]

Here, the "third world" is given an identity as a pure other space with a distinctive "otherworldly" aesthetics. The logic implied in this kind of reading is that graphicness and symbols, even though they may not be an accepted part of Western film, are an intrinsic part of "third world" audiences' reception. Instead of establishing the "third world difference" this way, however, I would argue that it is indeed in the graphic aspects of *Judou* that the historical conditions of "third world" cultural production are most pronouncedly truthful, but the graphic is truthful not because it represents "China" as such but because it signifies that which is not purely "Chinese." Another way of defining this impurity is to say that the "ethnicity" of contemporary Chinese cinema—"Chineseness"—is already the sign of a *cross-cultural* commodity fetishism.

Jean Baudrillard defines the semiological relation between commodity fetishism and ideology in these terms:

> The fetishization of the commodity is the fetishization of a product emptied of its concrete substance of labor and subjected to another type of labor, a labor of signification, that is, of coded abstraction (the production of differences and of sign values). It is an active, collective process of production and reproduction of a code, a system, invested with all the diverted, unbound desire separated out from the process of real labor and transferred onto precisely that which denies the process of real labor.[13]

For those intent on looking for the "third world difference," the dye mill would be one of those sites of "third world" labor that can be used to contrast with "first world" metropolitan centers. A predictable set of dichotomies would thus follow to oppose the "third" and "first" worlds in terms of rural versus urban life, manual versus mental labor, simplicity and innocence versus complexity and experience, and so forth. And yet, in *Judou*, the setting of the dye mill does not so much enable us to understand the labor of dyeing cloths in the Chinese countryside in the 1920s as it provides the metaphoric and cinematic staging for the romance, the physical violence, and the human tragedy that unfold in the course of the story. The dyed cloths that are hoisted to the roof of the village house, the visual effects of layeredness as pieces of brightly dyed cloths fall and fold upon each other at crucial moments (such as the lovers' first episode of lovemaking), the disturbed colors in the dye basin in which the two men die—all these are part of a kind of production that is *other than* the "realistic" portrayal of the labor of Chinese peasants living in the feudal countryside. Instead, an age-old labor activity is now given a second-order signification, that of cinema, in order to project a very different concept of labor altogether. This is the cultural labor of the "third world" in the 1990s, in which the "third world" can no longer simply manufacture mechanical body parts to be assembled and sold in the "first world." What the "third world" has been enlisted to do *also* is the manufacture of a *reflection*, an alterity that gives (back) to the "first world" a sense of "its" freedom and democracy while it generously allows the "third world" film to be shown against the authoritarian policies of "third world" governments.[14] But an "alterity" produced this way is a code and an abstraction whose fascination lies precisely in the fact that it is artificial and superficial; as Baudrillard says, "it *is the artifact that is the object of desire.*"[15]

Once we shift our thinking of production to that of image production, we can no longer theorize "labor" as purely physical or manual, that is, emanating from the human body and therefore more genuine and unalienated. The production of images is the production not of things but of relations, not of one culture but of *value between cultures*: even as we see "Chinese" stories on the screen, therefore, we are still confronted with an exchange *between* "China" and the West in which these stories seek their market. In the case of films from the People's Republic, this is especially evident when excellent films receiving applause outside China are banned at home. What this means is that the labor of Chinese filmmakers is, to use the language of classical Marxism, literally alienated from its home use. Contemporary Chinese film production serves in this instance to redefine "third world" cultural production as first and foremost alienated. Alienation is the very form of cultural production, which "third world" cultures, precisely because of their histories, make manifest. And the first symptom of such alienation is usually the emotional insistence on a "national" essence such as the "Chinese." It is as if the more indisputable the interference and intervention of the "foreign" have become, the stronger the insistence on cultural self-containment must be.[16]

The simultaneous fascination with traditional activities of physical labor and the abstraction of such labor in the form of beautiful images (as is the case with wine making in *Red Sorghum* and the nomadic livelihood of Tibetan people in *Horse Thief*) means that questions of "third world" cinema cannot be posed simply in terms of a uniform nationalistic opposition to the "first world." Instead, the production of images foregrounds the much more difficult issue of *value*, which, precisely because it is intangible, can be distributed, absorbed, and reproduced far more easily than actual objects. But in posing the question of "third world" cultural production in terms of images, I am not, I want to emphasize, making an argument for criticizing the "incorrect" images and finding the "correct" images of the West's others, since I would, in order to do that, need to presume the existence of an unalienated labor that can be matched onto a correct image. The much more disturbing issues of cultural exchange—the exchange of ideologies, values, and images—mean that what need to be fundamentally revamped are not so much positivistic representations as the critical bases on which "third world" cultures are currently being examined.

Here, the history of China vis-à-vis the West can be instructive in a number of ways. Unlike India or countries in Africa and America, most parts of China were, in the course of modern European imperialism, never territorially under the sovereignty of any foreign power, although China was invaded and had to grant many concessions throughout the nineteenth century to England, France, Germany, Russia, Japan, and the United States. Major political movements in China, be they for the restoration of older forms of government (1898) or for the overthrow of the dynastic system (1911), led by the religious (1850–64), by the well-educated (1919), by the antiforeign (1900, 1937–1945), or by the communists (1949), were always conducted in terms of China's relations with foreign powers, usually the West. However, my suggestion is that the ability to preserve more or less territorial integrity (whereas other ancient civilizations, such as the Inca, the Aztec, India, Vietnam and Indochina, Algeria, and others, were territorially captured) as well as linguistic integrity (Chinese remains the official language) means that as a "third world" country, the Chinese relation to the imperialist West, until the communists officially propagandized "anti-imperialism," is seldom purely "oppositional" ideologically; on the contrary, the point has always been for China to become as strong as the West, to become the West's "equal." And even though the Chinese communists once served as the anti-imperialist inspiration for other "third world" cultures and progressive Western intellectuals, that dream of a successful and consistent opposition to the West on ideological grounds has been dealt the death blow by more recent events such as the Tiananmen massacre of 1989, in which the Chinese government itself acted as viciously as if it were one of its capitalistic enemies.[17] As the champion of the unprivileged classes and nations of the world, communist China has shown itself to be a failure, a failure that is now hanging on by empty official rhetoric while its people choose to live in ways that have obviously departed from the communist ideal.

The point of summarizing modern Chinese history in such a schematic fashion is to underscore how the notion of "coloniality" (together with the culture criticisms that follow from it), when construed strictly in terms of the *foreignness* (that is, exteriority) of race, land, and language, can *blind* us to political exploitation as easily as it can alert us to it.[18] In the history of modern Western imperialism, the Chinese were never completely dominated by a foreign colonial power, but the apparent absence of the "enemy" as such does not make the Chinese case any less "third world" (in the sense of being colonized) in terms of the exploitation suffered by the people, whose most important colonizer remains their own government. China, perhaps because it is the exception to the rule of imperialist domination by race, land, and language involving a foreign (external) power, in fact highlights the effects of the imperialistic *transformation of value and value production* more sharply than in other "third world" cultures.

Karl Marx, we remember, defines value in relation to labor. What exactly is this relation? In her illuminating readings of Marx through Jacques Derrida, Gayatri Chakravorty Spivak criticizes the view, assumed by many to be unproblematic, that value is labor's "representation." Taking from Derrida's notion of writing as différance, Spivak redefines value not as the representation (i.e., completed symbolic replication) of labor but as difference: "The basic premise of the recent critique of the labor theory of value is predicated on the assumption that, according to Marx, Value represents Labor. Yet the definition of Value in Marx establishes itself not only as a representation but also as a differential. What is represented or represents itself in the commodity-differential is Value."[19]

Value, in other words, functions in the same enigmatic manner (in Marx) as "writing" (in Derrida). Although value is supposed to be secondary and derivative (because it occurs as the result of labor, as writing is thought to occur after "natural" language—speech), it seems shamelessly usurping: it acts as a primary determinant, an agent that creates and stabilizes value/worth. Like writing, value poses the question about origins: does the value/worth of value come from what "precedes" it, namely, labor, or does it come from itself? Is it not scandalous to assume that value is self-originating when, supposedly, labor is? And yet we cannot think (labor) without thinking in value. Reading Marx after reading Derrida, Spivak is thus able to force the paradoxical heterogeneity of value—what she calls the "economic text"—to emerge: like writing, value is both inside and outside; its "being" comes from its being in circulation, but in order to "own" or "have" it one must take it outside circulation, outside the process in which it becomes value/valuable. Value functions both as "culture" (the agent of capitalism, the general equivalent overriding all others) and as "nature" (the mysterious contentless thing that seems "originally" there, before cultural exchange begins), but this functioning, while dependent on the clean conceptual boundary between culture and nature, also violates that boundary.

Spivak's reading is especially useful for the production of value that is "national culture." The predicament faced by many "third world" nations becomes lucid once we see national culture as a kind of economic text—a kind of value-writing. While the history of Western imperialism relegates all non-Western cultures to the place of the other, whose value is "secondary" in relation to the West, the task of nationalism in the "third world" is that of (re)inventing the "secondary" cultures themselves as primary, as the uncorrupted origins of "third world" nations' histories and "worth."[20] In the case of China, for instance, the state authorities insist to this day on the separation of China from the West as summarized in the nineteenth-century dictum *zhong xue wei ti, xi xue wei yong*—"Chinese learning for fundamental structure, Western learning for practical use." This dictum, often interpreted as a sign of the conservative nature of China's attitude toward the West, actually signifies in an elegant manner the difficulty inherent in the labor process/value-writing that is otherwise known as the construction of national culture among "third world" intellectuals. According to this dictum, "China" is the foundation of cultural value, a foundation that determines other cultures' relation or relevance to itself rather than the other way around. "China" was there "before" the West, which might be added on for practical purposes but cannot usurp China's place as the origin of value. And yet, the predicament of China in modern times is, of course, precisely that inscribed in the paradox of Marx's economic text: the notion that "China" is first and original is already a *response* to the exchange with the West, a claim that is made *after* the onslaught of the West has become irreversible. If an original "Chineseness" somehow persists and thrives as collective belief, it is only because "China" continues to be circulated among entities that are not-Chinese. To prove the "Chineseness" of the Chinese culture, the only way is through difference, which means inserting "China" among others in processes of cross-cultural production—processes that render the fantasy of an original "Chinese" value untenable.

Precisely because the processes of labor's alienation—exchange, commodification, circulation—are inevitable and indispensable to the definition of value, the insistence on an original "Chinese" culture is the insistence on a kind of value that is *outside* alienation, outside the process of value-making. The wish to return a culture to an original (native) value is thus the wish to remove that culture from the process in which it appears "original" in the first place. In modern Chinese texts, filmic or literary, this kind of predicament and paradox of the production-of-national-culture-as-original-value repeatedly occur. Unlike, say, modern India, where the British left behind insurmountable poverty, a cumbersome bureaucracy, and a language in which to function as a "nation," but where therefore the sentiment of opposition can remain legitimately alive because there is historically a clearly identifiable *foreign* (external) colonizer, the Chinese continue to have "their own" system, "their own" language, and "their own" problems. Chinese intellectuals' obsession remains "China" rather than the mere opposition to the West. The cultural production that results is therefore narcissistic and self-conscious, rather than purely oppositional, in structure. Whatever oppositional sentiment there exists is an oppositional sentiment directed internally toward the center that is itself—"China," the "Chinese heritage," the "Chinese tradition," the "Chinese government," and variants of these.

This structure of narcissistic value-writing explains the current interest on the part of Chinese filmmakers to search for *China's "own" others*. The films about the remote areas of China such as Tibet, about emperors, empresses, and eunuchs, and about the agrarian lives of the nameless and voiceless peasants in the past, as well as about the lingering forces of feudalist oppression that persist in spite of the revolutions—all such films partake of what we may call a poststructuralist fascination with the constructedness of one's "self"—in this case, with China's "self," with China's origins, with China's own alterity. In the wish to go back to "China" as origin—to revive "China" as the source of original value—the "inward turn" of the nationalist narrative precisely reveals "China" as other-than-itself. This narcissistic structure then *(mis)translates* into the more familiar paradigm of "China as oppositional alterity to the West" through the international cinematic apparatus and the not so innocent apparatuses of cross-cultural interpretation.

In the following sections, I examine the problems that surface in such a narcissistic exploration of a "native" culture. Foremost among my questions is how narcissism informs the reconstruction of origins, the truncating of libidinal economies, and the imaginary reinvestments that make up the "labor" moving within a "third world" culture as well as between the "first" and "third" worlds.

The Futurity . . . the Futility of the Nation

The film I will discuss now is *Lao jing*, or *Old Well*, directed by Wu Tianming and produced in 1987. Like many contemporary Chinese films, *Old Well* is based on a novel by the same name.[21] The author of the novel, Zheng Yi, also wrote the film script.

Old Well is a village located far into the Taiheng Mountains. There are endless stony mountains, but no water. Over the generations, the Old Well villagers have dug 127 wells, but they have all been dry. The deepest was over fifty meters. The greatest hope of all the villagers is that they will find water on their own land. The protagonist is an educated youth called Sun Wangquan ("Sun," his family name, also means "grandson," and "Wangquan" means "auspicious for flowing stream"). When the film begins, Wangquan has returned to his village and is determined to use his knowledge to find water. His own family is very poor. To reach his goal and to help his brothers get married, he marries Duan Xifeng, a young widow with a daughter, and gives up his love relationship with another woman, Zhao Qiaoying. After many failed attempts, including one in which Wangquan and Qiaoying are trapped at the bottom of a well, where Wangcai, Wangquan's younger brother, is killed, Wangquan finally succeeds in digging a well by applying his newly acquired hydraulic knowledge. For the first time in many generations, Old Well village has water.

Old Well can, of course, be read as a "national allegory." According to this type of reading, everything in the film would be assigned a national—that is, Chinese—significance. The struggle of the protagonist and the village would then be microscopic versions of the "nation" and its people struggling to consolidate their identity.[22] It would be a story with a positive ending. But what if the supposedly "national" sign "Chinese" itself is more than the "third world nation" that is conferred upon it by modernity? Once we stop using the "nation" to unify the elements of the film text, other questions begin to surface. A careful *allegorical* reading of *Old Well* would demonstrate that the allegory of the "nation" is, paradoxically, the nation's otherness and nonpresence.

The "nation" reading is impossible because a national *enemy* is absent. Instead, the space of an enemy, which is crucial for the unification of a community, is occupied by two "others"—the dry well and the romantic woman. Why would a "Chinese" film of the 1980s concentrate on enemies other than "national" enemies?

In the readings of recent world events, it is commonly recognized that the breakdown of communism in Eastern Europe since 1989 has not led to democratic prosperity in accordance with anticommunist beliefs but has instead caused the resurgence of old ethnic conflicts that were neutralized and covered up under communism. The prominence of nationalistic sentiments in the states previously dominated by the USSR indicates that nationalism was actually the repressed side of communism, a repressed side that boils over once the lid of communism is removed.[23]

Digging an Old Well

In China, where ethnic differences are relatively undisruptive (except in Tibet) and where the centrality of the Han culture remains relatively uncontested by other ethnic groups, many of whom have been assimilated for generations,[24] nationalism functions in the past forty years to fuel communism rather than as communism's repressed side. As communism gradually loses its hold on the populace (even though it is still the official policy), what surface as the "social disorders" that are repressed under communism?—Two related things: sexual difference, which communism neutralizes, and "the West," which is communism's adversary but also its founding source. The surfacing of these disorders means the relative indifference not only to communism but also to communism's ally in China—nationalism itself.

Female Sexuality and the Nation

The eruption of romantic love in contemporary Chinese cinema continues the modernist interest in the controversies of love and sexuality among Chinese intellectuals since the beginning of the twentieth century. Why is romantic love such an issue? In the early twentieth century, the interest in love among popular literature writers (those of the Mandarin Duck and Butterfly School) was partly a result of the *ideological* rather than actual disintegration of the Chinese kinship family. The ongoing protest against the oppression of women and junior members of *jia*, the traditional family, meant that alternative spaces for human relationships had to be sought. During that period, when China's participation in anti-imperialism meant that resistance against Western and Japanese aggression had to be conceived in the form of nationalism, the "internal" battle against the family became allied with the promotion of Chinese culture as the "nation," which was literally conceived of as the state-family, *guojia*, the large organizational unit that would give China a place among the nations of the world.

If the conception of "woman" was in the past mediated by women's well-defined roles within the Chinese family, the modern promotion of the nation throws into instability all those traditional roles. How are women's sexuality, social function, economic function, contribution to cultural production, and biological reproduction to be conceived of outside the family and in terms of the nation?[25] This is the historical juncture when, in what appeared to be a sudden "liberation" of the traditional constraints on Chinese women's identity, romantic love became a leading social issue. For what is "romantic" about romantic love is not sex but the apparent freedom in which men and women could choose their sexual partners, in a way that differed from arranged marriage. And since the traditional family system was paternalistic—that is, resting on the sexual stability, chastity, and fidelity of women while men were openly promiscuous or polygamous—the new freedom meant first and foremost the production of a new female sexuality. In other words, because the conception of the nation sought to unify the culture regardless of sexual and class difference, it left open many questions as to how women's sexual identities, which were carefully differentiated and monitored within the kinship system, should be *re*formulated. This is why, one could say, in the discourse of modernity, the Chinese woman suddenly became a newly discovered "primitive"—a body adrift between the stagnant waters of the family, whose oppressiveness it seeks to escape, and the open sea of the nation, whose attention to "woman" is only such that her sexual difference and history become primarily *its* support (i.e., become erased).

The emotional as well as economic forms of the family, on the other hand, die a slow and drawn-out death. Especially because the modern discourse of the nation has not really provided real alternatives other than an apparently emancipated "body" with no constraints, the tenacious bonds of the family live on. And this is ironically even more so under the communist revolution. When Mao Zedong upheld women as "equal" to men in the public spheres of work and economic production for the nation, and when Western feminists were delighted to see Chinese women being honored without discrimination with the same tasks as men, the family continued to thrive in the ideological vacuum left by the creation of the communist nation, simply because women's *labor* in the home, unlike their kinship roles and positions, which could be taxonomically classified, remained real and material but traditionally unclassified and unpaid, and hence much more difficult to reclassify in the new system. The consequence is that the oppressiveness resulting from such labor is left intact to this day, leaving their imprints on cultural productions even when such productions are not overtly about gender, sexuality, or women.

Digging an Old Well

In *Old Well*, the kinship-bound and modernized female sexualities are represented by Wangquan's different relationships with Xifeng and Qiaoying. From the beginning, the two women are portrayed *stereotypically*, in accordance with the literary and historiographic conventions of understanding Chinese modernity. While Qiaoying is, *like* Wangquan, coming back to the village after having been in the outside world, Xifeng is the woman who remains at home. Qiaoying's attractiveness is associated with her "novelty": she brings back with her such modern items as a television set. Xifeng, although widowed, is clearly more "stable": her stability is represented by the support she has from the multiple roles she plays within the kinship system, in which the women are as strongly functional as the men.

Xifeng has a mother, who supervises her sexual life, and is herself a mother. All she needs is a husband who would make her female social identity complete. Qiaoying, on the other hand, is an unknown entity: one of the reasons Wangquan's grandfather disapproves of her is that he thinks she would not stay put in the village. Even though, in terms of social progress, Qiaoying is much closer to man himself than to the woman at home, in the rural village her avant-garde ontological proximity to masculinity is eyed with suspicion and distrust. The modernized, educated woman signifies romantic freedom—that is, "choice" over her own body—and thus social instability. Qiaoying is represented as without family relations. Like a mysterious signifier unleashed from centuries of anchorage to kinship, she does not know where she is heading.

What is most remarkable, however, is the way this *convention* of understanding modernity—the convention of exorcizing the romantic woman and romantic love from traditional society—surfaces in post–Cultural Revolution cultural production. What does this convention do here?

First, it helps consolidate the traditional female sexuality represented by Xifeng and her relation to Wangquan, whose genealogical as well as career stability is guaranteed through marriage. In Chinese, "digging an old well" conjures up idioms and expressions that carry sexual connotations. *Gujing qingbo* (the stirring of ripples in an old well) and *tao gujing* (dredging an old well), for instance, are expressions that allude to the renewed sexual activities in a woman who has been without them for a long time. The man who has sex with such a woman is then an old-well-digger, which is the role played by Wangquan, who "receives" not only food, cigarettes, and money from Xifeng but finally, though reluctantly, her body. Toward the end of the film, Xifeng is pregnant. By contrast, the romantic woman is turned into an outcast. Qiaoying is the "enemy" to the economic basis of the village community, who must be exiled.

Second, in the aftermath of the Cultural Revolution, the affirmation of traditional family values comes as an attempt to mask the lack created by the bankruptcy of communism *and* nationalism, even though nationalism may persist by reinscribing itself in traditional forms. The main point is that the central roles played by the family and village community are here signs of the *dismantling* of the modernist revolution from "family" to "nation." "Woman" is now caught between the bankruptcy of nationalism and communism, in which the sexes are "equal" and women's problems do not exist, *and* the resurgence of older patriarchal forms of community, in which female sexuality is strictly managed for purposes of kinship reproduction.

A film such as *Old Well* demonstrates that the "Chinese nation" itself does not have to exist in order for the social and sexual issues to be circulated and negotiated. Like the female body emancipated from traditional kinship bonds, the "nation"—that imaginary anchorage for primitive passions—is *nowhere* except in the politics that uses it to fight the past (be that past primitive, ethnic, feudalist, or colonized). Like the female body thrown into "romantic love," the nation is theoretically capable of all kinds of dangerous libidinal possibilities. Because it is fundamentally empty, the "nation" must be controlled by a more locally grounded production and reproduction. In their relative silence on the subject of the nation, contemporary Chinese films seem to say: "It is the 'nation' with all its extravagant promises that has led to the internal catastrophes in modern China. But—still, we must continue to seek such extravagant promises elsewhere!"

The Barrenness of Romantic Love

If the decline of the "nation" is as elusive as its rise, this elusiveness finds a convention of staging itself in the romantic woman.

Digging an Old Well

In spite of Wangquan's marriage to another woman, Qiaoying loves him, and we feel, through his silence and guilty expressions, that he still loves her. After Wangquan is married, Qiaoying has been going out with Wangcai, who earlier had a quarrel with Wangquan about his own lack of everything, in particular his lack of experience with women. Qiaoying's association with Wangcai is clearly presented as futile and futureless: Wangcai is an example of the "decadent" younger generation of contemporary China, who, unlike his brother, has neither the stamina nor the altruism to persist in a quest for the communal good. Instead of digging for water, he is more interested in stealing women's underwear and ridiculing women performers in ways that are clearly sadistic and misogynistic. A hilarious scene shows Wangcai leading a group of young people dancing wildly to the noisy tunes of Western rock and roll music played over a transistor radio at the site of an attempted well drill. In Wangcai, the "dangers" of Westernization threaten to become destructive. Here is a youth with no long-term plan and no concern for society's future. During a well-digging accident, Wangcai is killed by rubble falling into the well.

Because of the accident, however, Qiaoying is finally able to "consummate" her love for Wangquan. In this love scene, we have perhaps one of the most romantic portrayals of romantic love in contemporary Chinese cinema. Its romanticism lies in an excessiveness that can only belong to film.

From under the well, the image of the two lovers kissing in passion is superimposed with the cosmic landscape—the sky, the mountains, the trees—in a series of shots that are, like the accompanying music, in motion rather than still. The lovers' entrapment inside the well thus becomes, in a dreamlike fashion, the freedom one can find in "nature" outside the confines of human wants and desires. If this moment captures romantic fulfillment, it is also, I suggest, a capturing of the uncapturable through the juxtaposition of what is temporally and geographically specific—romantic love—with what is timeless and placeless—the cosmos. As that which is here and now, love does not and cannot reproduce itself outside the circuit of the two lovers. The sacrifice it requires, as well as the meaning of its intense presence, is that of an unrecuperable death. Romantic love is thus literally experienced as death, at a moment when the lovers have lost hope of getting out alive. It is in death that they can dream of being at one with each other and with the cosmos, in a way that—thanks to the imaginary possibilities of cinema—transcends the constraint of the specific here and now. This transcendence is fantastical and antisocial. Romantic love becomes the signifier of emptiness—the emptiness and emptying of the social.

After this death, society goes on. The fantasy of romantic love is from now on remembered with nostalgia, as what happened at a different time in a different place. Importantly, it is the woman, Qiaoying, who carries death with her. She eventually leaves the community and donates her dowry to the cause of continual well digging. Wangquan, who found himself a mistress in the depths of his failed social labor, reemerges as a cultural hero who is aided not only by his mistress but also by his wife, who calls upon the entire village to give what they can to help his cause. While one woman gets nothing and the other retains her husband, Wangquan keeps his family, the memory of love,[26] and leaves himself a name.

The futility of the nation is thus signified by the barrenness of romantic love, the consummation of which takes place in the depths of a dry well at the moment of a collapsed effort at drilling. Romantic love is barren not because it is impoverished but because it is surplus: its excessiveness threatens economic productiveness because it prevents that productiveness from being stabilized. Another way of putting this is to say that the sacrifice of romantic love is pure: unlike the attempt to drill a well, it cannot be rewarded or "completed" in the way that the "In Memoriam" plaque, as I will go on to argue, completes and rewards the sacrifices of men's lives down the centuries. If well digging generates the "value" that compensates for the loss of lives, the barrenness of romantic love lures modernity against itself and back toward the long-disputed family.

The Labor of Social Fantasy

> Ethnicity *can* mobilize the vast majority of its community—
> provided its appeal remains sufficiently vague or irrelevant.
> E. J. Hobsbawm, *Nations and Nationalism since 1780:*
> *Programme, Myth, Reality*

Digging an Old Well

> How is one to interpret the fact that large numbers of people
> collectively hold beliefs that are false?
>
> Partha Chatterjee, *Nationalist Thought and the Colonial World:*
> *A Derivative Discourse?*

If one "foreign enemy" to the community is the romantic woman, who must be cut off, the other "foreign enemy" is the lack that is inside Old Well village—the dry wells themselves. This lack awaits being filled and, once filled, will give meaning to the community.

The theme of dry wells repeats the obsession that has characterized "Chinese modernity" since the nineteenth century: the power of technology. Although we are familiar with the many technological inventions that owe their origins to the Chinese—the compass, paper, printing, fireworks, gunpowder, deep drilling,[27] to name just a few—in the modern period, notably after Western imperialism became unavoidable, one might argue that "technology" situates the Chinese culture vis-à-vis the West in the form of a lack. Political trends in the twentieth century vascillate between the desire to fill this lack and the pretense that China needs nothing. In the post–Cultural Revolution period, following Deng Xiaoping's modernization campaigns, we see once again the openness to technology, from the most mundane items for household use to computers. Contemporary Chinese films necessarily reflect these developments.[28] One of the narratives that have sustained China's relationship with Western modernity can thus be described as a quest for technology—a quest for that "power" without which China cannot become strong.

At the same time, in this film, the quest for technology is legitimated not so much in terms of the elusive "nation" as in terms of a post–Cultural Revolution *humanism* that tries to preserve the traditional in modernization. As such, the film also repeats one of the basic fantasies that have run throughout the course of Chinese modernization since the nineteenth century, which is expressed in the aforementioned phrase "Chinese learning for fundamental structure, Western learning for practical use." The fantasy is that the Chinese can have part of the West—technology—without changing its own social structure. Today, this fantasy continues in the evident split between official Chinese rhetoric, which still remains loyal to the classical themes of Marxism, Leninism, and Maoism, and Chinese social practice, which now includes all kinds of Western and capitalistic ventures and enterprises. Such fantasy is crucial to the narcissistic value-writing that I suggest as the alternative way of understanding "third world" cultures.

This narcissistic value-writing is, moreover, masculinist. *Old Well* begins with shots of part of a naked male body against a dark background hammering away in sweat. We read "determination" into these signifiers. The ending of the film *completes* these opening signifiers with an "In Memoriam" plaque indicating the lives (presumably all male) that have been lost in the centuries of failed attempts at well digging. The completion is the completion of the sacrificial process: finally, the film seems to say, the sacrifices pay off.

From the perspective of Wangquan, technology is strictly a means to an end. Technology is instrumental in fulfilling the mandate that is loaded on him and that he cannot resist. He cannot protest against that mandate because in it lies a communal meaning of responsibility; he cannot decline it because in it lies the very personal identity he receives from society as a reward. The mandate not only takes from him his life energy; it also gives him his life and his immortality.

What is interesting is not the simple affirmation of humanistic values and a process of identity production through stamina, effort, and willingness to self-sacrifice but how such an affirmation is at the same time part of that cultural narcissism that exoticizes its own alterity, its own otherness. The fact that the affirmation of humanistic values takes place not in metropolitan centers such as Shanghai and Beijing[29] but in backward villages in remote mountains suggests that the reinvestment in humanism in contemporary Chinese cultural production is at the same time an uncanny *ethnographic* attempt to narrate a "noble savagery" that is believed to have preserved the older and more authentic treasures of the culture, in ways as yet uncorrupted by modernity.

At the center of the treasures to be preserved is a system of production in which the will to work will be duly rewarded—if not in the form of an immediate gratification to the individual, then definitely in the form of the reproduction and continuance of the life of a community. The fascination not only with technological production or genealogical reproduction alone but with the welding of the two in the successful perpetuation of a culture is probably the most important fascination of the post–Cultural Revolution period, in which the diversion from the mindless destructiveness of the previous two decades needs to graft itself onto something substantial and concrete. These two kinds of production together make up the economy of the third kind—the production of value/ideology, a production that is at the same time a series of translations, decodings, and recodings between "contemporary" and "rural" China, between communism (with its emphasis on loyalty to the party) and humanism (with its emphasis on loyalty to the clan and the family, and on individual effort), between China's status as other to the West and the status of the "other" cultures of China's past and unknown places to China's "present self." In *Old Well*, the "lack" of China (in terms of technology) is projected onto the "lack" of China's rural area, which is further projected onto an actual lack, the lack of water. In this series of projections and substitutions, the "lack," always at once frustrating and empowering, finally gives way to a filling that stabilizes signification for survival.

At this point, we need to say, But wait, it's not only the "filling" and the production of water that enable the survival of the community. The *failure* to produce water is what has already sustained the culture of Old Well village for generations!

What indeed is the old well?

In terms of narrative structure, the old well is, of course, nothing: it is the lack that makes narrative possible. The old well is the obsession that, precisely because it remains unfulfilled, perpetuates itself in the village as a kind of collective memory, collective responsibility, and collective desire. Do the men in Old Well village know what they really want? Or do they continue digging simply because their ancestors have formed that habit—simply because it has become a *tribal ritual*? The sense of absurdity that figures in what looks like a revered tradition is clearest in the scene where villagers from a neighboring village attempt to close up a well that the Old Well villagers claim to be theirs. This competition over the rights to the well leads to the question as to the whereabouts of the plaque indicating the well's "ownership." Finally, it is the women who produce the "original" plaque, which has, it turns out, long become a latrine stone.

But the absurdity of this discovery does not change the powerful impact that the obsession has on the village. And such is the power of social fantasy: even when the "original" plaque has been turned into a latrine stone and is thus shown to be, after all, *no more than a (shitty) stone*, the belief that it is *more* persists. In a discussion of Eastern Europe after the collapse of communism, Slavoj Žižek writes about the fantastical nature of what he calls the "nation-Thing" in a way that is equally applicable to the old well:

> The Thing is not directly a collection of these features [composing a specific way of life]; there is "something more" in it, something that *is present* in these features, that *appears* through them. Members of a community who partake in a given "way of life" *believe in their Thing*, where this belief has a reflexive structure proper to the intersubjective space: "I believe in the (national) Thing" is equal to "I believe that others (members of my community) believe in the Thing." The tautological character of the Thing—its semantic void, the fact that all we can say about it is that it is "the real Thing"—is founded precisely in this paradoxical reflexive structure.[30]

This fantasy turns all accidents—events that are real but somehow cannot be accounted for coherently—into *mere* accidents, mere errors, which have no place in the actual functioning or *labor* of the fantasy. Similarly, all the lives that have been sacrificed in the course of searching for water are simply meaningless until the first well is successfully dug. Until then, we can say that the lost lives do not *matter*: they remain chance components waiting to be materialized into the full-blown fantasy peopled with real bodies. Instead of describing the history of Old Well village as one in which the villagers are united by a hope for the future (when water will be found), therefore, we should describe it this way: the discovery of water validates the sacrifices *retroactively* as parts of a concerted communal effort at well digging. This is the paradox of the ending, at which we are shown a close-up of the plaque "In Memoriam" of all the well-digging martyrs with the dates of their failed efforts and their deaths. Superimposed upon the rolling image of this plaque is the author's/director's inscription documenting Sun Wangquan's accomplishment: "January 9, 1983: Water was found, and fifty tons of water were produced every hour from the first mechanized deep well." The current "success" proves by its chance occurrence that "it" is what all the previous generations have been slaving for and that, moreover, their deaths were finally *worthwhile*.[31]

Digging an Old Well

The act of discovering water, in other words, is like a signifier that enigmatically constitutes the identity of the past by its very *contingent presence* or *randomness*. If, because of its success, this act becomes endowed with the value of a "primary" act, then "primary" value itself must be described not as an absolute origin but instead as a supplementary relation: like all previous attempts of well digging, the latest attempt is a random event; at the same time, this latest attempt is marked by an *additional* randomness—the discovery of water, the accident of "success." This additional randomness, this accident that is more accidental than all the other accidents, marks the latest attempt of well digging apart from the others, thereby constituting in the same moment the "necessary" structure that coheres the entire series of events in a meaningful signifying chain, a signifying chain that I have been referring to as social fantasy. The labor of social fantasy, then, comprises not only the random physical efforts at well digging and their failures but also the process of retroactive, supplementary transformation in which the random and physical becomes the primary, the necessary, and the virtuous, and henceforth functions and reproduces itself ideologically as such.

Crucial to this social fantasy is the danger represented by the romantic woman and the recurrent dry well, both of which are "taken care of" at the end. The fantasy is that the village can have the technology of the running well without the technology of the new (running) woman, that the village can turn into a self-sufficient community with only as much outside help as *it wants*—precisely at a time when Chinese countryside self-sufficiency, like that of other "third world" rural areas, has been irredeemably eroded by modernized production and distribution, and the permeation of global capitalist economics.

A film such as this, which demonstrates the fundamental nothingness of the labor of social fantasy, inevitably lends itself to a reading that is exactly the opposite. Attesting to that is *Old Well*'s warm reception by Chinese audiences at home and overseas, and its success at the Second Tokyo International Film Festival of 1987,[32] in contrast to the regular official censorship of films by the Fifth Generation directors that are consciously critical of Chinese culture. The intense appeal of a film that celebrates the rewarding of a communal, collective effort makes little sense unless we understand the magnitude of the fantasy of collectivity on the largest scale—the Cultural Revolution—and its collapse. The emotional vacuum left behind by the latter awaits the legitimating *work* of some other thing. This other thing is increasingly being sought in China's old and remote areas, where social fantasy, whose creation of a present identity is always through a nostalgic imagining of a permanent other time and other place, can flourish most uninhibitedly. And so, beyond the futility of the nation and the barrenness of love, the labor of social fantasy, like the muscular, masculine arms at the film's beginning, hammers on.

2

Silent Is the Ancient Plain: Music,

Filmmaking, and the Concept of Social Change

in the New Chinese Cinema

During a talk he gave at the University of Minnesota in the summer of 1989, the Chinese director Chen Kaige described his interest in filmmaking as that of "reform." These words, spoken during the immediate aftermath of the Tiananmen massacre, when Chinese intellectuals could not safely return to China, were deeply resonant with the hopes and despair that the Chinese have been feeling toward their culture since the mid–nineteenth century. Merely a year before, during an interview with the Chinese edition of *Playboy*, Chen had said this in response to questions about his work: "As someone who thinks, as someone who has emerged from a 5000-year old culture, you are bound to feel that you should do something, and bound to hope that your people do not have to go through yet another, greater tragedy."[1]

The films Chen had directed up to 1989—*Huang tudi* (*Yellow Earth*, 1984), *Da yue bing* (*The Big Parade*, 1985), and *Haizi wang* (*King of the Children*, 1987)—were produced in the midst of the "Modernization" campaign that was launched by Deng Xiaoping after he returned to power in the late 1970s. The emergence of a remarkable group of directors known as the Fifth Generation, who include Chen, Zhang Yimou,

Some Contemporary Chinese Films

Tian Zhuangzhuang, Wu Ziniu, and others, is generally considered a sign of the post–Cultural Revolution booming of aesthetic experimentation. Since June 4, 1989, however, the hope raised by Deng, which Chen expressed as the hope that the Chinese do not have to go through "yet another, greater tragedy," has been dashed. What promised to be an era in which China had learned from the wounds of the Cultural Revolution and opted for a greater political openness collapsed as the Chinese government resumed control, after a mindless show of military violence, over all channels of cultural production. During the latter half of 1989, while many who had been involved in the peaceful demonstrations for reform continued to be killed, arrested, imprisoned, or sent off to remote areas, the Chinese government launched a full-scale "back to the left" reeducation program for its citizens, labeling those who oppose it "counterrevolutionary."

In the years since 1989, as the leaders of the democracy movement continue to live in exile in the West, China seems to have bounced back to "normality," with an increasingly thriving economy and a consumers' market that most of the world's capitalist nations, even if they had at one time expressed disapproval of the Chinese government's violence, are eager to seize for their own trade. While Chinese official rhetoric remains loyal, as it has for the past four decades, to the dictates of Marxism, Leninism, and Maoism, the material bases of mainland Chinese life seem to be undergoing changes that were until now unimaginable in a communist country. As real estate speculations and investments rise, and stock markets revive after an absence of more than forty years, the future of intellectual life in China remains a huge question mark. Will the enthusiastic "opening" of China mean the opening of its intellectual life, or will Chinese intellectual life continue to be one of those jealously guarded areas of Chinese "essence" that must remain aloof to the barbaric forces from the outside? What will happen to the work that has been started by directors such as Chen, and to the innovative critical insights that have only begun to be recognized? At a paradoxical historical moment like the present one, Chen's 1980s films, all of which confront the destructiveness of Chinese culture as *human* culture, speak with particular poignancy. In this chapter I concentrate on one of them—his first—*Yellow Earth*.

Paradigms of Social Change in Current Critical Thinking about "Third World" Cinema

Social change is an alluring topic. When discussed by way of "third world cinema," it is often conveniently confounded with the dominant politics of reading that dictate the production of knowledge, especially knowledge about our "others," in the "first world." No discussion of "third world cinema" can therefore afford to ignore the role played by such politics in influencing the way we understand these "other" films.

One notion of social change that has surfaced with great explanatory power in the discussions of Chinese cinema derives from what I shall call the politics of identity formation—that is, a politics that confers upon the "other" the right to exist by a taxonomic differentiation such as is often intended by the ethnic label "Chinese." This, to be sure, has everything to do with the general cultural ambience that has made it possible for "third world cinema" to emerge with some interest for audiences in North America and Western Europe in the first place. This is an ambience in which, in order to debunk the West's claim to universality in every type of representation, the identities of the West's "others" are increasingly called forth, even though, as some Chinese critics have begun to argue, "the other," too, is equally caught up in the processes of othering and fragmentation. For instance, speaking of the exotic, unfamiliar rural landscapes that have become such a popular mise-en-scène for major works by China's Fifth Generation directors, Yuejin Wang comments: "To the average urban Chinese, these landscapes are equally alien, remote and 'other-looking,' as they presumably appear to a Western gaze—and urban Chinese may well be struck by their ethnic difference and otherness while the Western mind might immediately 'recognize' their ethnic distinction as a presumably unified Chineseness. They are a cinematic representation of a cultural order both to the Western eye and the Chinese eye."[2]

In spite of the shrewd problematizing of the term *Chinese* implied in a passage like this, the bulk of work done on Chinese cinema is still largely trapped in a dichotomy between China and the West as distinct entities. While it serves to give "third world cinema" the acknowledgment it deserves, the politics of identity formation is ultimately limiting if not reductionist. The "third world" remains locked within a Hegelian dialectic of overcoming that would finally, as it were, allow it to "come into its own." It is as though if the hackneyed search for identity no longer works in the West, then let us have the others do it—after all, they have been behind us all this time, so they can afford to waste some time attempting what we have long determined to be impossible. At the one extreme of this socially progressive or "reformative" ambivalence toward the cultural productions of the "third world"—an ambivalence that may be paraphrased as "letting them speak on condition that they do so within paradigms that have gone out of order in the West"— is the position of Fredric Jameson, articulated in his well-known statement that "all third world texts are necessarily . . . to be read as . . . national allegories."[3] As I argued in the previous chapter, regardless of what meanings may be intended by the theoretically packed term *allegory*, what remains unallegorized in Jameson's pronouncement is the word *nation*. A statement such as Jameson's presupposes a semiological transparency between the individual identity of the third world subject, be he or she the character in or the writer of a novel, on the one hand, and the collective identity of the "third world" culture or nation on the other. While giving credit to the sense of struggle and hardship that is expressed by many a "third world" text, this position also lodges such texts, ideologically, within a specific politics of representation in which the meanings of the "third world" are read more or less realistically for the content of national or ethnic "identity," which is what such texts must, for the Western critic, be primarily about.

At the other extreme of this progressive ambivalence, when enthusiasm for "third world" texts is spurred by white liberal feminism's own involvement in a long history of identity establishment, we find a tendency to pursue "cross-cultural inquiry" by zooming in on the other women's "subjectivity." E. Ann Kaplan writes, for instance, that "the underlying issue for women in China, then, from a Western point of view, would seem not to be entry into the public sphere—the right to work, to equal pay, to equal participation in the work force (issues that preoccupied Western feminists in the sixties and seventies), but a new, as yet not fully articulated, realization about subjectivity."[4]

But why should the right to work, to equal pay, to equal participation in the work force not be part of that problematic of subjectivity? When liberal feminist identity politics has, through its dealings with Freud, learned the necessity to include the "unconscious" in its struggles, what is questionable is not the category of "subjectivity" itself but how it is investigated. Kaplan's reading of "the case of women in recent Chinese cinema" suggests that subjectivity is to be explored in terms of hetero-sexual erotics. Speaking of the films she has seen by Chinese women directors, she sums up their aesthetic interest by way of a key scene in which the signified is romantic love and sexual union: "Each of the films contains a key scene in which the heroine's erotic gaze is finally met by the male's returned desire. In each, the desire cannot be expressed or consummated; in all cases, the heroines are left yearning to meet this 'gaze' again—a gaze that is the sign for romantic love and sexual union."[5]

A passage like this leaves us wondering what the differences in libid-inal organization in a Chinese film might possibly be. As Kaplan notes throughout her article, cross-cultural readings are "fraught with dan-gers." One of these dangers is our habit of reading the "third world" in terms of what, from our point of view, it does not have but wants to have. Once this axis of *possession* is established, our analysis is likely to remain bogged down in a predictable direction, with texts from the "third world" serving as the latest exotic objects, always confirming what makes sense for us (as subjects) and for us alone.[6] What happens if we shift our attention from what China and the Chinese "want to have" to what and how they *produce*? The first thing we will have to notice is how stunning it is that such productions *have been made* in spite of the dire material restrictions, both economic and ideological, under which most Chinese directors work.

The story of *Yellow Earth* is a simple one. The film's opening lines tell us that in 1937, the socialist revolution had begun in Western China, but most other areas were still under the control of the Kuomintang. Some soldiers of the Eighth Route Army were in the highlands of Shaanbei col-lecting folk songs for army use. The action of the film begins in the spring of 1939. Gu Qing, an Eighth Route Army soldier, arrives in a vil-lage where a wedding is taking place. Watching with interest is Cuiqiao, the unmarried daughter of a local peasant at whose cave home Gu Qing will stay while doing his work. Cuiqiao has a brother, Hanhan, who does not speak much. During the course of Gu Qing's stay, Cuiqiao becomes interested in the army's life. As Gu Qing leaves, she asks him to take her with him. He states that he must ask for permission from the army leader first, and that he will return. Soon after Gu Qing leaves, Cuiqiao is married. At Yan'an, Gu Qing watches peasants waist-drum dancing for new party recruits going off to fight the Japanese. Back in the village one day, Cuiqiao helps Hanhan fetch water from the Yellow River and tells him that she is going to join the army. As her boat moves away from the shore, her voice is heard singing the army song that Gu Qing taught her, but it is soon drowned by the roaring sounds of the river. Gu Qing returns to the village the following spring, when the male peasants are praying for rain. In the chanting horde only Hanhan notices he has returned. Hanhan runs toward the soldier but is trapped amid the mass of dancing peasants moving in the opposite direction. The film ends with Cuiqiao's singing voice in an empty landscape: the words are from the army song, but the music is the "sour tune" we associate with her many times before.[7]

Insofar as *Yellow Earth* explores an early moment of the communist revolution with interest, and insofar as it tries to locate that interest in the possibility of social change brought by the soldier, we can say that there is a strong idealism in this film. If one side of this idealism is invested in the revolution, which is indicated by details as small as the soldier sewing, then the other side of it is invested in the "formidable energy and force of the peasants" that Chen wanted the film to express: "Although that energy is still blind and undirected, as long as it exists it has great potential if properly tapped and directed."[8] This double-edged idealism, however, is steadily undercut by the materiality of the film itself. At a time when "rural China" means not only poverty and illiteracy but the depletion of natural resources and massive ecological catastrophes, an exploration of the origins of "modern Chinese culture" cannot but be a questioning rather than a teleological end. Mythically and historically (since the Loess area is the oldest area where the Han Chinese civilization began), as well as politically, the film's "representation" of the "origins" of the communist party does not consolidate those origins but instead challenges the self-evident, idealist meanings that have been attached to each of these words—"Chinese," "communist," "party"—in official propaganda and popular patriotic thinking. The issue of social change is thus, from the very beginning, an undecidable one. Should social change continue to follow the party line, represented by the soldier? But the soldier's work is ineffectual; in the words of Paul

Clark, it leaves untouched a "people stuck on an earth that will not give them a livelihood."[9] If the party's conception of social change—"communism"—has failed, what does it mean for "Chinese" history, to which the party has supposedly brought the most fundamental changes in the past forty years? What does "Chinese" mean, and where does it go from here?

In an essay called "*Yellow Earth*: Western Analysis and a Non-Western Text," Esther C. M. Yau offers a careful reading of the film in terms of "narrative strands."[10] By pointing out the ambiguities of cultural production in an era "when China becomes a phenomenon of the 'post,' " Yau captures the difficulty facing directors who are concerned with the impossibility of political reform in a land that is "stubbornly resistant" (p. 26). Yau's analysis emphasizes the film's deployment of Daoist aesthetic principles in imagistic terms: "Consistent with Chinese art, Chang Imou's cinematography works with a limited range of colors, natural lighting, and a non-perspectival use of filmic space that aspires to a Taoist thought: 'Silent is the Roaring Sound, Formless is the Image Grand' " (p. 24).[11]

Although I fully agree with the predominance of a Daoist metaphysics in the film's use of graphic space, I feel uneasy about calling the appearance of that metaphysics on the movie screen simply "Chinese." This is not because the term "Chinese" does not matter. On the contrary, it is precisely because it does that it cannot be used in a such a way as to disregard the medium in which "what is Chinese" appears. In a way that is typical of the difficulty of cross-cultural criticism, Yau's reading enacts *in its mode of analysis* the tensions that underlie the articulation of ethnicity as agency. As her essay's subtitle ("Western Analysis and a Non-Western Text") indicates, Yau reads the film by separating her own enunciation from that of the film: hers is Western; the film's is Chinese. The question that arises, then, is this: how does a Westernized Chinese critic write about a "Chinese" film?

From the perspective of a taxonomically dichotomized "East versus West" as that espoused in Yau's essay, there is obviously nothing "Chinese" about, as Yau puts it, "sets of contemporary Western methods of close reading—cine-structuralist, Barthesian poststructuralist, neo-Marxist culturalist, and feminist discursive" (pp. 24–25). This tension between the "raw material" of the filmic text and the ineluctability of the Western analytic "technology" at the Westernized Chinese critic's disposal is expressed in the ironically apologetic remarks with which Yau prefaces her reading:

> This essay will address the above questions by opening up the text of *Yellow Earth* (as many modernist texts have been pried open) with sets of contemporary western methods of close reading—cine-structuralist, Barthesian poststructuralist, neo-Marxian culturalist, and feminist discursive. This will place *Yellow Earth* among the many parsimoniously plural texts and satisfy the relentless decipherers of signifieds and their curiosity for an oriental text. (pp. 24–25)

But are "native" critics not "relentless decipherers of signifieds" and curious about oriental texts as well? This passage polarizes West and East in the form of interpretation (subject) versus ethnicity (object), which can only result in the reduction of ethnicity to something that has no real active status in the production of interpretation.

My second objection: why should "native" critics reading with the instruments they have at hand—even though these instruments are Western—feel guilty about what they are doing? If these instruments are bloodied with the history of Western imperialism, it is our task to confront that history rather than pretend that there is some pristine, as-yet uncorrupted, ethnic "raw material" on the other side of the Western world. Pushed to its extreme, the guilt-ridden logic of Yau's rhetoric would have to mean only one thing—that we should not and cannot read a Chinese text in the West at all.[12]

The impasse resulting from this self-consciously well-intentioned but, to my mind, unnecessarily apologetic attitude on the part of the Westernized "native" critic toward using Western methodologies is an impasse that exists beyond any individual critic's responsibility and that impinges on the problems of cross-cultural criticism in general. This impasse leads to contradictions in the very terms of analysis themselves. In order to show the "Chineseness" of *Yellow Earth*, for instance, Yau alerts us to the analogy between the film and Daoism, reserving an implicitly privileged place for the latter because it is what frustrates the expectations of hermeneutical suturing in Western classical cinema: "Within the text of *Yellow Earth*, one may say, two kinds of pleasures are set up: a hermeneutic movement prompts the organization of cinematic discourse to hold interest, while the Taoist aesthetic contemplation releases that narrative hold from time to time" (p. 27).

And yet, this opposition between hermeneutics and Daoism is posed in a reading that, in spite of Yau's declared wariness of dominant Western theories of signification, discusses the film primarily as *text* and chooses *narrative* as its predominant explanatory mode. The four "narrative strands" offered by Yau—the peasant, the daughter, the soldier, and Hanhan—together produce a hermeneutics that subsumes even those elements that resist narrative because of their elusiveness, their extranarrative meanings.[13]

This privileging of narrative leads Yau to read the film, in a fashion typical of the contemporary identity politics in the West, as a "search for meaning" (p. 22) and, as she puts it in another essay, as a "process of intense struggle for identity."[14] Even though it is implicitly distrusted for its overtones of desire, then, it is hermeneutics that occupies the space of the critic's gaze at the film, while what is supposedly "Chinese" difference—the emptiness of space and the silence that are such a cardinal part of Daoist aesthetics—remains caught in the logic of a cultural symbolic to which it exists as the Other, the Unconscious, and the Beautiful. The logic of this cultural symbolic, because it rests on an absolute distinction between the "self" and the "other," helps legitimize the continued "othering" of the "third world" in the two paradigms, one leftist masculinist and the other liberal feminist, that I mentioned above—the paradigm of the other *nation* ("national allegory") and the paradigm of the other *woman-as-sexed-subject* (heterosexual erotics). Narrative is here not simply hermeneutically instrumental but politically so, imposing on nonnarrative filmic elements a mode of critical organization whose ultimate demand is that the "third world" own up its meanings.

The Problem of the Image

The dilemma of reading faced by the Westernized Chinese critic is in fact homologous to that faced by Chinese filmmakers in the 1980s. How to "make" films about China with a technology that is, theoretically speaking, non-Chinese?[15] This, I think, is precisely where the question of social change lies. If this is so, however, it would also mean that we need to pry social change from its conventionalized location in the politics of identity, which is bound to the representational strategies of narrative and subjectivity described earlier. The issue of ethnic agency—of the film's "Chineseness"—must instead be posed as a question and an uncertainty, which is the beginning, rather than the end, of cultural production. In what follows, I will show how, in the formal aspects of the film, it is the filmic image, often taken in isolation as a self-sufficient locus of meaning, that tends to be aligned with the politics of identity. In order to gauge the film's conception of social change, then, a mode of inquiry that takes us not only beyond narrative and subjectivity but also beyond the image is necessary.

Take what most reviewers consider to be the chief formal (and ethnic) interest of *Yellow Earth*—its Daoist aesthetics of nonpresence. Yau, for instance, says:

> Centrifugal spatial configurations open up to a consciousness that is not moved by desire but rather by the lack of it—the "telling" moments are often represented in extreme long shots with little depth when sky and horizon are proportioned to an extreme, leaving a lot of "empty spaces" within the frame. The tyranny of (socialist) signifiers and their signifieds is contested in this approach in which classical Chinese painting's representation of nature is deployed to create an appearance of a "zero" political coding. (p. 24)

Though entirely sympathetic with the film's imagistic effect, this passage leaves unasked the question as to the complicity between this " 'zero' political coding" and the technological aspects of production. What exactly has been "zeroed"? A zero political coding—which I would rephrase as a politically nonsignifying coding—is something we would have to abstract out of the film's materiality and idealize ahistorically through the realm of classical art. According to such a reading, the ethnic value of *Yellow Earth* would have to be argued along lines like these: Daoist aesthetics, that which is the most "Chinese" aspect of the film, is part of a post–Cultural Revolution critique of the communist revolution; if communism is "politics," then Daoism signifies the apolitical aestheticism of China's younger generation seeking refuge in pure form. (To this extent, one can understand why the film raised suspicions among mainland Chinese censors when it was first released.) Theorized as the site of a traditional, politically "zero" aesthetics, ethnicity is consigned to the place of an absolute "other" and guaranteed to be ineffectual.

On the other hand, if we consider the film in terms of its material makings, we would need to rethink the cognitive values of "emptiness" and "blankness" that are such a crucial part of the graphic representation in question here. There is, in a rudimentary way, something incompatible between the notion of emptiness and the notion of representation—especially graphic representation. In order to talk about "emptiness," art historians must do so by way of "arrangements of space" that are understood to be the counterpoints to *filled* representation. Even so, the understanding of space in graphic terms is bound to remain caught in a rigid binary opposition between presence, represented by visible objects, and absence, represented by blanks. The viewer, if he or she tries to make sense of "space," would still have to "view" space from a position whose *locality* would "see" nonsignifying blankness in terms of representational presence itself.

Similarly, in film criticism, "space" and "emptiness," though visually nonsignifying, are bound to become occasions for a *narrative* filling. Why belabor this paradox? Because in it lies the reason why an alternative (in this case ethnic) agency, in order to be politically effective, cannot simply be argued by way of imagistic *nonpresence* alone. The argument of "blanks" must be supplemented by a different kind of perception—one that understands space not as a graphic entity *captured* visually but as an *emptying* of representation, an experience-in-motion that is not particularized. It is in this context that I propose a reading of *Yellow Earth* in terms of music.

What Is Music?

Music here is not only the sound track that we hear but what defines the status of the image as well. The image becomes a kind of alibi, with its full signifying power giving way to a significance that is musical in effect. How?

If we ask why it is that certain images have left their effect on us, we notice that it is because they have been repeated in one way or another. For instance, Cuiqiao's "labor" is often indicated by the image of the bucket into which she pours the water from the Yellow River. Several times in the film, we see a still image of the bucket alongside the shore for such a duration of time that we begin to realize it is the only thing available to the eye. But what kind of "seeing" is possible here—with a bucket of water? Similarly, the interior of the peasants' cave home is repeatedly filmed against a background of light from the outside, so that instead of the fullness of lit representation, what we "see" in the foreground are subdued motions in relative darkness.

As that which repeats, however, music does not only structure the generation of specific images as described in these examples; it also motivates the plot. At the most obvious level, music is what the "story" is about: Gu Qing is collecting folk songs for the revolution. "Chairman Mao and all the army leaders like folk songs," he says. "We collect folk songs—to spread out—to let everyone know what we suffering people are sacrificing for, why we peasants need a revolution." Through the soldier's act of transcribing in a notebook, music becomes the site where the transparency between national identity, here represented by the party, and individual identity is forced: the peasants, the army, and the chairman merge into one.

But who are the peasants? This description by the twentieth-century Chinese woman writer Xiao Hong in the 1930s stands in stark contrast to the beefed-up images offered by official propaganda in the decades to come:

> They are the kind who don't know where light lies, but they truly feel the chill on their bodies. As they try to fight the chill, sorrow comes.

> Since they were born, they have never had hope. The only hope is having enough food and warm clothes. But there is not enough food, nor are there warm clothes.

They endure whatever ill fortune that comes. As for good for-
tunes—there is not a single one in their entire lives.[16]

Historically, what distinguished Chinese communism's strategies was
Mao's shrewd recognition of the need for allying with Chinese peasants
in order to accomplish the party's political goals. The peasants' sufferings become useful not only in the processes of economic production
but in ideological production as well. Unlike, say, Lenin, who repudiat-
ed rural blindness and superstitiousness, Mao's stated party aim was not
to "expose" the people's errors but to educate them.[17] By a crude theoretical reversal, the party and the entire nation were also to be "reedu-
cated" by the peasants through direct contact in the countryside. Like
their ancestors who compiled the earliest books of poetry from the people, the Chinese communist party seized upon peasant backwardness
and let it "sing." The collecting of folk songs carries with it this principle of unearthing and organizing an unconscious that is not psychical but
ecological: the peasants' naïveté, poverty, deprivation, and hopelessness
become tools of party propaganda and the backbone of party power. In
this sense alone, one can already argue that the "sparseness" of *Yellow
Earth*'s Daoist "aesthetics" is politically inscribed: this is the sparseness
of material well-being, a sparseness that has been tirelessly tapped for
the purposes of revolution.

The way music politically structures the development of all civilized
societies has been examined by Jacques Attali.[18] Music is, for Attali, an
appropriation of political power through its control of noise. By chan-
neling noise, which is violence, music effects "a sublimation, an exacer-
bation of the imaginary" that is at the same time "the creation of social
order and political integration" (p. 26). Among the ancients he quotes is
the Chinese historian Sima Qian in *Shi ji* (*Historical Record*): "The sacrifices and music, the rites and the laws have a single aim; it is through
them that the hearts of the people are united, and it is from them that
the method of good government arises" (p. 29).

How remarkable it is that *Yellow Earth* should, in spite of its idealism,
take as its starting point this time-proven means of political centraliza-
tion endorsed by the most highly revered historian in the Chinese tradition—for a deconstruction of the "origins" of the Chinese communist

party! This deconstruction leads to a fundamental questioning of politics and culture, a questioning that takes us beyond the national boundary of China, even though, when asked whether his intention in filmmaking is that of criticism, Chen restricts his response largely to the culture with which he is most familiar:

> If I must criticize, I'd much rather criticize culture—Chinese culture. Take the example of the Cultural Revolution. I've always felt that what accounts for the Cultural Revolution is traditional culture itself. . . . The Cultural Revolution repeats, continues, and develops this traditional culture. The emperor-like worship that was bestowed upon Mao Zedong, the devastation of basic human rights, the forced indoctrination of revolutionary reasoning—how do these differ from feudalist society? You can't simply call them a cancellation of culture; they were actually the malicious expansion of the worst part of our culture. (*Playboy*, pp. 46–47)

Chen's remarks make it clear how pointless it would be to view a film such as *Yellow Earth* in terms of the politics of identity formation. If the film begins with a *certain* identity—a party identity—in formation, it no sooner delivers that identity as a "narrative" than it plunges it into an openness that, arguably, enables criticism and change. From a radical point of view, the "worst part" of traditional Chinese culture, which prides itself on the strength of history and historiography, is precisely that which is explicitly dramatized from the beginning in *Yellow Earth*: the systematic transcribing of life into a record, which then assumes authority over life itself. Gu Qing's presence in the village is an extrapersonal presence that signifies the thorough nature of political intervention in civilian life. The form of such intervention? Recording.

Attali defines "recording" as follows:

> Recording has always been a means of social control, a stake in politics, *regardless of the available technologies*. Power is no longer content to enact its legitimacy; it records and reproduces the societies it rules. Stockpiling memory, retaining history or time, distributing speech, and manipulating information has always been

an attribute of civil and priestly power, beginning with the Tables of the Law. . . . The reality of power belonged to he who was able to reproduce the divine word, not to he who gave it voice on a daily basis. Possessing the means of recording allows one to monitor noises, to maintain them, and to control their repetition within a determined code. In the final analysis, it allows one to impose one's own noise and to silence others: "Without the loudspeaker, we could never have conquered Germany," wrote Hitler in 1938 in the *Manual of German Radio*. (p. 87; my emphasis)

Those of us watching the ways in which both the Western media "captured" the China crisis of June 1989 and the Chinese government's "reeducation" campaign afterward cannot but shudder at the descriptive accuracy of this passage.[19] Attali discusses recording in the more technical sense of machine recording, but we may generalize his argument to include activities of recording in different historical periods. Recording, which was invented to preserve representation (i.e., to protect a preceding mode of organization), becomes a technology that imposes a new social system—the social system of repetition and mass replication. The symbiotic relationship between representation and recording suggests that it is always a power struggle. Ultimately, the mode that repeats and that derives its power from mechanicity rather than from "spontaneity" is the one that reigns supreme over the other.

In a strictly modernist setting, Attali's argument reminds us of Walter Benjamin's "The Work of Art in the Age of Mechanical Reproduction,"[20] which argues that reproduction for resemblance—a human practice with a long history—finally reaches perfection in the days of the camera. And yet, Benjamin argues that man's arrival at reproductive perfection as such changes the nature of reproduction once and for all. If the point of reproduction has always been that of increasing resemblance or proximity to the original work, then reproduction in the age of photography replaces the notion of the "original" altogether. The "original" now becomes significant only for people like the collector, who Benjamin tells us is a species that is becoming extinct. Jean-Louis Comolli makes a similar argument in his essay "Machines of the Visible": "At the very same time that it is . . . fascinated and gratified by the multiplicity of scopic instruments which lay a thousand views beneath its gaze, the human eye loses its immemorial privilege; the mechanical eye of the photographic machine now sees *in its place*, and in certain aspects with more sureness."[21] In other words, by intensifying reproduction *numerically*, the processes of mechanical reproduction change reproduction from being a technique to a technology. This is the technology of *repetition*, which radicalizes every type of social relation in the form of "copies" or "simulacra."

What is fascinating about Chen's film is that, while it partakes of this posttechnological perceptiveness to recording, reproduction, and repetition, it uses that perceptiveness to critique the founding myths of the Chinese communist party.[22] By presenting the problem of recording at an "originary" moment of a socialist revolution such as the Chinese one, Chen reveals the fascistic (because mechanized) control of mass society that Western theorists are able to capture more readily in their own cultural contexts through the palpable forms of technical apparatuses but that are equally imminent in a modernized non-Western state.

The deeply thoughtful challenge that is put to the origins of the party takes place, however, not only at the level I have just described, which is the level of "thematic" motivation, but also provocatively through the film's self-consciousness—that is, its consciousness of its own implication in technology and history. Take this statement by Chen: "My thinking about culture begins the moment it is in ruins" (*Playboy*, p. 48). What is "in ruins" is not only the myth of communist progressiveness but also the notion that critique itself can stand independent of the machines that allow its articulation. Because *Yellow Earth* uses the cinematic apparatus inherited from the West, and because it circulates in the world film market, it becomes, like other films, an instrument for representing a certain China. The filming of the remote Shaanbei area *liberates* it from its geographical specificity and delivers it as an image to metropolitan areas. In Benjamin's sense, what constitutes the "aura" of the Loess landscape—the earth, the sky, the peasants, and their quiet way of life—disappears the moment we see it on the cinema screen, because what we see is already the result of a reassembling (of the "original") through technology and commodification. When the Chinese censors distrusted the film's ambiguous representations of peasants, who lack the usual positiveness given to them by official propaganda,[23] *Yellow Earth* was quickly acquiring international acclaim that silenced the derogatory opinions at home. The "value" of the film—as a "Chinese" product, as a representation of "China"—thus already exists in the form of alienated labor, which returns triumphantly to its home base only after its exchange function is established abroad. Since then, *Yellow Earth* itself has been reproduced in a variety of forms in other films. In a long list of titles made during the 1980s, including *Dao ma zei* (*Horse Thief*), *Xiang nü xiaoxiao* (*Girl from Hunan*), *Hong gaoliang* (*Red Sorghum*), and the previously discussed *Lao jing* (*Old Well*), the fascination with "old China" takes on spectacular dimensions. The exotic rural landscape, peasant life, women's subjugation to the patriarchal economy, and so forth become ingredients of a new "Chinese" commodity that has only recently begun circulation but is fast becoming popular worldwide.

Woman Asymmetricalizes

In its self-consciousness of the tension between itself as "product" on the one hand and as "technology" on the other, *Yellow Earth* remains unique in a way that is not equaled by other contemporary Chinese films. It uses a narrative but does not depend on narrative for its revelations; it delights in the literalness of the images it produces but continues to combat that literalness. The resistance to both the narrative and the visual hold on signification is finally a refusal to concede to a conception of social change that uses "identity" as its stomping grounds.

This is most evident in Cuiqiao's struggle against her fate. On this point Chen says:

> In a sombre mood if we meditate on the fact that this river gives life to all things, but by the same token can destroy all things, then we realise that the fate of Cuiqiao, who lived among the people of old China, had an inevitable tragic cast. The road she chooses is a very hard one. Hard, because she is not simply confronted by the malign forces of society in any narrow sense, but rather by the tranquil, even well-meaning, ignorance of the people who raised her.[24]

The historically loaded sadness of this fate is not expressed through any significant narrative. We never directly know Cuiqiao's feelings about her life. Her most direct expression is given in the tune that is filled with a different set of words each time. For instance:

> *In the sixth month the ice in the River hasn't thawed,*
> *It's my own father who is dragging me to the wedding board.*
> *Of all the five grains, the bean is the roundest,*
> *Of all the people, daughters are the saddest.*
> *Up in the sky pigeons fly, one with the other,*
> *The only dear one that I long for is my mother.*[25]

The words of Cuiqiao's song tell of the victimization of women in rural China. They confirm the cruelty expressed by Cuiqiao's father in his conversation with Gu Qing while they are ploughing the land. In that conversation, we learn that Cuiqiao's sister has already experienced the same fate and that the old man thinks that women would be happy as long as they have food. The oppressive overtones of what in a different context would be straightforward misogyny must be understood here as part of the chronically impoverished nature of the lives of Chinese peasants. In a land where no one is spared, one seeks "relief" by displacing oppression onto the ones who have some exchange value—hence the fate of marriage that awaits peasant girls like Cuiqiao.

The significance of Cuiqiao, then, is aligned with her singing. But how? In an article that explores the problem of the "feminizing" of music in film, Carol Flinn defines music as "cinema's irrational and theoretically recalcitrant contributor."[26] Flinn argues that music occupies an uncertain place in film because it is always understood in terms of dominant representational aesthetics. While music is, through feminized metaphors, equated with raw emotionalism, direct expression, and a kind of meaninglessness, it also is "forced to take as its starting point the image" and "serves to anchor and reinforce—even in counterpoint—the visual meanings of the film."[27] Flinn's argument enables us to see the difficulty of interpreting a character like Cuiqiao. Because her awareness of her fate—an awareness that we might call "subjectivity"—is given to us primarily in the songs she sings, it occupies the uncertain status that music has in cinema in the terms suggested. Is Cuiqiao's song simply a reinforcement of the narrative/imagistic signification of the film—as "Chinese" difference (the "national allegory" reading)? Or is it the direct expression of her emotions—her subjectivity as "woman" (the "heterosexual erotics" reading)?

It is, I think, neither. As she sings for Gu Qing, Cuiqiao's voice becomes, in the words of Kaja Silverman, "doubly diegeticized"[28] in the sense that it is a voice heard in a recording within a recording—the recording of the Eighth Route soldier that is within the recording of the filmic apparatus. Silverman associates the female voice with the "interiority" that "implies linguistic constraint, physical confinement—confinement to the body, to claustral spaces, and to inner narratives."[29] This association of sound and femininity would apply in *Yellow Earth* if we, for the time being, isolate the *words* of Cuiqiao's song for interpretation. As we do this, we would be describing her significance in terms of a speaking subject whose inner narrative has been suppressed. The meaning of this inner narrative is its own futility. Thus, as she performs passionately for the soldier in the scene in which they say goodbye ("Brother Gu, take out your notebook!"), Cuiqiao's concluding words are "Even folk songs cannot save me." The musicality of her song, however, takes us beyond this paradigm of "interiority." The uniqueness of Cuiqiao lies somewhere else.

It lies, one may say, in the way Chen refuses the facile optimism of giving Cuiqiao's "fate" a humanistically signifying power. Like the "empty" scenes of the land, the sky, and the river, Cuiqiao's tune punctuates the "narrative" of the film. The scenes of her singing are almost always done away from the light. As Cuiqiao sings, we often do not see her mouth moving with the words of the song: it is as if the song, which occurs because of the quest/request of the socialist program, breaks away from the humanly specific and emanates from nowhere and everywhere.[30] The status of Cuiqiao's singing must therefore be understood as much through its pitch, its rhythm, its lyrical elusiveness, and its referentless resonances as through its verbal content. Its significance is to be found *between* exteriority and interiority, in an interplay between the "subjective, immediate realm" and its "external representation."[31]

The reader would sense that I am going against the lessons we have learned from Western feminism in the way I accede to a certain equation between music, femininity, and what might be called the nonsignifying. But the assertion of woman's rise to speech would be a false approach to the problems raised in this context. Indeed, one of the challenges posed by the new Chinese cinema is precisely this: not the search for a particular alternative agency but the acceptance of the radicalness of "elusiveness" in a context where politics, as the omnipresently agential, systematically wipes out the elusive.

What the elusiveness of Cuiqiao's voice suggests is that "woman," especially the rural woman, cannot (yet) be collapsed into the happy narrative of a new nation in formation. Rural women are not simply the other but rather the other of the other of the other (if one starts with the West and moves from there to China, to China's remote areas, then to the women in these areas). The status of the rural woman, apart from the definite but coerced contribution she has been making to the economy of the land, is uncertain. The diegesis shows that her singing is triggered by the soldier's organization of culture. But she has been suffering and singing for centuries unheard, and will continue doing so. What can be collected and recorded?

Instead of making Cuiqiao's songs the loci of her "subjectivity," I propose understanding them as instances of the *objet petit a*[32] whose import is both political and metaphysical. Jacques Lacan, we remember, defines the *objet petit a* as "bound to the orifices of the body."[33] The partial object is "something from which the subject, in order to constitute itself, has separated itself off as an organ."[34] The constitution of the subject is, in other words, impossible without some process of displaced longing, or "fetishizing."

If, going against the predominantly *visual* and *narrative* logic in which Freud's argument about the fetish is cast,[35] we locate the imaginary recaptivity of our "lack" through music, which we receive through the orifices of the ears and the skin, then what kinds of things can be said about partial objects and fetishism? The voice, considered this way, is not necessarily the locus of a metaphysical "presence" that Jacques Derrida's early work on the logos, in an attempt to emphasize and deconstruct the culturally loaded nature of an inscriptive paradigm (the paradigm that privileges the human voice), argues that it is.[36] Rather, like Derrida's "writing," this music already embodies the segmentation and disappearance of presence, in a way that is definable only in terms of "différance."

The music of Cuiqiao's voice should be understood as the struggle between politics as record and politics as the production of difference. As a performance for the soldier, her singing is a fetish for the elusive plenitude that is the vast peasantry in the hinterland and that the communist party uses for its defense against the eruption of ideological disorder. In Attali's words, music fetishized this way is describable as a "primary function" that is "not to be sought in aesthetics . . . but in the effectiveness of its participation in social regulation" (p. 30). Cuiqiao's performance epitomizes the process in which peasant labor is commodified and undergoes a "passage from usage to stockpiling" (p. 126).

On the other hand, Cuiqiao's music is also where the origins of political organization are deconstructed and revealed most powerfully—in what I would call a cognitive slow motion. The "fetish" of sensual music is not only the occasion for the party's documentation but also where the visual, narrative logic of fetishizing with its tendency toward particularization, localization, and fixed identification—all of which contribute toward party authority—is combatted. Cuiqiao's singing moves, lives, can be heard, yet cannot be seen. It is a singing in which she longs for her mother; but her mother, like the music itself, is not particularized or particularizable because she is dead. A singing unheard by specific ears, a longing unanswered by specific objects: this is the way "woman" is musicalized for a fundamental questioning of the party's logic.

In the scene where Cuiqiao is crossing the Yellow River, she sings the army song that Gu Qing taught her, but the song fades with the roaring sounds of the river, which drown the final words, preventing the completion of the phrase *gongchandang*—"communist party." Does Cuiqiao die? Does she cross the river and join the party? We do not know. "Common sense" suggests the former. The only certainty we have is that she bravely rejects her traditional role in the rural family and her implication in the land, the unconscious that is the raw material for socialized production and that reduces her to a reproductive function in a submissive relation to patriarchy. This "No!" is displaced, in a nonparticularized, nonpartialized way, onto the singing that subsequently disappears with her personal disappearance but returns to end the film against a scene of the land and the sky.

In sharp contrast to other scenes in which sound is produced by traditional folk music, performance, or amplification of people's eating and breathing noises, Cuiqiao's singing is frequently followed by an orchestral score, the kind of musical backing that the rest of the film fastidiously avoids. If orchestration, insofar as it evokes an emotional response from us, means the return of a narrative and thus some kind of collective "identity," what is the effect of such orchestration here? Precisely because it always occurs when Cuiqiao is the loneliest (singing by herself), the score can be regarded as a stylized, conventionalized way of conjuring empathy at a place—Cuiqiao's life—where, in fact, the oppressiveness of history needs to be confronted head-on rather than sentimentalized. In the guise of "accompanying" and "supporting" Cuiqiao, the orchestrated backing functions rather like an ideology that tries to subordinate her story to a false—because artificially produced and amplified—sense of harmony with the community.[37]

For Chen, Cuiqiao's singing thus signifies, through femininity but not at the expense of femininity, that refusal to concede to the literalness of the "sad woman's story" that comes across accessibly through the filmic image. As such, "woman" *asymmetricalizes*: she intensifies the feelings of oppression and victimization and enables a politicized understanding of the film's "aesthetics," but she does not allow for any definite identification. The idealism of Chen's conception of "woman," we may say, lies in an ultimate split between her words and her music: though the words that fill Cuiqiao's singing voice at the end harmonize with the "story" of the soldier ("The people's salvation all depends on our communist party"), her reverberant music disembodies those words, dissolving in them the "logical machinery to secure emotive particularity."[38] Chen's idealism is evident in these comments: "Cuiqiao is Cuiqiao; Cuiqiao is not-Cuiqiao. She is both concrete and transcendent. From her we can see the hope for our people."[39]

Partial Defense, Cultural Crisis, and Composition

If, in Silverman's words, "classic cinema has the potential to reactivate the trauma of symbolic castration within the viewer, and . . . puts sexual difference in place as a partial defense against that trauma,"[40] then the system of defense set up by a film such as *Yellow Earth* is not sexual difference but the Daoist principle of nonpresence. This system, as we know, has fascinated Western artists and intellectuals on visual terms because of its divergence from the pictorial perspectivism that characterizes Western art. Such fascination has led to laudatory descriptions like this one: "Chinese landscape paintings . . . avoid leading the eye into a single depth, stretching out the viewpoint instead along the entire panorama, so that their mountains and water-falls all appear to be moving toward us."[41]

As I have been trying to argue, however, the conception of ethnic "difference" ("Chinese," "Eastern," and so forth) purely in terms of a visual nonpresence or a pictorial aperspectivism—a pure space—remains politically ineffectual because of the predetermined—that is, presence- and perspective-oriented—nature of the criteria used. In this sense, the "visual difference" set up in *Yellow Earth*, like all systems of defense, is partial. The point, though, is not to come up with a "whole" and "foolproof" defense. The significance of "music" here is not that it replaces one defense system (the visual) with another (the auditory) but that, by putting pure space in motion, it accentuates the contradictions inherent in representation-as-reproduction.

On film, features of Daoist principles that create the effect of a nonanthropocentric "emptiness" come to the fore so visibly and *largely* (in a way that is not matched by classical Chinese painting) can do so because of a repetition—through the camera—that also ruins its originariness and its purity. Through the intervention of the camera, the quietistic principles of Daoism are now juxtaposed with the noise of the mass market. The nonanthropocentric Daoist aesthetics now meets the inhuman mechanicity of photographic technology face to face—in collision. Tradition is not simply there, but invoked idealistically, at a time when it is "in ruins"—for what is already a technologized mass defense against the imminent processes of appropriation.

In this regard, aesthetically minded critics who notice the persistence of Daoism in the new Chinese cinema but who see cinema as a "preservation" of Chinese cultural patterns[42] are, precisely by ignoring the film's technological materiality, repeating the "recording" principle of governmental culture that Chen's film so remarkably challenges. The film becomes in the "preservation" reading merely a modern-day transcript of the aesthetics that is eternal. Ironically, on the other hand, the literary historian who does not look for an eternal aesthetics but reads film primarily in terms of the *literary* tradition is rightly distrustful—from his elite, cultivated point of view—of the fascination with the mechanical that the new Chinese films, in spite of their fondness for Daoist aesthetics, exhibit. Thus Leo Ou-fan Lee, in a statement that reveals (albeit in a way unintended by him perhaps) that the interest in Daoism is not the heart of the matter in the new cinema, writes: "The obsession with sheer mechanical technique is a reflection of the 'modernization' drive—yet in my view a very 'vulgar' way to modernize."[43] Because of his fine breeding and his dedication to the scholarly tradition, the literary historian is not easily distracted by the Beautiful that appears on the movie screen: he immediately senses the danger of a much more drastic change, a change that threatens the very conception of the aesthetic as refinement, as literary cultivation, as good taste itself. As Paul Clark observes with regard to *Yellow Earth*: "Here is a film that knows it is a film."[44] In other words, what is often thought of as a major factor of the "Chineseness" of the new Chinese cinema—its deployment of "traditional" Daoist aesthetics—is in fact the rendering of that traditional aesthetics *in film*, which turns classical good taste into "vulgar" mass culture and puts ethnic and national "origins" in crisis.

This notion of crisis is nowhere clearer than in two scenes of music toward the end of the film—the peasants' waist-drum dance at Yan'an and the prayer for rain back in the village. As musical events, these scenes demonstrate what Attali calls the "channelization of noise" by primitive societies as a way to effect social order and political integration (p. 26). At the same time, there is another, less obvious sense of music in operation here—music as repetition and recurrence. In both scenes, a sensitivity to the limits of the image (as representation, as graphic record of culture) transforms into a self-conscious *replication* of the image itself. Because the images are repeated not simply over the duration of time (which is the usual meaning of repetition) but also through identical arrangements of the mass in single picture frames, what comes across is a physical sense of uniformity and of men in collectivity—what we might call *a making of music in recurrent space as well as time*. Like the final scenes of the People's Liberation Army marching in formation in front of Tiananmen Square in Chen's *The Big Parade*, these scenes enact sensations of orderliness that result from a *quantitative* representation, a simple duplication of numbers. But what happens after the orderliness of numbers? No sooner is the sensation of orderliness accomplished than an awareness of repetition as "the stockpiling of sociality" (Attali, p. 88) becomes inevitable. Such stockpiling is the ultimate transformation—the ultimate crisis—of traditional Chinese life in the modern age. In Attali's words:

The crisis of repetition announces a form of crisis different from the one to which we are accustomed in the schemas of representation. Crisis is no longer a breakdown, a rupture. It is no longer dissonance in harmony, but excess in repetition, lowered efficiency in the process of the production of demand, and an explosion of violence in identity. It is far less easy to conceptualize, and much more difficult to circumscribe, than that of representation. (p. 130)

The busy and crowded images of the last scenes in *Yellow Earth* are therefore a musical way of signaling that "emptiness" toward which Daoist aesthetics gestures. But it is not emptiness per se but the act of emptying and struggling that confronts us. This act is poignantly present in the scene in which Hanhan runs toward Gu Qing. A residual idealism about the party is deconstructed in slow motion: as the speechless child—the stand-in for China's future—tries to go where the soldier is, the frantic mass traps him by moving in the opposite direction. Is the mass responsible for its own catastrophic fate? The blindness of the mass contrasts sharply with the clarity with which the figure of the soldier reappears on the horizon—alone, specific, directed. But is this particularized clarity not also questionable? From where does it arise? The film leaves us with a cognitive repetition and roughening of the oppression whose true origins remain ambiguous with historical weight.

Chen's consciousness of the crisis of the Chinese culture as a modern culture implicated in senseless repetition aligns him with modernist writers such as Samuel Beckett and Eugene Ionesco, and earlier, with the Gustave Flaubert of *Bouvard et Pécuchet*.[45] Chen himself explicitly compares the experience of his generation of directors with the post–Second World War writers and directors in Europe:

I feel that it is not an accident that we can make the films we do now. It's due entirely to the fact that we grew up during the Cultural Revolution. This is like the writers and directors who emerged after the Second World War. The war was their childhood and their adolescence, so they had a special sensitivity and perceptiveness toward the war and toward the lies brought by civilization. As for us, we were full of dreams to build a strong China;

we were full of ethnic pride and consciousness, and yet the Cultural Revolution suddenly made us understand that it was all nothing. (*Playboy*, p. 44)

What makes such comparisons with the European writers quickly unuseful, however, is the timing with which such expressions of crisis appear in China's new cinema. Instead of concluding that China, because it has closed its doors to the world until recently, is experiencing belatedly the existential angst and artistic experimentation that Europe and America already went through during an earlier chronological period, we may pose the problem differently: what is it that enables Chinese intellectuals on the mainland to produce works that are so relevant to the contemporary West *in spite of* the extremely limited resources with which they must work? How is it that a film such as *Yellow Earth* speaks so germanely to the repetitive logic of late capitalist society in its making, when China has not, properly speaking, undergone the full development of capitalism itself? These questions cannot be dealt with by relegating the new Chinese cinema to an "other" position. Instead, they point beyond the isolation of cultural exceptionalism to the global issues that "third world" cinema—precisely because its modes of articulation inevitably conjure the historical relations between "East" and "West"—forces us to recognize.

In his discussion of *Yellow Earth*, Clark says: "Yan'an and all that it implies in terms of heroism and austerity, may have become . . . remote and the stuff of dreams for the generations."[46] Are dreams a matter of looking back or of looking forward? *Yellow Earth* suggests that they are both. As a bold retrospective exploration of the founding moments of the Chinese communist party, it recasts the tyranny of cultural recording in the form, to use Martin Heidegger's phrase, of a "world picture."[47] But what distinguishes Chen's works from the primarily visual conception of modernity that Heidegger gives us is their refusal to submit to the literalness of the cinematic image, no matter how alluring that image is. This insistence on the significance of something *other* than the most accessible aspect of filmic production characterizes all of Chen's films up to and including *Life on a String*, in a way that puts him in great contrast to his equally remarkable contemporary Zhang Yimou. As I will argue in the following chapter, the fascination with technology in Chen's work is an inherent part of what Ma Ning, writing in a different context, calls the "process of deconstruction" in Chinese cinema.[48] Deconstruction is not destruction but a taking-apart of tradition as ideology that is at the same time a *production of differences*. Paradoxically, deconstruction understood in these terms is comparable to the notion of "composition" with which Attali concludes his book. Susan McClary comments: "Attali's usage returns us to the literal components of the word, which quite simply means 'to put together.' "[49] To compose is "to take pleasure in the instruments, the tools of communication, in use—time and exchange—time as lived and no longer as stockpiled" (Attali, p. 135). Attali describes "composition" as the musical practice that follows and outdates the monopolizations of power he respectively refers to as sacrifice, representation, and repetition:

> When power wants to make people *forget*, music is ritual *sacrifice*, the scapegoat; when it wants them to *believe*, music is enactment, *representation*; when it wants to *silence* them, it is reproduced, normalized, *repetition*. Thus it heralds the subversion of both the existing code and the power in the making, well before the latter is in place.

> Today, in embryonic form, beyond repetition, lies freedom: more than a new music, a fourth kind of musical practice. It heralds the arrival of new social relations. Music is becoming *composition*. (P. 20; emphases in the original)

The meanings of that weighty word *reform*, which Chen uses to discuss his vision of China in the future, may be glimpsed from the essentially *compositional* nature of his filmmaking. What emerges in this filmmaking is not a mode of resistance by way of a particular agency (which may be located in women, the proletariat, and so forth, with their alternative subversive "gazes") but rather one by way of a nonparticularized intervention that is based on a deconstruction of tradition as a production of difference. What kind of difference? If Western cinema (including some of its radicalized others such as women's films) is predominantly structured by desire, then in a film like *Yellow Earth* it is aphanisis, the "fading of the subject" as Lacan defines it, that becomes the organizing principle. When "subjecthood" has always been (within) the possession of the state with its weapons for eavesdropping, censorship, recording, and surveillance (Attali, p. 7), aphanisis means not the end of human action but a reopening of the avenues that have been foreclosed by official violence. It is another way of announcing, with deconstruction and composition, that which is "perhaps the most difficult thing to accept: henceforth *there will be no more society without lack*" (Attali, p. 147, emphasis in the original).

One may object, of course, that it is precisely the awareness of such "lack" that leads to the assertion of partialized meanings. This is the old story. For Chinese filmmakers in the 1980s, the awareness of lack has to mean something else. Most of all it means a conscious effort to resist the complacent, preemptive "self-sufficiency" or completeness that is fantasized at the national, cultural, and personal levels; it also means a putting together of new directions in which lived experience, however self-contradictory, rather than revolutionary rhetoric, makes way for social change. *This* awareness of lack—as incomplete, lived experience—is, as the ultraconservative members of the Chinese government call the protesters for freedom and democracy in 1989, *counterrevolutionary*. Instead of revolution, it indicates the necessity for an "abstract utopia" (Attali, p. 145) in a culture in which "politics" has so far meant only a devastating official presence in all aspects of personal life. When all conceivable spaces of social relations have for so long been occupied and thus demolished by centralized state power, the fading of the subject and the awareness of lack are not a matter of being apolitical; they are major ways of reconceptualizing the basis of political power itself. Attali writes: "Just as what is essential in a philosophy is not in what it says, but in what it does not say, the future of an organization is not in its existence, but in its opposite, which reveals its mutation. Today, the future is in our lacks, our suffering, and our troubles" (p. 44).

As if in an unconscious rejoinder to Attali, Chen instructed his film crew: "The quintessence of our style can be summed up in a single word: 'concealment.' "[50]

Thus *Silent Is the Ancient Plain*: this was the title for the original screenplay of *Yellow Earth*, which was adapted from a script written by Zhang Ziliang in 1983.[51] When the first work print of the film was produced, its beautiful colors led the producers to adopt the name *Yellow Earth*.[52] Like the generations of artists who, as Eisenstein tells us, were dazzled by the complex sensual meanings of the color yellow,[53] the Chinese filmmakers opted for a name that gives priority to the image rather than to sound, even when the original conception was musical and not imagistic. This naming, then, is the film's first concealment and difference from itself, directing critical as well as spectatorial attention to a location of illusionism that it nonetheless continues to subvert. Chen's work plays a "truly revolutionary music"—"not music which expresses the revolution in words, but which speaks of it as a lack" (Attali, p. 147).[54]

Male Narcissism and National Culture:

Subjectivity in Chen Kaige's *King of the Children*

Part 1: The Detour

How many [teachers] (the majority) do not even begin to suspect the "work" the system (which is bigger than they are and crushes them) forces them to do, or worse, put all their heart and ingenuity into performing it with the most advanced awareness. . . . So little do they suspect it that their own devotion contributes to the maintenance and nourishment of this ideological representation of the School.

Louis Althusser, "Ideology and Ideological State Apparatuses: Notes towards an Investigation"

The history of the "educated" ought to be materialistically presented as a function of and in close relation to a "history of uneducation."

Walter Benjamin, *Moscow Diary*

Like living things, words and phrases undergo fates inconceivable at their moments of birth. In contemporary Chinese writings, especially

Male Narcissism and National Culture

of the kind that we encounter in the media—newspaper articles, reviews in nonacademic journals, and popular political discourses—we run, from time to time, across this phrase, which is used to suggest the determinacy of hope: *lu shi ren zou chu lai de* (roads are made by men). Because of the phrase's popularized nature, I have no need to cite specific examples. (Those who read regularly in Chinese would recognize what I am saying immediately.) The by now idiomatic nature of this phrase shows us how an expression of hope can be standardized through mass usage.

The phrase originated in a passage from the ending of Lu Xun's "Guxiang" ("My Old Home," 1921). This is, among other things, a story that tells of the changed relationship between the narrator and his childhood friend, Runtu, a member of the servant class. Once equals in the world of children's play, the two adult men's reencounter is shaped by a class-consciousness that becomes painful for the narrator. Even though, on first seeing Runtu again, the narrator keeps to the old familial appellation *Runtu ge* (older brother Runtu), Runtu addresses him from the place of a servant: *laoye* (old master). As in all of Lu Xun's fiction, the gap between the intellectual narrator, who belongs to the educated class, and the oppressed "others" who make up the contents of his story-telling intensifies as the narrative progresses. In "My Old Home," this gap is "filled" at the end by a reflection on hope. Thinking of hope, the narrator becomes aware of its idolatrous nature. Does his reliance on "hope" not make him more similar to Runtu than he first imagined? The difference, he writes, is perhaps simply that between an accessible and an intangible idol: "The access of hope made me suddenly afraid. When Runtu had asked for the incense-burner and candlesticks I had laughed up my sleeve at him, to think that he was still worshipping idols and would never put them out of his mind. Yet what I now called hope was no more than an idol I had created myself. The only difference was that what he desired was close at hand, while what I desired was less easily realized."[1]

After asserting the equality between himself and a member of the lower class at the point of his departure from the place in which Runtu is probably stuck for life, the narrator concludes his tale with the passage on hope that subsequently gave rise to the idiomatic phrase "roads are made by men." Lu Xun's text goes as follows: "I thought: hope cannot be said to exist, nor can it be said not to exist. It is just like roads across the earth. For actually the earth had no roads to begin with, but when many men pass one way, a road is made."[2]

Why is Lu Xun's passage instructive for a discussion of contemporary Chinese culture? Thematically, Lu Xun's works stage the problems that continue to haunt Chinese intellectuals: the impossibility of effective social change, the unbridgeable gap between the educated class and the "people," and the fantastical nature of any form of "hope." What comes across in Lu Xun's passage is the awareness that hope is at best a form of wager. Hope is, by nature, indeterminate, but people can, if there are large numbers of them, consciously steer it in one direction. Lu Xun's text itself, however, does not do that. Instead it remains, in a way that is ironic to the positive interpretation that has been imposed upon it since, in a state that can be referred to in Chinese as *wuke naihe* (having no alternative), *wuke wubuke* (not caring one way or another), *moleng liangke* (equivocal or ambiguous). The text's originary indeterminacy, in other words, is what enables its subsequent politicized appropriation. The interpretative production of the affirmative phrase "roads are made by men" is thus itself a historical materialization of the arbitrary process of road making that Lu Xun describes: as more people pass one way, a road is made.

A return to the relationship between the elusiveness of an originary textual moment and its eventual honed version indicates a way of understanding the notion of the "people" and "mass" in political processes. One could say that the power of the people or mass lies in the form of an indeterminacy. Precisely because they are undecided, they can go one way or another. For something—history—to happen, it would take a forcing—an accident perhaps—in a definite direction. The new direction as such, however, always retains its originally arbitrary character.

Lu Xun's tactical understanding of the arbitrary nature of politics, though not directly stated, is implied in the way "hope" always appears as a figure of enigma in his fictional texts.[3] Because it is always *to be* decided—or arbitrated—hope cannot be known for certain in the present. We can now understand why there are often what appear to be inexplicable shifts in narrative moods in his stories. Marston Anderson comments that such narrative shifts have led Lu Xun's critics to classify his work in two apparently contradictory fashions, as satiric realist, and as reminiscent and lyrical.[4] This contradiction is a politically truthful one. In the subsequent reappraisals and criticisms of the writings from the 1920s and 1930s launched by the Chinese communists, such political truthfulness was threatening because it did not cooperate or conform with the absolute clarity of direction laid down by the party. One could say that the orthodox communist criticism of textual elusiveness such as Lu Xun's implies this question: if there is hope, why are you writers not more assertive? A more programmatic, indeed official, representation of the people and of hope therefore increasingly came to replace the kind of uncompromised incisiveness in Lu Xun's perception. However, the issues embedded in the "making of roads" do not disappear. Although the short-story form became impermissible with the new social orthodoxy in the decades after Lu Xun's death, the problems it poses, precisely because they pertain to fundamental questions of morality, "raise their head every time there is a political thaw."[5]

As a figure of wager, hope can, I think, be redefined through "subjectivity." "Subjectivity" is one of those "politically incorrect" words that conjure up notions of "bourgeois idealism" for orthodox Marxist critics. Terry Eagleton, for instance, disapproves of it from the viewpoint of a Western European, supposedly post-Althusserian Marxist literary criticism, as a category tainted with "intransigent individualism": "It remains the case that the subject of semiotic/psychoanalytic theory is essentially the *nuclear* subject."[6] While I disagree with Eagleton, I find his statement useful in helping to clarify the Chinese situation. In Chinese communist scholarship, it is common to hear the same kind of ideological objection to the "subjective," which is mapped onto such expressions as *zhuguan* (subjective view), *weixin zhuyi* (idealism; literally, "heartism"), and so on. In a period in which cognition is intertwined with issues of politics, and in which creative energies have to be channeled toward fighting for the national cause, the literary forms that can be viewed as paradigms of explorations of subjectivity, such as biographies, autobiographies, diaries, first-person narratives, and narratives that deal explicitly with issues of sexuality, tend to live brief lives and remain subordinated to the more conventionally "public" concerns of history and realism.

If, on the other hand, we dislodge subjectivity from the narrow "nuclear" mode in which Eagleton puts it and instead understand it in terms of the material relationships among human beings as participants in a society—relationships that are in turn mediated by the collective cultural activities of speaking, reading, and writing—then it is an issue that is as forcefully present in modern Chinese literature and culture as it is in the West, even if it is not named as such.

I suggest that the predominant subjectivity that surfaces in the May Fourth period (mid-1910s to around 1930) is not so much a dense psychic "self," impenetrable and solipsistic, as a relationship between the writer, his or her object of narration, and the reader. In political terms, this is the relationship between Chinese intellectuals, the Chinese national culture, and "the people." In the writing of fiction, this relationship always presents itself as a question rather than a solution: how do we write (construct images of our culture) in order to relate to "the people"—*especially those who are socially inferior and powerless, since they are the ones who constitute the "mass" of the nation?* As such, subjectivity, even when it appears in the most "subjective" or "privatized" forms (as for instance in Yu Dafu's writings), is incomprehensible apart from its fundamental implication in the question of national culture. At the same time, it is also this tenacious relation with national culture that makes the differences between intellectuals and the masses (differences generated by the activity of literary production) a continual source of tension between Chinese intellectuals and the party state, as both hold claims to the indeterminate "mass," for whom they both want to speak.[7]

If we rethink the history of modern Chinese literature along these lines, that is, if we regard "history" as a matter of the contending claims made by the state and Chinese intellectuals on "the Chinese people"—a figure as enigmatic as hope itself—then it becomes necessary to ask how "the Chinese people" are represented. Through what kinds of aesthetic displacements and idealizations are they "constituted"?

Typically, "the Chinese people" are displaced onto figures of the powerless. Hence, I think, the large numbers of social inferiors who appear in the texts of modern Chinese literature. Literature is no longer, in the modern world, about the lives of emperors; rather, it is about the oppressed classes—the wretched of the earth. Other than the positivistic view that these are "realistic portrayals" of modern history, what else can we say about such frequent—indeed epochal—representations of the underprivileged? In other words, why does the conception and construction of a modern national culture—if writing in the postimperialistic "third world" is in part about that—take the form of an *aesthetic* preoccupation with the figures of the powerless? What does it say in terms of the things that we have been talking about—hope, the making of roads, and subjectivity?

Of all the figures of the powerless, the child is at center stage. One would need to include here not only stories about children, whether from the lower or from the upper classes, but also the autobiographical narratives in which Chinese writers look back to their childhood as a source for their current literary production. (The list of writers here is long: Lu Xun, Ba Jin, Bing Xin, Ding Ling, Ye Shengtao, Guo Moruo, Xiao Hong, Shen Congwen, Ling Shuhua, Luo Shu, Zhu Ziqing, Xu Dishan, and many others.) It is as if the adult thinking about China and the Chinese people always takes the route of memory in which the writing self connects with the culture at large through a specific form of "othering"—the presumably not yet acculturated figure of the child. In this light, the continuity among Chinese intellectuals from the May Fourth to the present period could be traced in another one of Lu Xun's enigmatic narrative endings, that of "Kuangren riji" ("The Diary of a Madman," 1918): "Jiujiu haizi . . ." ("Save the Children . . ."). At Yan'an in 1942, Mao Zedong would end a speech on art and literature with a couplet from Lu Xun about children, to which he supplies his own politicized interpretation:

This couplet from a poem by Lu Hsun should be our motto:

> *Fierce-browed, I coolly defy a thousand pointing fingers,*
> *Head-bowed, like a willing ox I serve the children.*

The "thousand pointing fingers" are our enemies, and we will never yield to them, no matter how ferocious. The "children" here symbolize the proletariat and the masses. All Communists, all revolutionaries, all revolutionary literary and art workers should learn from the example of Lu Hsun and be "oxen" for the proletariat and the masses, bending their backs to the task until their dying day.[8]

Mao's interpretation empowers the figure of the powerless child by renaming it as the proletariat and the masses. Ultimately, it is by giving this enigmatic figure, "the Chinese people," a specific politicized shape that the party state succeeded in mobilizing popular sympathies. The "powerless" is thus turned around representationally and becomes the means to construct national culture on a "concrete" basis. The utilitarian nature of this process of empowerment is familiar to all of us. The "masses," because they are "powerless," should, ideally speaking, be users of intellectuals, who are now at their *service*.

But service here clusters around another figure—the ox/cow. Lu Xun uses this figure in a such a way as to recall not only China's agrarian origins but also the familiar and familial process, traceable to images in classical art and poetry, of the affectionate playing between adults and children in which adults act as toy cows on which children ride. The image of "intellectuals becoming oxen for the masses" is thus intertwined with the realm of meanings associated with children, parents, kinship, and genealogy—a realm of meanings that Mao removed—or at least shifted away—from Lu Xun's couplet in order to consolidate his own analysis of Chinese society and its need for revolution in terms of "class" and "class struggle."[9] In ways that exceed Mao's restrictive political purpose, however, Lu Xun's image stages the philosophical struggles between the state and intellectuals over the "Chinese people" in terms of *reproduction* that continue to this day.

The components of this image—intellectuals, oxen, the masses—are what make up Chen Kaige's *Haizi wang* (*King of the Children*; Xian Film Studio, 1987), a film based on the novel of the same title by A Cheng (1984).[10] The story of *King of the Children* takes place in the post–Cultural Revolution period in a rural area. Lao Gan, the narrator and protagonist, is posted to a school after spending years in a production unit. A Cheng's story focuses on Lao Gan's relationship with his young students and the changes he introduces in their methods of learning. Before he came, the students had "learned" by copying texts that their former teachers had copied onto the blackboard. Seeing how futile this is, Lao Gan teaches them how to read, character by character, and then proceeds to teach them composition. One student, Wang Fu, gradually emerges as the most outstanding one through his hard work. His special relationship with Lao Gan prompts the latter, as he is dismissed from the school at the end, to leave behind for Wang Fu the only available Chinese dictionary, which the students revere as "the teacher of the teacher."

Both the novel and the film draw attention to children as that class of social inferiors who continue to fascinate modern Chinese intellectuals. What distinguishes the children in King of the Children is that they pose a specific question about national culture: the status of education. They are thus not simply members—to use the psychoanalytic categories from Lacan—of a presymbolic infantile state but already participants in a major social institution, what for Althusser is the major "ideological state apparatus" of the school.[11] At the same time, the children are powerless, their future as yet undecided. This future raises the question of hope, and hope seems dismal in the aftermath of the Cultural Revolution. Although in his novel A Cheng never directly describes the Cultural Revolution as such, we feel its destructive effects unmistakably, through the impoverished state in which the Chinese education system now finds itself. What kind of a road can be made for these children? This is, I think, the primary issue in A Cheng's text; its force is a pedagogical one. As a socially powerless figure, the schoolchild becomes the site for cultural (re)production and its various levels of arbitration. In A Cheng, Lao Gan acts as the agent who steers these schoolchildren away from the reproduction of a destructive culture. By training them how to read and write from scratch, we are given to think, it might be possible to regenerate national culture in a positive manner. Instead of being associated with a particular political system, communism, this national culture would now be rooted in the humanistic principles of learning.[12]

For me, what makes Chen Kaige's film interesting to watch is not its faithfulness to A Cheng's novel but the way in which it departs from the novel through its translation into the film medium. This is not a translation in the sense of producing a "filmic version" of the same story. Rather, in the translation that is *filming*, we witness a significant shift from A Cheng's *script*. What this means is that, first, the translation from writing into film removes the story from the terrain of words into a realm in which verbal language is merely one among many levels of expression. Second, and more important, the shift from script to film is also a shift *away from* the primacy of writing. Because writing occupies the central position among representational forms in the Chinese culture (in which to draw or paint, for instance, is referred to as *xiehua*, literally "to write a picture"), and also because the content of the story itself is about the acquisition of the use of the written word, the translation into film, in which nonverbal cultural signifiers such as visual images and sounds play a primary role, poses all the questions about literature and national culture we have raised so far—questions that are condensed in A Cheng's story into the relationship between teacher and children in the school—in entirely different ways.

In an account of the relationship between literature and film, the Russian formalist critic Boris Eikhenbaum writes:

> The cinema audience is placed in completely new conditions of perception, which are to an extent opposite to those of the reading process. Whereas the reader moved from the printed word to visualisation of the subject, the viewer goes in the opposite direction: he moves from the subject, from comparison of the moving frames to their comprehension, to naming them; in short, to the construction of internal speech. The success of film is partially connected to this new and heretofore undeveloped kind of intellectual exercise.[13]

What Eikhenbaum refers to as "the construction of internal speech" can be restated simply as the verbal interpretation of the filmic image. That, however, is precisely the problem: how is "internal speech" to be constructed? How exactly do we undertake what was at Eikhenbaum's time a "new and heretofore undeveloped kind of intellectual exercise"—the "move," the translation from filmic images to words?

To begin to approach this problem, I think we need to think of "internal speech" not as a self-generating, self-sufficient monologue but rather in terms of the problematic of language and discourse as formulated in the works of Mikhail Bakhtin / V. N. Vološinov.[14] Instead of understanding discourse as simply a tool at the disposal of the individual user, Bakhtin and Vološinov argue that discourse, even when it appears to come from a single individual user, is in fact a plural or "polyphonic" phenomenon peopled with the intentions of others. Similarly, we may say that "internal speech" is always already a socially constituted discursive reality: it is dialogic in nature even if it is heard only as a single, monologic utterance. Its apparent "interiority" or "privacy" notwithstanding, "internal speech" is a site of struggle, a meeting ground between competing voices.

If Bakhtin's and Vološinov's understanding of the social nature of internal speech relies as its model on the medium of verbal language,

Male Narcissism and National Culture

Eikhenbaum's attention to the relationship between literature and film shifts the problematic of internal speech to a more complex level by posing the additional question of how internal speech is constructed when more than one type of medium is involved. In other words, Eikhenbaum's passage asks, *How is the sociality of internal speech to be understood through visuality, through the relation between visuality and words?*

The visual image, as we know, is characterized by two seemingly opposite features: obviousness and silence. While the obviousness of the image expresses an unambiguous presence, the silence of the image suggests, instead, nonpresence—that is, all those areas of "otherness" that are an inherent part of any single "presence." This "double feature" of the visual image means that, when considered in relation to visuality, the construction of internal speech must be posed in different terms. If, when we speak of the dialogicity of internal speech in the verbal sense, we must resort to figures of speech such as "a struggle between different voices"; when we deal with the dialogicity of internal speech in the medium of visuality, we have conveniently at our aid the "double feature" of the image itself. The silence of the image, which exists side by side with its imagistic obviousness, serves as an economical means of evoking all those subterranean elements that are not immediately present but are nonetheless implicit. This silence thus becomes a way of staging, in and beyond its visible form, the inter-*media*-ry nature of "consciousness"—of consciousness not only as a struggle between voices (as in Bakhtin and Vološinov), but also as a crossing between sign systems, between visuality and verbality. Precisely because this silence necessitates translation and interpretation (what Eikhenbaum calls "naming"), highlighting thus the *dis*continuity between visual signification and verbal signification, the image is, we may say, an especially germane illustration of the *media*ted nature (the construction and constructedness) of internal speech.

In the terms of our ongoing discussion, "internal speech" is also interchangeable with what I have been referring to as subjectivity, namely, the relationship between the individual as participant in social activity (for instance, film watching) and that which transcends the boundaries of his individualized physical apparatus—his own bodily vision/look. This is a relationship that is always *to be* articulated/constructed. The difference between responding to the printed word and responding to film that Eikhenbaum mentions is particularly relevant here because we are dealing with the translation of a novel into a filmic text. Where words have provided the clues to a possible relationship between Lao Gan and the world at large (he is, after all, the narrating subject in A Cheng's story), how are we to understand that relationship in film? What is the subjectivity or internal speech that reveals itself in the *King of the Children* by Chen?

One specific *filmic* feature that departs from the novel is the way Chen uses Lao Gan's look to reopen the question of pedagogy.[15] Throughout the film, we see shots of Lao Gan staring into the distance, sometimes as if he is surprised, other times as if in a daydream. For instance, after settling down in his lodgings at the beginning, we have a scene in which the camera, taking the shot from outside his cottage, shows him sitting by a window inside, with his hands hanging out leisurely. As he unconsciously touches himself by crossing his long graceful fingers, his eyes look into the distance. Following his look, we ask: what does he see? If the individual look is a response to a collective gaze, to what does his look respond? What is the larger realm that connects with this look? In the language of contemporary film criticism, this is a question about suturing—that process of subjective activation and reactivation through complex transactions between symbolic and imaginary significations, transactions that give rise to an illusory sense of unity with the field of the other and to coherence in narrative meaning. How is Lao Gan's stare sutured? In other words, with what does his look cohere?

The School

By following A Cheng's *script*, Chen shows that Lao Gan's look seeks its connection in the schoolchildren whose education constitutes his "appointment." The protagonist's look here is the specific device through which the issue of pedagogy is addressed *filmically*. "How does one teach in the aftermath of the Cultural Revolution?" becomes "How does one look into the eyes of China's future generation?" But because the question is now asked specifically in the form of vision, it leaves "subjectivity" a matter of construction, offering us that "new and heretofore undeveloped kind of intellectual exercise" that Eikhenbaum mentions.

Lao Gan's discomfort at the question about pedagogy is evident from the time he arrives at the school. First, he discovers to his surprise that he has been assigned to a higher grade than he thought he was qualified to teach. Then, on arriving at the door of the classroom, he drops his books. As if in a confrontation, he greets with great unease the little faces that await him. This mutually responsive relationship, back and forth between teacher and schoolchildren, directs the narrative development of the story.

When Lao Gan realizes that all he can do is to copy, a deep sense of frustration arises. With his back to the children, he copies standardized communist texts onto the blackboard, day in and day out. The children, on their part, copy everything mechanically into their notebooks. The sounds of chalk on the blackboard and pencils on notebooks fill many scenes. As this "collective" activity intensifies, we are forced to ask, What kind of cultural production is taking place here, with what future for these rural children? This series of copying scenes is followed by one in which Lao Gan goes home one night, holds a candle to his broken mirror, and spits at his own image. (I will return to the significance of this violent act of self-degradation later.)

Things change when Lao Gan begins to teach the copied texts. One of the students, Wang Fu, boldly reprimanding him for his incompetence, proclaims the principles of correct teaching. At this—what appears in every sense a public humiliation by a student, a member of the lower class in the school system—Lao Gan breaks into a laugh, as if he has finally made a connection with the schoolchildren. From then on, he proceeds to teach the students how to read and write, and slowly, each student learns to produce his or her own original thoughts in composition.

Wang Fu's persistence in copying the dictionary and his eventual "success" in producing a piece of coherent writing are the symptoms of the child who has been properly "interpellated" into the system of learning—to use the term from Althusser. Wang Fu's perseverance, seriousness, and ability to work hard are all part of the process by which the school as an apparatus of ideology solicits the voluntary cooperation of its participants.[16] The reproduction of a society, writes Althusser, is not only the reproduction of its skills but also "a reproduction of its submission to the rules of the established order, i.e., a reproduction of submission to the ruling ideology"[17] for those who are exploited.

Precisely because he is sensitive to how ideology works effectively not only through coercion (by the powerful) but more often through consent (from the powerless), Chen's film departs from the more straightforwardly humanistic direction of A Cheng's story. We see this in the way Chen handles the episode of copying. Whereas in A Cheng's novel Lao Gan leaves behind the dictionary for Wang Fu as a gift, in the film he departs with these words on the table: "Wang Fu, don't copy any more, not even the dictionary."

What Chen's film makes clear is that even though A Cheng's text is radical (because it affirms proper learning against the destructiveness of the Cultural Revolution), it leaves unasked the entire question of what it means to base culture on the kind of repetition that is copying. In reading A Cheng's text, one feels that it is not the act of copying that is really the problem; rather it is a matter of finding the right source from which to copy. The protest A Cheng makes, accordingly, is that the Cultural Revolution has destroyed such sources. Against such destruction, A Cheng shows how one should always write *after* (one has done) something (that is, one should copy from "life"), or else one may, as Wang Fu does, copy from the dictionary. Chen, on the other hand, does not attach to copying the value of a positive meaning as does A Cheng; rather, in it he sees contemporary Chinese culture's *deconstruction* of traditional Chinese culture. For Chen, the destructiveness of the Cultural Revolution is not an accident but the summation of the Chinese civilization, and the act of copying, to which the students are reduced, signifies the emptiness of culture itself. This is why he says: "Culture is precisely this: it's a matter of copying."[18] The following passages from the director's notes to the film script of *King of the Children* reveal the decidedly deconstructive turn Chen gives to A Cheng's story:

Many would say the Cultural Revolution has destroyed Chinese culture since numerous cultural relics were destroyed. However, intellectually, it was more a time when the values inherent in traditional Chinese culture were carried to a dangerous extreme. This was violently reflected in the behaviour of every individual— from their blind worship of the leader / emperor figure to the total desecration and condemnation of individual rights. These are mere repetitions of tradition.

Repetition is a characteristic of Chinese traditional culture. The children in the film copied the textbook, then the dictionary, without any comprehension. Man, in his preservation of himself, has developed culture, but in the end, the culture has become the master of man. The glory of past cultural accomplishments have left today's men impotent. With 5000 years of culture shining in our history, we had the frenzy of the "Great Cultural Revolution."

Thus, what is embedded in the film *King of the Children* is my judgement on traditional culture. The burning of the wasted mountains at the end of the film is a metaphor of my attitude towards traditional values. "Don't copy anything, not even the dictionary"; "Carry your head high on your shoulders and write your own essays" is what I require and expect of myself.[19]

Because Chen's understanding of copying is much more drastic, he also constructs his *King of the Children* in such a way that the success of the child-as-copyist is being scrutinized and challenged through a juxtaposition with other forms of subjectivity. While A Cheng's narrative offers a more or less completed circuit of suturing between Lao Gan and the schoolchildren, especially through his special relationship with Wang Fu, this process of suturing is only one of the several crucial elements in the film.

The drastic questioning of the traditional authority of the written word (and thus of the primacy of verbal language) is, I would contend, not a questioning of a moralistic kind. As I argue in the previous chapter, the film medium allows Chen to explore the much larger issue of technological reproduction in a modern "third world" culture. Here, a brief reference to Martin Heidegger's understanding of technology helps clarify the issues somewhat.[20] In his work, Heidegger dissociates the word *technology* from its more popular associations with instrumentality. Instead, he defines the essence of technology as the bringing-forth of being—a process of revealing truth and a mode of knowing. He locates this essence of technology in the Greek word *techne*, which for him does not mean mere technique or craft but the "bringing-forth" of that which presences into appearance. For Heidegger, modern machine technology does not depart in essence from the ancient concept of *techne*. Rather, modernity's mechanized, regulating, gigantic, and indeed dangerous apparatuses reveal *techne* as an "Enframing" and a "setting-upon" of nature in ways hitherto concealed from human apprehension. Because of this, Heidegger says: "Modern technology, which for chronological reckoning is the later, is, from the point of view of the essence holding sway within it, the historically earlier."[21] Having shown this about modernity, Heidegger also asks: is there a time when it is not technology (as we now know it) alone that reveals the meaning of *techne*? He finds his answer in art and especially in poetry.

In many ways, Chen's work (the three films he directed in China prior to 1989) can be seen as an exploration of the question of *techne* in the context of a devastated "third world" culture which is at the same time one of the most sophisticated ancient civilizations. The intense challenge posed by Chen's *King of the Children* to the written word is a challenge to the cultured origins of Chinese history. The written script with its stable, permanent cast points to that "Enframing" of being that Heidegger suggests as the essence of *techne*. Central to the power—indeed the violence—of writing is its ability to repeat itself. In China, where writing is seldom divorced from history—that is, from the notion of writing as recording and conserving—the written script is *techne* in its most basic form, through which the transmission and reproduction of culture is ensured. At the same time, writing is also *modern* technology in the hands of the communist state, which turns it into a pure machine for propaganda and thought control. These two aspects of writing—first as the cumulative, unbearable burden of the past (history) and then as the technologizing imperative to construct, in the modern world, a brand-new national culture (revolution)—are brought together succinctly in the mindless *copying* of the post–Cultural Revolution period.

On the night Lao Gan obtains and reads the dictionary for the first time, the scene takes on a surreal feeling as sounds of human voices reciting ancient texts are slowly echoed and magnified, creating a ghostly atmosphere of how tradition impinges upon human consciousness as so many indistinguishably repeating voices. The simple acts of reading and writing, performed here in the rural area, far away from the "centers" of urban civilization, nonetheless partake in this unmistakable sense of culture as copying, echoing, repeating. Instead of concealing it, the impoverished material circumstances help intensify the sheer mechanism of writing as cumulative recording.

In the urban setting, of course, the unstoppable terroristic power of technology is apprehensible in more palpable forms. Chen shows this in his second film, *Da yue bing* (*The Big Parade*, 1985). In this film, the portrayal of one of the most important bases of Chinese national culture—the People's Liberation Army—is done in an admixture of a fascination with discipline (which suppresses all symptoms of the human body such as crying, fainting, vomiting, or even the physical "deformity" of bowed legs) and an ultimate sense of emotional blankness that comes with this technologized discipline. The instrumentalization of human bodies into a "collective" purpose such as the army, to the point at which material impoverishment and deprivation, including deprivation in the form of a restraint of the body's reactions to disciplinary torture, is visible on the screen through the orderliness of soldiers and other production units marching in the "big parade" in front of Tiananmen Square. It is as if the sheer regimentation of human bodies—in uniform, their faces devoid of expression, their movements absolutely identical—provides a kind of pseudo- or mechanical "bridging" of the gap between the irretrievable past and the unknowable future. If this "bridging" indicates modern China's "successful" achievement of modernization, it is an achievement that, as we sense through the slow motion and funereal music in the last scenes of *The Big Parade*, requires from the individual a submission to the technologized collective goal—to technology as collective goal—in total obliteration of himself.[22]

The rural setting of *King of the Children* does not permit the demonstration of the workings of technology in the graphically striking form it takes in *The Big Parade*. In the absence of the industrialized, militarized, and urbanized forms of technology, Chen probes the roots of *techne* in a more basic manner—through the fundamental working of verbal language itself. Here, the power of *techne*, as what brings forth the ordering of being, is demonstrated with frugal means, through a practice of traditional learning—storytelling. One day, the friends from Lao Gan's former production unit come for a visit. Out of sheer playfulness, he has them sit down like students in the classroom, whereupon he proceeds to "teach" them. As he *repeats* his words, it quickly becomes clear that this is one of those narratives that uncover the mechanism of narrating from within, so that "form" and "content" are merged and thus revealed as one: "Once upon a time there was a mountain. In the mountain was a temple. In the temple was a Buddhist monk telling a tale.

What is the tale? Once upon a time there was a mountain. In the mountain was a temple. In the temple . . ."

His friends join him in what immediately becomes an uproar that reproduces the same story over and over again collectively. As they finally come to a stop, the schoolchildren, who have been eavesdropping outside the classroom, pick up from where the adults left off and run off into the distant hills repeating exactly the same narrative with rhythm. As they disappear on the horizon, the camera returns us to Lao Gan's look. This look is one of surprise, as if he has suddenly understood something. What is it that he has understood? What is the content of his sudden awareness? These are questions that the film medium leaves unanswered and that must be approached through the process of interpretation.

Such a moment of "awareness" is one of the undecidable moments of subjectivity that are crucial for the understanding of modern Chinese culture and literature. Instead of immediately supplying it with a definite meaning, such as "Lao Gan realizes how education is passed on," we should juxtapose it with other components of the film in order to grasp its range of significatory possibilities.

Nature

Side by side with the relationship between teacher and schoolchildren is another set of scenes that revolve around a character who does not exist in A Cheng's novel—a cowherd. This is, once again, a child figure; and yet unlike the schoolchildren, the cowherd belongs to "nature." Through him Chen's film creates a discourse that counters the institution of education. What is this counterdiscourse like? In other words, what is the function of the nature child in this film?

"Nature" supplies an alternative form of suturing for Lao Gan's look. Oftentimes, as he stares, what he "sees" is the expansiveness of the rural landscape. Though some might argue that "nature" as such is the unsuturing of the look and therefore, arguably, a non-Western type of cinematic intervention, I am, as I indicated in the previous chapter, reluctant to divide "West" and "East" in this facile manner by putting "nature" and "East" in the space of an "outside." There are two reasons for not taking this interpretative step. First, I see the elusiveness and fantasy that are part of nature-as-filmic-signifier as a major *political* means of resisting the overwhelmingly articulate, verbal, indeed verbose machinery of official Chinese communist discourse with its technologies of mass control through propaganda. By presenting a counterdiscourse in the form of a natural muteness, therefore, directors like Chen are not exactly nostalgic about a metaphysical beyond; rather it is a politically engaged way of searching for an alternative cultural semiotics—*a detour*. Second, "nature" fulfills the function of being the unconscious side of a male circuit of production. As such, it plays an indispensable role in reinforcing certain patterns of censorship, especially the censorship of the physical body and the biological reproduction through woman. This point will become clear in the second part of this chapter.

The cowherd first appears in the scenes of Lao Gan's journey to the school. He is dressed in white; a large straw hat covers his face so that we cannot see his features; he is leading a herd of cows on the mountain road. He is mute throughout the film, and his "communication" with Lao Gan takes the opposite form to that of the schoolchildren—the nonverbal.[23] Two scenes demonstrate the significatory power of this nonverbalness.

One day, as Lao Gan is teaching, he sees that the cowherd is doing something on the blackboard in the classroom next door. As he goes and looks, he finds that the cowherd has splattered dung on the board; meanwhile he has disappeared into the distance. A second scene shows Lao Gan meeting the cowherd face to face in the fields. He asks: "Where are you from, child? Do you go to school? Why not? I know how to read and write. I can teach you." The cowherd remains mute and goes away.

Why does Chen insert the figure of this mute child in this story about teaching? From the beginning, we feel that the cowherd's existence is a mystery, which belongs to the plane of fantasy rather than to the institutional reality to which Lao Gan is officially appointed. And yet this fantasy intrudes into his path of vision in spite—perhaps because—of its mysterious nature. Here, the use of cinematic image and sound together effects a forceful interplay between the pedagogical and the natural frames of reference. The film begins, after all, with *two* series of sounds—first, cowbells, then the sounds of writing with chalk on the blackboard. As Lao Gan travels with his friend Lao Hei to the school, the two men come across things that seem to startle them. Among these things is the cowherd. Typically, we are shown the seemingly slightly surprised look of the two male characters, especially Lao Gan; then the camera "sutures" the look by showing a scene from the mountains, a view of rocks falling from a cliff, of trees, and so forth. What kind of "suturing" is this? This type of scene, in which Lao Gan's human, individualized look is seen to be actively *looking*, only to be "connected" with something "natural"—that is, something mute, stationary, and uneventful—parallels his actual encounters with the cowherd, who becomes *a personified form of the nonverbal presence of a natural world* that exists side by side (rather than metaphysically beyond) the human institution of learning. Precisely because the cowherd is nonverbal, he belongs more appropriately to the medium that does not rely on verbal language alone to generate its significations. The cowherd's *bodily presence* signifies the challenge of nonpresence, nonparticipation—a form of life and a history of uneducation—which runs parallel but indifferent to the history of education.

If the pedagogical subjectivity in this film is the circuit that runs between Lao Gan's look to the schoolchildren (which is the dominant narrative in A Cheng's novel), then this mute presence of the cowherd alters this subjectivity significantly. Side by side with the pedagogical suturing—especially between Lao Gan and Wang Fu, the inheritor of book culture—is now another one, which is nonverbal *on the child's side*. The nonverbal nature of the cowherd's "response" to Lao Gan forces us to think: what is the use of education? How does it reproduce itself, and for whose benefit?

The status of nature in *King of the Children* carries with it the implications of a counterdiscourse that is situated not in human agency but in fantasy. On the night Lao Gan browses through the dictionary, I mentioned, the film supplies a chorus of muffled voices from the past reciting texts to accompany Lao Gan's reading. At the same time, this "rejoining" with the ancestral voices of education is interrupted by a noise from the outside. It is a cow, standing mysteriously in the dark and walking away as Lao Gan opens the door and discovers it.

I hope by now that I have clearly established the terms of this part of my argument. If we are to think of subjectivity in terms of the suturing of a perceiving individual and an undecidable external reality, then Lao Gan's subjectivity that emerges in the film is a bifurcated one. On the one hand, it retains the "good" Chinese tradition of a compassion for children as the socially powerless. This subjectivity directs its own "completion" in the other through the acquisition of the written word. This particular suturing process stands for the compliance with a *proper* sense of national culture, as that which must be built from the most basic technology—writing. This subjectivity takes us in the direction of a determinate and determinable form of hope. If the children are the "masses," then education through literacy represents the hope of a definite and definitive road.

On the other hand, Chen explores Lao Gan's subjectivity through another realm in which the teacher's impulse to reach out to the socially powerless child cannot materialize into an act of pedagogy. Instead, it is met with a defiance that one must describe as at once natural, silent, mysterious, and uncooperative. This other story of subjectivity punctuates Chen's film in the form of scenes that are placed halfway between reality and fantasy—the point is that the audience cannot tell the difference and that it does not matter. What matters is that the figure of the cowherd reappears persistently, as if in a dream, a detour, which swerves from the conscious and straightforward relationship between teacher and schoolchildren.

Along this detour is a nonexistent Chinese character. One day, as Lao Gan is copying texts on the board, he writes down a character that he subsequently erases:

Toward the end of the film, he recalls this episode of miswriting in his parting words to the students. Cows are stubborn animals, he says; you can scold them and hit them, and they just blink at you. But there are times when cows go wild—that is, when you piss. This is because cows love salt. (In A Cheng's novel, Lao Gan also tells us that once you have pissed for a cow, you can make it do anything you want, for they would respect you as if you were their parents.) It was this association of "cow" and "piss," Lao Gan explains, that made him write the imaginary character "cow water" the other day.

The significatory density of this nonexistent character is, structurally speaking, what counteracts the ferocity of Wang Fu's dedication to verbal language. The "cow water" fantasy exposes literate culture in a scandalously different manner—as excrement. This exposure takes place at various levels at once. First, the fantasy returns us to the origin of the Chinese civilization—peasant knowledge. As such, in a text that is critical of the destructiveness of the Cultural Revolution, tribute is paid to one of Chinese communism's most compelling pedagogical imperatives: intellectuals must learn from peasants. The way cows behave toward urine is an ecological fact that one acquires by being "exiled" in the countryside, not by being in the classroom.

Second, this fantasy is a story about the dialectic of submission and domination. The cows, in spite of their patient and uncomplaining nature, go wild at the rare physical pleasure of salt. Whoever provides this pleasure, in other words, also has the power to dominate them. From the human perspective, this understanding of pleasure and submission is profoundly disturbing because in it we recognize the acts of degradation and humiliation, indeed violence. An act of physical discharge, which eliminates that which stinks—how could this, from the perspective of the properly educated, possibly be a source of pleasure and an inducement to submission? To what can we compare this at the symbolic level? Is this story about animal nature also one about human culture? If so, what kind of blow has been dealt to the dignity of the latter?

The radicalness of "cow water" lies in the way it reveals the fundamental violence of culture as a process of production. The success of "culture" is the success of subjugating those who are in need (as, for instance, with salt in the case of cows) for productive purposes. The paradox is that not only would the act of subjugation not make them rebel but because its violence is at the same time what sustains and what nurtures, the dominated respond to it submissively—animalistically. To return to the making of roads, pissing is, in this light, the act that establishes a path, which is met with pleasure and followed henceforth with loyalty.

If submission as such, transposed onto the human cultural frame, is essential for the formation of identity, then this fantasy illuminates the unutterable inequality involved in that process. The silent, fantastical text of this *other* story about Chinese national culture reads, Are not the hardworking, uncomplaining masses of Chinese people like the cows—and is not "tradition," as represented and endorsed by official political orthodoxy, the pissing master? (In the modern economy, "work" is what generates "salary," which etymologically means "payment for one's work in the form of salt.") No matter how abusive this master becomes, the masses succumb to him as the source of their survival. The masses submit even as tradition and national culture crush them. Against this *equivalence* between cows and people, the direct political empowerment of the "masses" that appears in Mao's reading of Lu Xun—a reading that distinguishes between cows and people by making the former a symbol of those who should serve the latter—is at once a hope, a lie, and the making of a road by force, with blood and tears.

The conception of culture as violence and excrement also returns us to the question of copying and writing-as-reproduction. Unlike A Cheng's story, in which one feels that the point of learning is to identify the correct source from which to copy, Chen's film deconstructs cultural production itself as copying. With the insertion of the cowherd, words, texts, dictionaries, and verbal language—summations of the human learning tradition—exist on a par with piss, as the (waste) product of a violently subjugating act to which Chinese individuals, like the intelligent student Wang Fu, have no choice but to submit. The nature of this submission is that of copying and reproducing precisely the source of their subjugation—in other words, cultural violence through institutionalized education itself. It is only when this "originary" act of violence is completed through the act of submission and voluntary reproduction (because it includes the possibility of pleasure and physical survival) that it becomes fully effective as cultivation and culture. (In A Cheng, the hardworking cows are compared to philosophers.) This is why, on first discovering that he cannot teach the students anything except copying—that is, on discovering that he is not, properly speaking, helping to perpetuate culture, Lao Gan expresses physical violence toward *himself*, by spitting at his own image in the broken mirror. Meanwhile, as Wang Fu strikes back in words, he is happy: the circuit of teaching that he initiated has been properly completed by this young child's active response and can now regenerate itself.

But if human culture is violent, nature is more so. If the cows in Chen's film are not, as Mao's image suggests, the "intellectual servants" to be used by the proletariat, they are not icons of humanistic benevolence either. The cowherd's (and by implication, nature's) muteness is a form of subjugating presence to which Lao Gan, even though he is a teacher, submits. In the last scenes of the film, as he departs from the village, we are once again given what look like dream scenes of nature. Chief among these is a field of black stumps, which stand mysteriously and collectively. As these stumps meet our eyes, we hear cowbells and someone pissing. It is the cowherd, who faces the camera and pisses at us directly, his genitals exposed. The camera then shows us his eye under the broken straw hat—is he looking at Lao Gan or at us? With the amplification of cowbells in the wind, the cowherd disappears; we see the black stumps and his hat on one of them. The stumps are magnified, and the sounds of the cowbells increase. A moment of quiet. Then the face of the cowherd without the hat: a scruffy country child, turning around, looking at us.

The fantasy of the cowherd returns nature to the cosmic indifference described by the *Dao De Jing*: *tiandi bu ren, yi wanwu wei chugou* (the cosmos is without/outside human benevolence; it treats everything as mere straw dogs). It is the mute, natural world, forever untamable, which ultimately pisses at us without shame or guilt. Vis-à-vis this nature, human violence itself is, the film says, a mere copy and reproduction.

Part 2: The Road Not Yet Taken

We have found, especially in persons whose libidinal development has suffered some disturbance, as in perverts and homosexuals, that in the choice of their love-object they have taken as their model not the mother but their own selves. They are plainly seeking themselves as a love-object and their type of object-choice may be termed *narcissistic*. . . .

[The child] is really to be the center and heart of creation, "His Majesty the Baby," as once we fancied ourselves to be. He is to fulfill those dreams and wishes of his parents which they never carried out. . . . At the weakest point of all in the narcissistic position, the immortality of the ego, which is so relentlessly assailed by reality, security is achieved by fleeing to the child.

Sigmund Freud, "On Narcissism: An Introduction"

Male Narcissism and National Culture

The child is a metaphysical being.

Gilles Deleuze and Félix Guattari, *Anti-Oedipus:*
Capitalism and Schizophrenia

Ultimately, a thorough-going feminist revolution would
liberate more than women.

Gayle Rubin, "The Traffic in Women: Notes on the
'Political Economy' of Sex"

It is now possible for me to turn to the issue of "male narcissism" alluded to in the title of this chapter. Although I am sympathetic to the deconstructive reading of culture that Chen Kaige offers through what I have been calling the detour of nature and fantasy, I think such a reading leaves certain forms of human agency that are accountable for such violence unidentified and thus unquestioned. The detour, though it may fundamentally critique the violence of culture as pedagogical suturing, also becomes complicitous with such violence because the alternative it offers, through nature, is *silence*. It is at this point that a social criticism, however partial, of recognizable types of human agency that lurk behind cultural violence is necessary as a way out, even if such criticism does not yet lead to a new road.

By offering a feminist reading as a supplement to my analysis of the bifurcated subjectivity above, my point is not to belittle the political subversiveness at work under Chen's direction. It is, rather, to attempt a mode of reading that, in a way that is not autonomous from but involved with that subversiveness, locates certain excesses that fall outside Chen's detour. These excesses—what to me are possible signs of a new mass and new hope that exist in incomplete forms in the film—are to be found with "woman." By focusing on the question of woman, we will see that the structural interplay between the subjectivities in *King of the Children*—stranded between the pedagogical and the fantastic—is a closed circuit.

A major question results from this supplementary reading based on woman. Is this closed circuit, which I term male narcissism, at bottom a way to resist the reproduction of national culture altogether? If so, why? Why do the male subjectivities in Chen's film seek to connect with the child either through the school or through nature, while bypassing woman? What is the root of this "disturbance," which manifests itself as aesthetic symptom? In other words, does the *passive* role in which Chen casts his male protagonist reflect a response to a larger force of destruction at work, so that the exclusion of woman must be seen not simply as misogyny but as an effort to cope with what in Lacanian terms we would call symbolic castration?

To deal with these questions, let us now do a retake of interpreting *King of the Children.*

If subjectivity is possible only as the result of a certain completion of an individual viewer's look—even if that process of completion is an illusory one—the two types of subjectivity evident in Chen's film, which are held in a contentious relationship with each other, are also held *together* by the absence of women as productive agents. (The girl students are, strictly speaking, recipients, not producers.)

From the beginning, Chen gives us a world of male play. From Lao Gan's former production unit, to the school, to his special relationship with Wang Fu, to the mute cowherd, it is a world of men and men as children at play. In addition, we find several scenes in which Lao Gan is alone against the background of nature, moving his own body around aimlessly and enjoying himself. Between the continuation of human culture through verbal pedagogy and its discontinuation through the fantasy of nature, therefore, what disappears is woman. Moreover, this disappearance of woman occurs at a particular intersection: the woman disappears as the child appears.

We turn, at this point, to Laidi, the woman cook and singer in Lao Gan's production unit. Laidi's entrance is always a disruptive one. Take, for instance, the scene near the beginning in which Lao Gan and his friends gather for a meal before he departs for his new posting. Chen shows us—with what nuanced attention!—the men's comradeship in cooking: first the collective contributions to the menu, then the washing, cutting, chopping of meat and vegetables, then setting the rice to be cooked inside a section of bamboo, and finally the sharing of the cooked meal. The power of males in such a group is, as Gayle Rubin would describe it, "not founded on their roles as fathers or patriarchs, but on their collective adult maleness, embodied in secret cults, men's houses, warfare, exchange networks, ritual knowledge, and various initiation procedures."[24] By contrast, although Laidi is a cook, she is never shown to be cooking; instead she strikes one as always bursting onto the scene of male play, bringing with her some kind of disorder. When Laidi enters this first scene of a shared meal, she is announced by her loud voice, her plump body, her broad manners, and a very unfeminine question: "Why don't you ask me for a drink?" Although she is a singer, we never hear her sing; the voice that comes from her is rather always given in a clownish fashion, as shouting and as disharmonious *noise*.

By stripping Laidi of what are conventional feminine (erotic) qualities—submissiveness, shyness, slenderness, and reticence, all of which belong to Lao Gan instead—Chen leaves open the question of his attitude toward women's role in the production of national culture. To what extent does this exclusion of Laidi from the conventional feminine realm of significations constitute an exclusion of woman in the cultural symbolic? And to what extent does this *clowning* of her become a new type of signification, a feminine power that is in fact stronger than the male because of its libidinally uninhibited nature? Two episodes allow us to negotiate these questions.

Laidi's ambition is to become a music teacher at the same school where Lao Gan teaches. She wants the men to see that she is more than a cook. But this wish is met with patronizing criticisms from the men, who tease her for not understanding that she has none of the professional qualifications it takes to be a teacher. What she considers to be the most important qualification—her ability to sing and to compose through her voice—is thus immediately dismissed as irrelevant. Lao Gan, for his part, is honest enough to recognize that he is not properly qualified to teach, either. But this understanding of Laidi's equality with him does not prompt him to help her.

Meanwhile, Laidi is the one who, among all the people Lao Gan knows, provides him with the Chinese dictionary he needs for teaching. When she comes to his school for a visit, Lao Gan introduces her to Wang Fu as the real owner of the dictionary, whereupon Wang Fu calls her "teacher." In A Cheng's novel, Lao Gan writes down Laidi's name as well as his own as donors when he leaves behind the dictionary as a gift. What is interesting about the relationships among Laidi, Lao Gan, and Wang Fu, I think, is that they indicate the potential for a new type of genealogy or reproductive unit. The woman, the man, and the schoolboy form a kind of collective away from the familial reproduction restricted to "blood" and heterosexuality. But as woman is liberated from her erotic and biologically reproductive role, what does she become? What we see in the film is that she has been turned into a comic spectacle whose palpable physical dimensions exceed the closed circuit of male pedagogy and fantasy.

In what sense is this closed circuit narcissistic? I turn now to Freud's argument about narcissism for some definitions.

Narcissism, as we understand it in popular usage, is the "love of the self." Freud states that narcissism is not so much a perversion in the pejorative sense as it is a means of self-preservation. He distinguishes between two types of libidinal development in human beings—the ana-clitic, which is typified by the search for an object of love external to the subject and which he identifies as active and masculine; and the narcis-sistic, which is typified by the subject's seeking himself as the love object and which he identifies as passive and feminine. Freud's famous tableau of narcissists goes as follows:

[Narcissistic] *women* love only themselves with an intensity compa-rable to that of the man's love for them. . . . Such women have the greatest fascination for men, not only for aesthetic reasons . . . but also because of certain interesting psychological constellations. It seems very evident that one person's narcissism has a great attrac-tion for those others who have renounced part of their own nar-cissism and are seeking after object-love; the charm of a *child* lies to a great extent in his narcissism, his self-sufficiency and inacces-sibility, just as does the charm of certain *animals* which seem not to concern themselves about us, such as *cats* and the *large beasts of prey*. In literature, indeed, even the great *criminal* and the *humorist* com-pel our interest by the narcissistic self-importance with which they manage to keep at arm's length everything which would diminish the importance of their ego. It is as if we envied them their power of retaining a blissful state of mind—an unassailable libido-posi-tion which we ourselves have since abandoned.[25]

This passage from Freud clearly reveals his bias, that is, his exclusion of "man" from his tableau of narcissists. But if we disregard this sexual bias (which is obvious), a far more important feature of his argument that is relevant to our present discussion surfaces. We notice that those that he identifies as narcissistic share a common status, which is the status of the outsider—marginalized, mute, or powerless—beheld from a distance.

Because of this, I would defocus Freud's rigid sexual division between the male and female as anaclitic and narcissistic, and instead use his argument about narcissism for a *social* analysis that would include men as well as women as narcissists. Narcissism, seen in terms of the "outcast" categories in which Freud locates it, can now be redefined as the effect of a cultural marginalization or even degradation. The narcissist's look of "independence"—a self-absorption to the point of making others feel excluded—to which Freud attributes an aesthetic significance must therefore receive a new interpretation in the form of a question: is it the sign of a lack or one of a plenitude? Is it the sign of insecurity or self-sufficiency? Once we introduce the dialectic of social relation here and understand the "exclusionary look" as a possible result of (or reaction to) being excluded, it becomes necessary to think of certain forms of narcissism not in terms of independence but as the outward symptoms of a process of cultural devastation, which leaves the self recoiling inward, seeking its connection from itself rather than with external reality.

Freud's argument makes it clear that narcissism is not an intrinsic quality (even though we inevitably attribute it to others in terms of "personality" or "character") but a relation produced through the process of observation. In other words, the understanding of narcissism involves a viewing position from which others look narcissistic and exclusionary to us. Narcissism is thus a description of our psychological state in the other: as we feel excluded, the other becomes "narcissistic." In contemporary Chinese cinema, what does the creation of narcissistic male characters tell us about the making of film? In other words, why is narcissism *conferred upon these male characters*? Why does Chen make his male protagonist self-absorbed, passive, and thus "feminine"? How is this related to the question of national culture?

These questions bring us back to the one I raised earlier—namely, why does the writing of national culture in modern China typically take the form of an aesthetic preoccupation with the powerless? If the construction of national culture is a form of empowerment, then the powerless provides a means of aesthetic transaction through which a certain emotional stability arises from *observing* the powerless as a spectacle. In this spectacle, the viewer can invest a great amount of emotional energy in the form of sympathy; at the same time, this sympathy becomes the concrete basis of an affirmative national culture precisely because it *secures the distance from the powerless* per se. The projection of narcissism—an exclusionary self-absorption—onto the other becomes thus a way (as we notice in Freud) of stabilizing, or empowering, the viewing subject's position with an inexplicable aesthetic and emotional pleasure. Such pleasure gives rise, through the illusion of a "solidarity" with the powerless, to the formation of a "unified" community. What distinguishes Chen's film from, say, classical Hollywood narrative films, is that it is male, rather than female, figures who make up the spectacle(s) of the powerless. Moreover, it is "maleness" that sutures each point of the aesthetic transaction within the director's control, from (using the male character as) spectacle to (using the male character as) viewer, from feelings of devastation to feelings of solidarity.

According to Freud, a person may love, in the narcissistic manner, the following:

1. what he is himself (actually himself)
2. what he once was
3. what he would like to be
4. someone who was once part of himself

These descriptions define the world of male play, which provides much pleasure for the men in Chen's film. Laidi, on the other hand, makes it impossible for them to play merely as sexless children; her difference reminds them that there is a world of brute biological reproduction in which they, as the inheritors of Chinese culture, are supposed to participate. Hence, for instance, an attempt at swearing at the beginning of the film is preceded by the question: "Is there any woman around?" If this question is one pertaining to social decorum, then social decorum is an indicator of the functioning of the unconscious. The question points to a shared understanding on the part of the men that swearing, which as a rule alludes to sex or sexual organs, brings out a reality that signals human reproduction and that is thus on a par with "woman." As long as women are not present, however, that reality is not materialized and can remain at the level of empty male talk.

On Lao Gan's return visit to the production unit, Laidi touches him. As he refuses such touching, she retorts: "Even if you were to teach for one hundred years, I'd still know what's between your legs!" This reminder of "nature" is as defiant as the trees, the cows, and the cowherd, and yet because it is spoken by a woman—because, shall we say, it comes from a human voice other than that of the male—it cannot be relegated to the realm of fantasy and has the potential of erupting as an alternative symbolic order. Unlike the mute nature child who allows the male "look" to wander in a happy mood of self-exploration and self-projection, the woman's harsh voice keeps calling him back to the world of human culture and to the burdens that await him there. For Chen, it is as if these burdens cannot be shaken off unless one becomes per-verse—by taking off for the world of fantasy.

Instead of following the road opened up by the female voice, then, Chen's work follows a detour that is, seen in a feminist analysis, a well-trodden philosophical one. This detour heads for the child, voiced or voiceless, a stand-in for culture or nature, who becomes the recipient of what in psychoanalytic language is the process of idealization.

If Lu Xun's call to "save the children" provides the continuity through modern Chinese literature and culture, we need to ask whether the emotional insistence behind such a call is not at the same time an insis-tence on forgetting and excluding women. While the child occupies a position in modern Chinese literature and culture similar to other fig-ures of social oppression, because of his association with infancy he also offers the illusion that he is "freer" and more originary than the others. By contrast, woman, as the recipient of every type of social structura-tion, is a heavily "corrupted" space—a densely written script—which offers no such illusion of freedom. Because of this, it is much easier to project onto the child the wishes that cannot be fulfilled precisely because of the oppression of culture, through the illusion that the child occupies a kind of beyond-culture status that is superior because out-side. The extreme form of this projection, as we see in Chen's film, is to use the child to personify nature's original, amoral violence. The mute, pissing cowherd is, in this light, Chen's supreme invention of a doubled narcissistic relation. He is the silent beast confronting the feminine man, the ultimate narcissist—nature—beheld by the human narcissist.

The idealization of the child contains in itself a violence that is self-directed. This violence disguises itself as love of the self, as "narcissism." As Freud says, "At the weakest point of all in the narcissistic position, the immortality of the ego, . . . security is achieved by *fleeing to the child*."[26] Fleeing to the child—what this means is that what appears to be a love of the self, which generates the look of complete self-absorption, is actually a desperate flight to another figure, who is powerless and inferior but therefore safest for the realization of otherwise unenactable fantasies. In the Chinese context especially, this process of flight is a complex one. The child onto whom cultural hope is projected is not simply a figure of Chinese sentimentalism. Rather, he is the formation of an ideal, and, as Freud says, "The formation of an ideal would be the condition of repression."[27]

What is repressed, and why does it need to be? The answer to this question must be sought historically and collectively rather than within the space of one chapter or even one book. For now, I can only point to the visible avoidance of the physical sexuality as embodied by woman, an avoidance that aesthetically intersects with the acceptance and idealization of the child. This is, as I already mentioned, not misogyny *tout court* but symptomatic of a more profound disturbance.

In the sexual economy, "woman" represents that place in which man is to find his mating other in order to procreate and perpetuate the culture of which he is the current inheritor. "Woman" therefore serves as a reminder of the duty of genealogical transmission—of *chuanzong jiedai*. The question implied in Chen's film is this: do Chinese men in the post–Cultural Revolution period want to perform this duty?

In the idiomatic Chinese expression for the "mating other," *duixiang*, we find a means of understanding the sexual economy in psychoanalytic terms. *Duixiang*, in contemporary psychoanalytic language, is that mirror image that would correspond to one's self, so that when we are looking for a mate, we literally say *zhao duixiang*—"to look for the corresponding image."

In the narcissistic subjectivity, this *duixiang* is internally directed. The "natural" *duixiang* for Lao Gan would have been Laidi, who loves him and wants to be with him—her aspiration to be a music teacher is, one could say, an expression of her wish to "correspond" to him. And yet in Chen's film, the strong woman's love is presented as now farcical, now threatening. The possibilities it offers—heterosexual love, marriage, reproduction—are refused by the film. Instead, the male subjectivity takes another route and joins children as figures of idealization. It is the children, then, who have come to take the place of the corresponding image, in a way that bypasses the woman (even though she is kept in an affectionate light, as a mother or sister who tends). In bypassing the woman as the figure of reproduction, what does the film project? It projects, as I stated, two types of subjectivity, each of which can now be understood in terms of a narcissistic male circuit of reproduction. Reproduction is either strictly through education or through a submission to the awesome muteness of nature. In each we find a "suturing" between the male protagonist with a male child. The "sublimated" message of the film is that the world is generated in this interplay between pedagogy and fantasy, between "culture" and "nature"—that is, without woman and without the physical body!

In Freud's text, narcissistic gratification, involving repression, can be secured through the ego-ideal, which, besides the individual side, also has a social side, in the form of "the common ideal of a family, a class, or a nation": "The dissatisfaction due to the non-fulfillment of this ideal liberates homosexual libido, which is transformed into sense of guilt (dread of the community). Originally this was a fear of punishment by the parents, or, more correctly, the dread of losing their love; later the parents are replaced by an indefinite number of fellow men."[28]

Would it be farfetched to say that the narrative of modern Chinese history, culminating in the catastrophe of the Cultural Revolution and more recently in the Tiananmen massacre of 1989, represents precisely this "dissatisfaction" of the ego-ideal in the form of the nation? The guilt felt by the educated Chinese toward their fellow men generates the massive "censorial institution of conscience"—a feeling of being watched by other men—which makes it difficult, if not impossible, to engage in the conventional procedure of searching for the "corresponding image." Instead, *zhao duixiang* becomes a process not of finding the one who loves one but of self-observation, self-watching, and self-censorship. The displacement of narcissistic emotion onto "corresponding images" that are not women—difficult partners in biological reproduction—but idealized figures of children is symptomatic of a dissatisfaction with the failure of culture at large and an attempt nonetheless to continue to bear its burden conscientiously, by *disembodying* the reality of culture's reproduction and displacing that reality onto the purely institutional or fantastic level. Contrary to Freud's way of dividing the sexes, a film like *King of the Children* shows us that it is in male subjectivity that the need to secure emotional stability through narcissism is most evident. We can only speculate that this is in direct proportion to the burden of cultural reproduction that publicly or symbolically falls on men. Ironically, in spite of their obviously oppressed status, women seem more exempt from this desperate route because they are considered superfluous from the outset. In this "ironically" lies what I would call "the road not yet taken."

I understand that by equating Laidi with the physical body I seem to be going against one of the major lessons we have learned from feminism—that "woman" is not about biological reproduction alone. But my point in emphasizing the reproductive function of woman in this context is rather to show how a criticism of the cultural violence in Chinese culture cannot be undertaken without a vigilance of how the physical aspects of life are as a rule suppressed. Because women are traditionally associated with such physical aspects, their (women's) exclusion from the symbolic realm becomes a particularly poignant way of exposing this general suppression. My insistence on the biological, therefore, is not an attempt to reify it as such but a means of interrupting the tendency toward what I would call, for lack of a better term, *mentalism* in Chinese culture, a mentalism that we witness even in a subversive film such as *King of the Children*. Because the Chinese national culture reproduces itself biologically by means of the machinery that is women's bodies even while continuing to dismiss them on account of their femaleness, and because the Chinese communist state controls the population by controlling women's bodies, upon which forced abortions at advanced stages of pregnancy can be performed as "policy"—I think we must belabor women's reproductive role somewhat, even at the risk of "biologism."

In Laidi, we find the suggestion of a healthy narcissism that comprises an assertiveness, spontaneity, and fearlessness to seek what she wants while at the same time letting the other be. Because of this latter ability to let the other be, Laidi's love for Lao Gan is expressed not in the exclusive form of sexual desire and conquest but rather in that of a general affection in which one feels the presence of the caring sister, mother, and fellow worker as well. This alternative form of narcissism does not evade the other's difference (through specularization) in order to achieve its own stability. In it we find a different form of hope, toward which the film, caught in the closed circuit of male narcissism, nonetheless gestures, even though it never materializes into a significant new direction.

King of the Children continues, in the formalist manner of Lu Xun, the exploration of the cluster of issues involving Chinese national culture that has haunted Chinese intellectuals since the beginning of the twentieth century. To the literary incisiveness of Lu Xun's conception of hope—not as a road but as a crossroads—Chen's work brings the complexity of the filmic medium, in which the suggestively speculary process of *zhao duixiang*—of finding that which gives us "self-regard" and "self-esteem"—takes on collective cultural significance. If Chinese intellectuals in the twentieth century have consistently attempted to construct a responsible national culture through an investment in figures of the powerless, Chen's film indicates how such an investment, because it is inscribed in the formation of an ego-ideal in the terms I describe, excludes woman and the physical reality she represents. Chen's film offers a fantastic kind of hope—the hope to rewrite culture without woman and all the limitations she embodies, limitations that are inherent to the processes of cultural as well as biological reproduction. The subjectivity that emerges in Chen's film alternates between notions of culture and those of nature that are both based on a lineage free of woman's interference. As such, even at its most subversive/deconstructive moments (its staging of the unconscious that is nature's brute violence), it partakes of a narcissistic avoidance of the politics of sexuality and of gendered sociality that we will call, in spite of the passive "feminine" form it takes, masculine. This masculinity is the sign of a vast transindividual oppression whose undoing must become the collective undertaking for all those who have a claim to modern Chinese culture.

The Force of Surfaces:

Defiance in Zhang Yimou's Films

The decisive element in every situation is the permanently
organised and long-prepared force which can be put into the
field when it is judged that a situation is favourable (and it can be
favourable only in so far as such a force exists, and is full of
fighting spirit).

Antonio Gramsci, "The Modern Prince"

This chapter centers on three films by Zhang Yimou—*Red Sorghum*
(*Hong gaoliang*; Xian Film Studio, 1988), *Judou* (co-directed with Yang
Fengliang; Star Entertainment, 1990), and *Raise the Red Lantern* (*Da
hong denglong gao gao gua*; China Film Co-Production Corporation,
1991). I will not, however, offer "close readings" of these films in the
manner of the previous chapters but will instead use Zhang's films as a
way to raise some issues in cross-cultural interpretative politics. This
does not mean that I will neglect the specificities of Zhang's films. On
the contrary, my argument is that these specificities can be fully appre-
ciated only when we abandon certain modes and assumptions of interpretation.

Elements of a New Ethnography

The three films in question constitute a distinctive type. Their characteristics have become the "trademarks" of Zhang's style.[1] The "background" in these films is uniform: it is an oppressively feudal China. The historical details are blurred, even though we know from the original novellas from which the films are adapted that the events take place in the precommunist period.[2] The oppressiveness of feudal China is usually personified by an unreasonable, domineering older male figure, such as Jiuer's leper husband in *Red Sorghum*; Judou's husband, Yang Jinshan, the owner of the dye mill; and Chen Zuoqian, the landlord who owns several wives in *Raise the Red Lantern*. Because they are powerful within their class, these old men have the license to be abusive: they purchase wives, use them for both perverse sexual pleasure and reproduction, and sometimes murder them when they become disobedient or inconvenient. In terms of representing the maltreatment of women, the blurriness of historical background in Zhang's films is matched by an obliviousness to class differences. The mental or psychical suffering of Songlian, the new concubine in *Raise the Red Lantern*, is as intense as that of Judou, even though Songlian has attended university and Judou is an illiterate peasant. For Zhang, woman is very much a typical sexual body that is bound by social chains and that needs to be liberated.

As I mentioned in part 2, chapter 1, these tales of gothic and often morbid oppression are marked by their contrast with the sensuous screen design of the films. Zhang's film language deploys exquisite colors in the depiction of "backwardness." The color red in *Red Sorghum*, the bright solid colors of the dyed cloths in *Judou*, the striking, symmetrical screen organizations of architectural details, and the refined-looking furniture, utensils, food, and costumes in *Raise the Red Lantern* are all part and parcel of the recognizable cinematographic expertise of Zhang and his collaborators such as the talented cinematographer Gu Changwei.

In many respects, these three films can be described as constituting a new kind of ethnography. The first element of this new ethnography is that it presents the results of its "research" in the form not of books or museum exhibits but of cinema. Zhang's films have become a spectacular and accessible form of imaginative writing about a "China" that is supposedly past but whose ideological power still lingers. While many of the ethnic customs and practices in Zhang's films are invented,[3] the import of such details lies not in their authenticity but in their mode of signification.[4] Such import makes up the second major element of the newness of Zhang's ethnography: the use of things, characters, and narratives not for themselves but for their collective, hallucinatory signification of "ethnicity."

Roland Barthes theorized this type of signification in terms of what he called "mythologies" in the 1950s. With his characteristic good humor, Barthes gives a comically precise example to explain what he means by mythical speech:

> I am a pupil in the second form in a French *lycée*. I open my Latin grammar, and I read a sentence, borrowed from Aesop or Phaedrus: *quia ego nominor leo*. I stop and think. There is something ambiguous about this statement: on the one hand, the words in it do have a simple meaning: *because my name is lion*. And on the other hand, the sentence is evidently there in order to signify something else to me. Inasmuch as it is addressed to me, a pupil in the second form, it tells me clearly: I am a grammatical example meant to illustrate the rule about the agreement of the predicate. I am even forced to realize that the sentence in no way *signifies* its meaning to me, that it tries very little to tell me something about the lion and what sort of name he has; its true and fundamental signification is to impose itself on me as the presence of a certain agreement of the predicate.[5]

The "imposition" of this other significance—other to the obvious meaning the sentence seems to denote—is, for Barthes, the activity of myth: "In myth there are two semiological systems, one of which is staggered in relation to the other: a linguistic system, the language . . . which I shall call the *language-object*, because it is the language which myth gets hold of in order to build its own system; and myth itself, which . . . is a second language, *in which* one speaks about the first."[6]

I will return to the full implications of Barthes's analysis of myth later. For now, his example of the lion suffices in providing a parallel to

The Force of Surfaces

the type of signifying activity we find in Zhang's films. Like Barthes's loquacious lion, the ethnic details in these films are not there simply to "mean" themselves; rather, they are there for a second order articulation. They are there to signify "I am an ethnic detail; I am feudal China."

The difference between the ethnic detail as such and its self-conscious articulation is not the kind of difference that separates the time of the ethnographer's "fieldwork" and the time of her writing. Rather—and here we come to the third major element of the newness of Zhang's ethnography—because the ethnographer here is himself a "native" of the culture he is transcribing, the difference made conscious by the second order articulation becomes in effect a culture's belated fascination with its own datedness, its own alterity. Although Zhang may think that he is making films about China, what he is doing is representing a timeless China of the past, which is given to us in an imagined because retrospective mode. This "China," which is signified mythically, is the China constructed by modernity—the modernity of anthropology, ethnography, and feminism. It is also a "China" exaggerated and caricatured, in which the past is *melodramatized* in the form of excessive and absurd rituals and customs.[7]

In his mythical construct, what Zhang accomplishes is not the reflection of a China "that was really like that" but rather a new kind of organization that is typical of modernist collecting. The chaotic, overabundant elements of the past are now (re)arranged in a special kind of order.[8] In this way Zhang's films enact cinema's capacity, described by Paul Virilio, for gratifying the wish of those away from home for a dreamy "homeland" at the same time that it turns everyone who watches into a kind of migrant:

> The cinema gratified the wish of migrant workers for a lasting and even eternal homeland. . . . The cinema auditorium would not be a new city agora for the living where immigrants from the whole world might gather and communicate with one another; it was much more of a cenotaph, and the essential capacity of cinema in its huge temples was to shape society by putting order into visual chaos. This made cinema the black mass necessary for the country to achieve *a new aboriginality* in the midst of demographic anarchy.[9]

Some Contemporary Chinese Films

Mandarin Ducks and Butterflies, Oedipus, and the Tactics of Visuality

Zhang astutely places the center of interest on femininity in his construction of this "new aboriginality." Femininity in his films is the place where the contradictory nature of culture-writing—as a retrospective capturing of the past's violence and chaos, and as a progressive, forward-looking investment in the possibilities of rewriting and enlightenment—becomes clearest. Women are here the prototype of "the primitive" in all the ambiguities of that word—they are the bearers of the *barbaric* nature of a patriarchal system that has outlived its time and place; their abuse is a sign of China's *backwardness*; through them we come to understand the *fundamental* horrors about a culture. At the same time, women's sufferings reveal a larger human *nature* that has been unjustly chained and that seeks to be liberated; they are a kind of wronged, maligned, exploited *noble savage* whose innocence must be redeemed.

Insofar as they melodramatize womanly events in what often turn out to be trivial, hackneyed narratives, Zhang's films are, in terms of ethnic lineage, inheritors of the popular Mandarin Duck and Butterfly fictional modes that run throughout Chinese literature and film in the twentieth century. I have argued elsewhere that the predominant feature of Butterfly fiction is that women's problems serve as the hinges of many narratives.[10] If we translate the Butterfly novelists' narrative strategies into cinematic terms, we may say that it is women who are the objects of cinematic close-ups and slow motions, and that it is women who provide the suturing points at which the narratives "hang together." Unlike Butterfly novelists who had to focus on women with the abstract means of verbal language, however, Zhang has in the film medium an obvious means of visual display. Whereas Butterfly novelists must devise strange plots in which women characters' loved ones mysteriously disappear so that they are left alone for dramatization, Zhang has at his disposal a much more palpable means of externalizing and thus reifying women's oppression. If the subject matter of these films is the kind long decried by canonically minded critics as feminine and thus insignificant, Zhang makes us realize anew the fascination of such trivial matter. His films do not change the mundane nature of the stories but enlarge the possibili-

ties of our enjoyment of precisely those unspeakable, at times pornographic fantasies that are, shall we say, a culture's "shame."

Furthermore, whereas in the traditional Butterfly novels, the enjoyment of such fantasies still had to be "covered up" by moralistic prefaces
and didactic justifications, in Zhang such a "cover-up" is not necessary
because film, at the same time that it provides him with a palpable
means of expressing womanly contents, also provides him with an alibi:
he is merely showing such (pornographic) contents in order to give a
"realistic" picture of China. The didactic excuse, which the Butterfly
novelists had to insert explicitly into their narratives, is already there, in
the silence and ambiguity of the filmic image.

Indeed, there is every indication that whatever Zhang does, he does
in order to emphasize not the thematic concerns or even characterization but the filmic or visual nature of his films. This is where the prominence of womanly content—that conscious invention of an ethnic primitivism—must be seen as part and parcel of the cross-cultural significance, the emergent ethnographicity, of his practice. This practice is,
above all, a conscious and tactical mobilization of every kind of event
toward visual display, a display that is most effectively achieved through
women. Hence, even though Zhang's interest is not inherently in
women's problems themselves, he relies for his culture-writing on a
focalization, a "zoom-in" on the women characters.

To this end—that of skillfully displaying women as bearers of his
filmic ethnography—Zhang makes full use of the modernist conceptual method that many have called, after Freud, *Oedipalization*. Examples:
In *Red Sorghum*, Jiuer's husband was mysteriously murdered before "my
grandpa" shows up to claim her. In *Raise the Red Lantern*, there is the suggestion that the eldest son of Songlian's husband, the young man called
Feipu, might be romantically attracted to her but there would be no
hope for such a romance since his father is alive and well.[11] The woman's
body/sexuality becomes, in both films, the place where Oedipal rivalries—rivalries between men—are visually, visibly staged.[12]

In *Judou*, Oedipal rivalries literally take the form of incest: Judou
lives her life between her husband and his nephew Tianqing. Apart from
the background of a dye mill, Zhang introduces a significant number of
changes in the Judou story in order to enhance the Oedipalist focus on
femininity. First, the title of the story is changed from the name of a
mythic male figure in Liu Heng's novella—Fuxi is the mythic emperor

who invented the *bagua* (octogram) and the weaving of nets—to that of a poor and insignificant woman, a female subaltern, in modern times. Second, Zhang rewrites Liu Heng's plot in such a way as to connect the dramatization of femininity with patricide. Whereas in Liu Heng's novella, the old man Yang Jinshan dies a quiet natural death with a smile on his face and Tianqing, Judou's lover, commits suicide in a vat, in Zhang's film these two men, both of whom are fathers to the youngster Tianbai, are killed by him (accidentally in Jinshan's case and deliberately in Tianqing's). Third, instead of living to a great old age as she does in the novella, Judou burns down her house in what seems to be a revolutionary but suicidal ending. The implications of Oedipalization are the twin deaths of the father and the mother. If fathers are often murdered, mothers, if not murdered, commit suicide or go mad.

Together, the repeated associations of patricide typical of Oedipalization—the physical impotence, symbolic castration, and ultimate death of fathers—constitute a reading of China's modernity and "ethnicity" that is a *self-subalternization*: we are made to feel that, being fatherless, China is deprived of power; China is a subaltern in the world of modern nations. At the same time, this self-subalternization is unmistakably accompanied by the fetishization of women—a fetishization that can, I think, be more accurately described as a *self-exoticization* through the tactics of visuality.

Such tactics of visuality are apparent once we examine other alterations Zhang made in the literature he borrowed.[13] In my brief discussion of *Judou* in part 2, chapter 1, I already mentioned, for instance, that the background of a dye mill in *Judou* was not present in the original story by Liu Heng but added in the film so that the audience can see the drama on the screen as primarily a drama of colors. In *Raise the Red Lantern*, the eye-catching family ritual of lighting lanterns in the courtyard of the favored concubine is not present in Su Tong's novella "Qi qie cheng qun" [Wives and concubines], from which the film was adapted. Moreover, in Su Tong's story there is a well in which concubines were thrown previous to Songlian's arrival. The well, located in a neglected part of the garden, is a symbol both of femininity and of the inevitable death that awaits women in the Chen family.[14] In Zhang's film, the well disappears. Instead we find an architecturally spectacular rooftop where various members of the household make their presence and where stylized singing, conversations, and conflicts take place. The space of murder is changed to a small house locked up on one side of the roof. Unlike the well in Su Tong's novella, this house, in which concubines who commit adultery are hanged, is much more prominently visible on the screen.

Examples like these indicate that what Zhang performs here is not really a liberation of sexuality—neither a vibrant male sexuality nor a repressed female sexuality—in the narrow sense but, first and foremost, a production of filmic signs. To return to Barthes, Zhang is building one semiotic system on another, in such a manner as always to bracket the denotative meaning of the "raw" first level of signification.

The Art of Seduction

While Barthes uses the word *myth* to describe the bracketing of this first level, Jean Baudrillard, in a more dramatic manner, calls it death, a death he associates with seduction: "To seduce," writes Baudrillard, is "to die as reality and reconstitute oneself as illusion."[15]

Borrowing from the etymology of the word *seduction*, which refers to the act of leading astray or leading away, Baudrillard defines seduction as the turning of a sign away from meaning, from its own truth.[16] Following Baudrillard, we may say that what we see in Zhang's films is a "transubstantiation of sex into signs that is the secret of all seduction."[17] What is displayed is not so much woman or even feudal China per se as the act of displaying, of making visible. What Zhang "fetishizes" is primarily cinematography itself. If we speak of a narcissism here, it is a repeated playing with "the self" that is the visuality intrinsic to film. *This* play is *the* sexuality of Zhang's works.[18]

Barthes writes that "myth is not defined by the object of its message, but by the way in which it utters this message."[19] Baudrillard writes that "seduction . . . never belongs to the order of nature, but that of artifice—never to the order of energy, but that of signs and rituals."[20] Accordingly, the seduction of Zhang's films—the appeal of his visual ethnography—is that they keep crossing boundaries and shifting into new spheres of circulation. The wish to "liberate" Chinese women, which seems to be the "content," shifts into the liberation of "China," which shifts into the liberation of the "image" of China on film, which shifts into the liberation of "China" on film in the international culture market, and so on.

With the shifting of attention from "message" or "nature" to the form of utterance and to artifice, meaning—that culturally loaded thing—is displaced onto the level of surface exchange. Such a displacement has the effect of emptying "meaning" from its conventional space—the core, the depth, or the inside waiting to be seen and articulated—and reconstructing it in a new locus—the locus of the surface, which not only shines but *glosses*; which looks, stares, and speaks.

In the light of this seductive locus of the surface, which constitutes the space of a new culture-writing, Zhang's modesty about his own work becomes very interesting.[21] Speaking in regard to *Red Sorghum*, for instance, Zhang has said that he has not really thought too clearly about how to shoot the film (or films in general) and that he likes discussing with friends in "theory circles" because they can help him figure out many problems. Speaking guilelessly thus, Zhang is like the seducer described by Baudrillard—the seducer who does not consciously know that he is seducing even though he is fully engaged in the game of seduction. Zhang's films, it follows, are the seducer's snares—the enigmatic traps he sets up in order to engage his viewers in an infinite play and displacement of meanings and surfaces—and, most important, to catch these viewers in their longings and desires, making them reveal passions they nonetheless do not fully understand.

The Search for Concreteness

Oppressive feudal practices, ethnic details, myth making, magnificent cinematography, female sexuality—these elements I have summarized as the recognizable trademarks of Zhang's films are also those that have most interested his critics, whether or not they are sympathetic with his projects. What I find most revealing about readings of Zhang's films is that regardless of their evaluation, they all tend to revolve around assumptions about depths and surfaces. I will begin with the readings that are critical of his works, readings that fall into three main types.

First, we hear that Zhang's films lack depth, a lack that critics often consider as *the reason* why his films are beautiful. For instance, in a short review of *Red Sorghum*, David Edelstein writes that "Zhang's superb eye masks his lack of interest in his subjects' psychology." Edelstein concludes that the film is a "robust crowd-pleaser from mainland China" and that "the depth of its dumbness must have been a secondary consideration, a small price to pay for sweep and novelty and unimpeachable politics."[22] H. C. Li writes that *Red Sorghum* is "a film intended to please the eye and excite the senses, and a film endowed with superficial brilliance but not deep content."[23] Wu Ruozeng says that one should not talk about *Red Sorghum* in terms of "profundities" (*shenke*) but should simply understand the strong feeling (*ganjue*) it puts forth for a return to human nature.[24]

Second, Zhang's "lack of depth" is inserted in what become debates about the politics of cross-cultural representations. The beauty of Zhang's films is, for some critics, a sign of Zhang's attempt to pander to the tastes of foreigners. Yang Zhao, for instance, writes that the visual design of *Judou* is specially made to cater to those who are familiar with the established rules of American film culture, which is characterized by a kind of "tourist's psychology" (*guanguang xintai*).[25] Dai Qing, who charges the crew of *Raise the Red Lantern* for taking "outrageous liberty with such details as decor, dialogue, and diction," writes that "this kind of film is really shot for the casual pleasures of foreigners."[26] For Paul Clark, who is speaking about 1980s mainland Chinese films in general, the international awards won by films such as Zhang's suggest that "the strong visual qualities of these films could reach across borders," even though "for the comparatively tiny Chinese audience who followed these films . . . the new movies were distinctively Chinese."[27] There is in these remarks a feeling that the use of appealing visual qualities exoticizes China and that it is such exoticization, rather than the genuine complexities of Chinese society, that accounts for the success of such films in the West.[28] Even though Zhang and his contemporaries are "orientals," then, they are explicitly or implicitly regarded as producing a kind of orientalism.[29]

Third, this lack of depth, this orientalism, is linked to yet another crime—that of exploiting women. Zhang's films are unmistakably filled with sexually violent elements, such as the kidnapping of Jiuer by "my Grandpa" in *Red Sorghum*, Jiuer's eventual submission to him, the voyeuristic treatment of *Judou*, and the commodification of women in *Raise the Red Lantern*, in which wives and concubines are portrayed as jealous enemies preying upon one another in order to win the favor of the despotic husband who dominates them all. It is said that by fetishizing the female subaltern, or the female-as-subaltern, Zhang is simply reinforcing the patriarchal interests for which women are merely sex objects. Hence feminist critics such as Esther Yau and Peter Hitchcock write of Zhang's films: women such as Jiuer are "being engaged in excessive sexist exchanges motivated by male desire";[30] Zhang and Chen Kaige "remain remarkably mute about how reactionary technologies of gender may inform their own discourse"; Zhang's "close-ups of [Jiuer's] face and soft focus are entirely traditional in their aesthetic effects";[31] and so forth.

I would like to clarify at this point that I am fully in agreement with the feminist intent of critics such as Yau and Hitchcock. Insofar as he adopts a traditional, mainstream understanding of male-female relations, it is clear that Zhang's films do not depart at all from the politics of the polarization of male gaze versus female body that was problematized by Laura Mulvey's influential essay "Visual Pleasure and Narrative Cinema."[32] On the contrary, Zhang's films provide a demonstration, from the perspective of a non-Western culture, of Mulvey's incisive observation of what in many ways is still the predominant heterosexual problematic. It seems to me, however, that rather than simply reinscribing Zhang within this problematic (and condemning him for it), we need to go further and ask what we would be disabling and prohibiting from surfacing once we adopt, as we must from time to time, the moral overtones of this admittedly justified feminist position. The reason why we need to go further is that, in criticizing Zhang's "traditional" or "patriarchal" treatment of women, feminist criticism may unwittingly put itself at the service of a kind of conservatism that values depths over surfaces, and nativism over universalism, in a manner that is, ultimately, antifeminist. How so?

Jia chou bu ke wai yang

To explain what I think is the central problem here—the universal prejudice against exhibitionism and self-display—let me return to one of the most reactionary responses to Zhang, such as that coming from the mainland Chinese authorities. Apart from the explicit sexual contents of Zhang's films, it is believed that the Chinese authorities are displeased by Zhang because his films transgress the "Chinese" taboo, *jia chou bu ke wai yang.*[33] The English equivalent to this Chinese expression would be something like "Don't air your dirty laundry in public." But the Chinese phrase is much more precise in that it points to the exact area that is being tabooed—not the "dirty laundry" itself but *wai yang*, the act of showing, brandishing, exhibiting (to the outside). The point, in other words, is not that there should not be such dirty laundry around—*that* is taken for granted, as a matter of course about *jia*, the family. The point is rather that such shame and dirt should not be flaunted.

In the language of visuality, what the Chinese authorities' disapproval signals is a disciplinary surveillance from above, but it is not exactly a surveillance over the "content" of backwardness in Zhang's films as is often assumed (many mainland films of the past few decades also use such content to point their morals).[34] Rather, the surveillance is over the act of exhibiting and displaying. The reactionary response of the Chinese authorities in fact contains much more intelligence than most of their critics are willing to grant them, for in their disapproval lies the correct intuition that Zhang's films are not simply about backwardness but about a different kind of signification. Hence even though all the settings of Zhang's three films date back to the 1920s, 1930s, and 1940s—the period before the People's Republic of China was established—the authorities remained firm for a long time in their prohibitive resolve. Zhang's casual remarks about his filmmaking are revealing in this regard, for they point precisely to this deliberate flaunting, this defiant display of difference that disturbs the authorities:

In *Red Sorghum* I did not deliberately try to combat or contradict the traditional way of making film. . . . [However] that was indeed the purpose when we made *One and Eight* [*Yi ge he ba ge*] and *Yellow Earth*, and especially when we made *One and Eight*. At that time I was filled with anger whenever I set up the camera. All of us were basically fed up with the unchanging, inflexible way of Chinese filmmaking, so we were ready to fight it at all costs in our first film. I would set down the camera and take a look, and [say to myself,] Oh, god, the composition is still the same as the old stuff! No! Turn the lens around—just turn it around, raise it, just for the sake of raising it. Actually *if you ask me whether there was any concept in this kind of incomplete composition, the answer is no; but the point was simply and deliberately to be different.*[35]

What the Chinese authorities sense is perhaps exactly this kind of *gestural* force that, according to Zhang, has nothing "beneath" it. In its "emptiness," Zhang's filmmaking challenges the deep-rooted attitude of approval, ingrained in the understanding of representation across cultures, toward depth, profundity, and interiority. This attitude, which associates depth, profundity, and interiority with "virtue," is also the preference for a *somethingness* in representation.

Shi versus *xu*: The Ethnic Paradigms of Evaluation

It is well known to the practitioners and scholars of Chinese literature and culture that this attitude toward deep meanings is part of a pervasive bifurcated moralism of *shi* (fullness or concreteness) versus *xu* (emptiness), which are often used as criteria for judging virtues of aesthetic representation. Ultimately, such criteria must also be seen as major ways of *producing value in a culture*. For the purposes of our discussion, a table schematically contrasting the associations commonly attached to *shi* and *xu* may be drawn up as follows:

SHI	XU
full	empty
concrete	abstract
deep	shallow
earnest	superficial
authentic	fake
real worth	cosmetics
content	form
history	fiction
male	female

The notion of *shi* is linked to an approved concreteness of content in any representation, a concreteness that by extension would also be described with metaphors such as *shendu* (depth) and *neihan* (inner meaning).[36] On the other hand, with the exception of philosophical discussions (typically, of Daoism) in which *xu* is attributed with the significance of the nonsaid, and with the exception of moralist advice of modesty and open-mindedness,[37] the notion of *xu* is almost always invoked pejoratively in the language of cultural evaluation, as a way to express contempt for the kinds of associations listed in the right-hand column of our table. We think of expressions such as *xuruo* (weak, debilitated), *xuwei* (pretentious), *xufu* (superficial, slick), *xurong* (vanity), *xuhuan* (illusory), *xuwang* (fabricated), *xujia* (fake, artificial), *xu you qi biao* (superficial; literally, "possessed only with the surface"), *xuqing jiayi* (hypocritical display of affection), and *xu zhang sheng shi* (much ado about nothing; literally, "making empty noises and gestures").

When Zhang's critics criticize him for a lack of depth and an empty display, they are hence simply reinvoking the criteria of the reactionary *xu/shi* structure. As we will see in the following, precisely because this structure has to do not only with evaluation but with the production of value itself, it becomes even more crisis-laden once it is confronted with the politics of cross-cultural interpretation.

The Eyes of the Foreign Devil

In postcoloniality, this traditional or ethnic polarization of the criteria for aesthetic merit is complicated by the presence of that entity called the *foreign devil*. What may be added to our table now are "China" and "native" in the left-hand column and "the West" and "foreigner" in the right.

Among the Chinese, as among many non-Western peoples, there is a *postcolonial way of expressing contempt for one's fellow "natives"*: *zuo gei waiguoren kan*—such-and-such is done "for the eyes of the foreigner," with "foreigner" usually meaning those from the advanced industrial West. (See remarks from critics such as Dai Qing, cited earlier.) One thinks of expressions of contempt such as *chongyang* (worshiping the foreign) and *meiwai* (fawning on the foreign), which allude to the obsequious ways in which "natives" identify with the foreign devil rather than with their own culture and countrymen. These expressions, however, also reveal a highly ambivalent attitude toward the foreign, for the contempt they proclaim is, in fact, not possible without a keen observation or imagination of the foreigner's gaze and what may be done to attract or please that gaze. In other words, these expressions of contempt already contain *in themselves* the acts of looking at foreigners—of natives looking at or imagining the foreigner looking, of natives looking at or imagining fellow natives being looked at by foreigners, and so forth. And yet, while clearly recognizing in the foreigner a power to authenticate and endow value themselves, those who harbor such contempt are frequently quick to repudiate such acts of looking *in others*. Their contempt for fellow natives' looking is thus, we may say, ultimately an attempt to censor or prohibit this exchange between native and foreigner, even though, in their very mode of proclamation, they have already attested to the inevitability of this exchange.

Very often, and I think this is the case with the reception to Zhang's filmmaking, the expression of contempt is really the expression of an envy or jealousy at the success enjoyed by those who *have* captured the gaze of the foreigner. These ambivalent sentiments, which are laden with the injustices of history and politics, and which are transindividual, nonetheless manifest themselves prominently in the behavior of many individual "natives," in academia as much as in other circles, who look upon their fellow "natives" with suspicion, belittlement, and scorn, even while the same people who accuse others of pandering to the foreign devil remain themselves subserviently respectful to the foreign. Whenever the phrase *zuo gei waiguoren kan* (or its equivalent) is invoked, therefore, it is always the symptom of a self-contradictory sentiment, the meaning of which is "They have made it! They are actually being seen by the foreign devil!"—followed by a moralistic type of dismissal and self-assurance: "But of course they did it only by improper, shallow means." The fantasy that lies at the heart of such contempt is that we must prove "from within" that we are worthy of that foreign gaze and that if we do it properly, the foreign devil will look closely and deeply "inside" us for our authentic value.[38]

Zhang, Too, Is Concrete, Not Empty

Although no books are written on how these postcolonial sentiments translate into aesthetic criteria, it is possible to see in the attempts to evaluate an artist like Zhang the inscriptions of the dilemmas of cross-cultural interpretative politics. If the more reserved of these evaluations tend to focus on the "superficial" quality of Zhang's films, the laudatory evaluations, too, are symptomatic of the bifurcated structure of moral-aesthetic criteria. These laudatory evaluations, which come by and large from male critics, would show how *meaningful* Zhang's films are.

For instance, H. C. Li writes that *Red Sorghum* is "a Dionysian ode to life . . . a tribute to the heroic spirit of the Chinese people."[39] Yan Xiang-lin praises *Red Sorghum* for its portrayal of a nonidealized humanity, which "returns aesthetic truth to values of simplicity and authenticity" [*dui yishu zhendi de fanpuguizhen*];[40] while Wu Ruozeng, who rules out using "profundities" as a criterion for *Red Sorghum*, praises the film for returning us to the forces of human nature.[41] Others draw on authors such as Bakhtin and Racine to compare the carnivalesque atmosphere and intensity of Zhang's films.[42] Perhaps the most articulate of this type of reading is Yuejin Wang's, who sees *Red Sorghum* as a return of the collective repressed and an evocation of the cultural unconscious. Basing his interpretation of feminine sexuality entirely on Jiuer's looks, which he describes as "autonomous ecstasy," Wang upholds the film as containing a theory about a strong femininity as well as a marginalized but transgressive masculinity.[43] These critics' interpretations are close to Zhang's own. Among Zhang's favorite descriptions of *Red Sorghum* are *reqing* (passion) and *huoli* (energy). When speaking about Mo Yan's *Red Sorghum Family*, on which his film was based, Zhang repeatedly refers to the "sensuous motion of life," the "enthusiastic human pursuit of life," and the "eulogy of life" signified by the narrative.

In their laudatory mode, the masculinist reviewers disprove the more negative conclusions of Zhang's critics but not their premise, which they in fact share. This is the premise that the value of a work of art consists in the concreteness, the "somethingness," of its content. What these enthusiastic reviewers uphold here is the "somethingness" of what we might call primitivism. In a way that reminds one of the eulogies of "nature," "life," and "sexuality" that characterize male modernist writers such as D. H. Lawrence and Henry Miller, we find in the positive readings of Zhang an overwhelming consensus about "energy" and "human nature" *in spite of* the apparent superficiality of his films. Instead of accusing Zhang of a lack of depth in the mode of being *xu*, then, these reviewers affirm, by their identification of the "energy" in Zhang, that his films are *shi*——that is, sanguine, earthy, instinctual, close to the people. Together they produce a reading based on male homosocial bonding, a reading that says, Zhang, too, is concrete, not empty.

Feminist criticism, when confronted with the basic masculinism of this kind of "pro-life" clamor, has little choice other than pointing out the untenability of Zhang's "energy." Once it does this, however, it is putting itself at the service of the *xu/shi* interpretative machinery. Against the kinds of *shi* qualities affirmed by male critics, feminists must charge that Zhang's films are false representations of women's sexuality, that they fictionalize women's sufferings, and so on. In other words, feminists must *demystify* Zhang's films by saying that they are inauthentic representations of women. In the words of Yau, for instance, *Red Sorghum* is an example of China's "filmic fantasies" whose "defenses" are to be undone by "history."[44] Another way of putting this would be to say that Zhang has left out the truth (*shi*) that is female subjectivity in favor of the lie (*xu*) that is the (fetishized) female image. In a manner perhaps unintended by most feminist critics, this type of feminist criticism would then, by implication, be helping to consolidate the kind of conservatism that would distrust all filmic representation on account of its superficiality, or that would repudiate all Westernized ethnic representation on account of its eagerness to cater to "foreign" consumption.[45]

Whether positive or negative, therefore, evaluations of Zhang's films tend to leave the central problem of the moral-aesthetic polarization of *shi* and *xu* intact, allowing the values espoused therein to return under multiple guises. Despite their otherwise different or opposed politics, these readings have one thing in common——the assumption that there is a hidden truth, a core of meaning that is other than or interior to what we see on the glossy surfaces of Zhang's films. In Michel Foucault's terms, all these interpretations, regardless of their race, class, or gender perspectives, share the symptom of the "repressive hypothesis"——the hypothesis that some fundamental secret or nature has been "repressed," that human beings are awaiting emancipation, and that the representation of sexuality equals the revelation of truth:

> This oft-stated theme, that sex is outside of discourse and that only the removing of an obstacle, the breaking of a secret, can clear the way leading to it, is precisely what needs to be examined.

Does it not partake of the injunction by which discourse is provoked? Is it not with the aim of inciting people to speak of sex that it is made to mirror, at the outer limit of every actual discourse, something akin to a secret whose discovery is imperative, a thing abusively reduced to silence, and at the same time difficult and necessary, dangerous and precious to divulge? . . . What is peculiar to modern societies, in fact, is not that they consigned sex to a shadow existence, but that they dedicated themselves to speaking of it *ad infinitum*, while exploiting it as *the* secret.[46]

The "repressive hypothesis," in other words, does not so much affirm the truth of sexuality or its need for emancipation as it testifies to the complex institutional networking of power through "discourse." Whether in terms of a modernist reading of China as an impotent old man chaining his descendants to his rigid ways, or a Marxist-masculinist reading of vibrance and energy, or a feminist reading of the still-unarticulated truths of female sexuality and subjectivity, the tropes of prohibition, repression, and liberation that run consistently throughout readings of Zhang's films in effect load them with power—the power of interpretative ideology, of *discursive meaning-ful-ness*.

My primary objection to these interpretations is not that they do not tell the truth about Zhang's films—they do, and with great sensitivity and sophistication—but rather that, in concentrating on the search for concrete meanings, they seem to miss the predominant fact that filmic images operate as images, as surfaces whose significance lies in their manner of undoing depth itself. In order to deal with the problem of reading that Zhang's films cause, it is hence not enough simply to provide alternative analyses and hermeneutical exegeses of the "deep meanings" of the films.

This is the place where a kind of reading different from those legitimated by the "repressive hypothesis" must intervene and where a reference to someone such as Baudrillard is necessary. As is characteristic of all of his writings, Baudrillard's target in his book *Seduction* is Western culture's ingrained beliefs in production, depth, and the metaphysics of interiority. He argues that even ground-breaking, subversive modern theories such as Marxism, psychoanalysis, and feminism are complicitous with such beliefs when they systematically *avoid* seduction in favor of interpretation.[47] While I do not find Baudrillard's deliberately scandalous rhetoric unproblematic—this rhetoric is itself an example of seduction, aimed at turning the reader away from even the most intimately held "truths"—I think that in a context in which the "deep" and "concrete" tendencies of interpretation are adamant, such as the present one, Baudrillard's theoretical excessiveness can be useful. Baudrillard's mistake lies in his assumption that "deep" interpretative tendencies are diseases of "the West" only. His orientalist romanticism about non-Western peoples[48] blinds him to the fact that what he is criticizing is also a firmly cultivated legacy of the non-West, in this case China.

Approaches to Illusion: Zhang and Chen Kaige

Inherent in Zhang's tactics of visuality is an astute, almost militaristic understanding of the way *time* works in cinema and, even more so, in mass culture. In order to be successful, film must communicate as if it is automatic and unmediated, in such a way as to make people feel that they can follow without having to make an effort. In their crudity and simplicity, Zhang's films contain this shrewd grasp of the essential illusion of transparency that film audiences are after. The following lucid remarks reveal his mastery of what makes film not only a formally specific medium but also a mass event:

> [In film adaptation] even very good literature . . . has to become filmlike. The first thing I can do is to reduce the complexity of the events, and make the story simple and popular [*tongsu*]. Film is a "one-time deal." The form of its watching is compulsory: there is no time for turning back, and there is no time for thinking; you must follow the screen. When it is a matter of concise, charming words, you can keep reflecting; even when you have arrived at the last chapter [of a book] you turn back to the front. Film [however] is a one-time deal, and very few ordinary people watch the same film two or three times. Everywhere else in the cinema it is dark and silent; only the screen has light and sound. Watching can

only follow screen time. You can't let people pass without having understood what is going on.[49]

In other words, the irreversible time (or speed) of watching imposes itself on the filmmaker as a strict discipline. For Zhang, filmmaking is about learning and submitting to the *dominance* of this "one-time deal."[50]

Zhang's pragmatic and disciplined (pragmatism-cum-discipline) approach is one of the major differences between him and his contemporary Chen Kaige. Whereas Zhang makes maximal use of the limited but predominant mode of time on the screen to construct the kinds of images that would be accessible to a large number of people, in Chen's films there is, as my foregoing discussions indicate, a fundamental distrust of the positivity of screen images. Hence the images in Chen's films are much less accessible and much more "allegorical" in the sense of not saying everything.[51] This approach to the image is part of Chen's way of bringing a traditional Daoist understanding of (visual) presence—as only the partial truth if not altogether a distraction—to bear upon his use of a medium that, ironically, is predominantly defined by visuality. Juxtaposed with Zhang, Chen can be described to have put into play the *philosophical* meaning of *xu*, as a steady *emptying* of presence. In Chen's films, blanks signify and silences speak: this is why they invite *interpretation*. Moreover, interpretation must supplement the predominant imagistic and narrative presences in the films with nonimagistic and nonnarrative significations such as (as I demonstrated in the previous two chapters) music and nature.

As a result, however, Chen's films demand from their audiences a kind of attentiveness that automatically excludes a large number of people. Juxtaposed with Zhang's, Chen's approach presents itself as a more traditional scholarly belief in truth as that which is inward and invisible,[52] and which can be apprehended but not positivistically seen. Zhang, by contrast, does not rely on the audiences' philosophical perceptiveness, patience, or fondness for contemplation to get his films across; instead he operates at an obvious and crude level that guarantees him an audience. Instead of an idealist and idealistic notion of truth as that which resides inside his own mind, inside the nuances of his films, or inside his characters' or the audience's subjectivities, Zhang, like popular novelists and mass culture–producers, relies on attention-seizing strategies that seduce audiences away from whoever they happen to be and whatever they happen to be doing. If "plot" has become weak in both Chen and Zhang, it is for entirely different reasons. In Chen the weakening of the plot has to do with the distrust of storytelling as a means of arriving at the truth; it is the distrust of a convention because it is too conventional, because it has already been used by too many people and has thus become uninteresting.[53] In Zhang the weakening of the plot is really a heightening of effects. Zhang's films do rely on storytelling, but it is storytelling purged of its more cumbersome complexities. The story is now used for the most direct purpose of generating and sustaining interest. If storytelling is mobilized in the most conventional way, it is simply because convention is where the crowds are.[54]

If Chen's way of critiquing culture is deconstructionist, in the sense of a careful, meditative, vigilant disassembling of culture's components *from within* its structures, Zhang's critique comes from a more popularized Marxist and Maoist idealism, in the sense of a belief in the force of the masses and in the changeability and adaptability of cultural production.[55] Zhang, who bought his first camera by selling his own blood,[56] often speaks of a close identification not only with China but in particular with China's peasants,[57] and of art as a liberation from oppression.[58] In other words, Zhang's social critique follows Chinese communism's way of discrediting tradition *from below* rather than from within culture's core of coherence. If Chen has inherited the traditional Chinese literati's way of doing "culture" through philosophy and poetry, Zhang's lineage is that of the popular dramatist, novelist, and street performer whose modes of enunciation are inseparable from the masses. For Chen, even a simple act like that of pissing becomes, as I indicated in the previous chapter, an occasion for philosophical reflection (on the animalistic truth about human culture). For Zhang, piss is, as it is in *Red Sorghum*, what unexpectedly makes wine taste better, what enhances the quality of a collective form of production.

These differences also mark their respective treatments of women. While Zhang uses women for the obvious, conventional, pornographic purposes of representation—as fetishized body parts[59] complete with the melodrama of mental suffering—in Chen women occupy a much less clear-cut, because *much more idealized*, space. Cuiqiao's brave determination to change her life leads her to her death in *Yellow Earth*; women do not appear in *The Big Parade* except in idyllic scenes that are brought about by feverish daydreams; Laidi in *King of the Children* appears in the role of a coarse, fat sister and mother; the women in *Life on a String* are either mysteriously motherly or frustrated and suicidal. The hardly visible or hardly material place women occupy in Chen's works is the symptom of an idealism that regards truth as that which is hidden, which is *other* than the here and now. Chen's critique of traditional Chinese culture stems from a belief in the invisible inward depths that have been veiled and distorted by culture's untrustworthy surfaces. Zhang's critique stems, instead, from the material force of such surfaces—from their vulgar womanly focus, their seductive accessibility, their irreversible time, their illusion of transparency.

The Deep Habits of Ideology-Criticism

What Zhang's films force and dare us to do, ultimately, is to see ideology in terms other than those of a moralistically denounced "illusion"— what Barthes calls mythical speech. As my brief overview of Zhang's evaluators shows, we can be so caught up in our habits of thinking by way of depth that we would read even those discourses that are meant to be critical of depth in a deep way. When the truth is thought to be something lying behind, beneath, below, and beyond ideology, ideology becomes simply a mask and a veil to be indignantly stripped away. But ideology is seldom, if ever, that.

We can now return to the implications of Barthes's *Mythologies*. In retrospect, we realize that ideology-as-mask constitutes what is the "content" part of Barthes's inquiry. For Barthes, the mass culture phenomena of France in the 1950s—from detergent advertisements to plastic to the cover pictures of popular magazines—were a kind of mythologized language, a second order signification that was saturated with the ideology of the bourgeoisie. This mythologized language entices the masses with wishes for those things that, precisely because of the hierarchical class structure of bourgeois society, they will never be able to possess. Barthes's chief reference here is Marx's and Engels's *German Ideology*, in which ideology is defined as an upside-down version of reality, a camera obscura.[60] Accordingly, myth for Barthes is a kind of veil that naturalizes, that hides the real social conditions of their making.

Some Contemporary Chinese Films

Even though Barthes was writing about French society in the 1950s, the problems crystallized by his remarkable little book remain germane to this day. Central to these problems is the age-old tendency, among intellectuals in particular, to distrust surface phenomena. As a result, whatever is glossy, beautiful, or glamorous always takes on the status of the suspect. Depending on the type of criticism being mobilized, myth or ideology is alternately mapped onto "the culture industry" (Theodor Adorno and Max Horkheimer), masculinist "visual pleasure" (Laura Mulvey), or orientalism (Edward Said), but the rhetorical move remains the same: what is ideological remains the illusion that prevents us from seeing or knowing the truth; and criticism's task, it is believed, lies in unveiling that illusion. We see how this is the case in some of the interpretations of Zhang's films: all the talk about his lack of depth and his pandering to the tastes of Westerners is part and parcel of this universal distrust of surface phenomena, phenomena that tend to be treated as myth, error, and deception. To put it in the terms of our ethnic paradigm, such attitudes amount to a continual repudiation of the associations of *xu*.

Toward the end of *Mythologies*, Barthes realizes that the demythifying activity he has been pursuing places him in an impossible situation: he would either have to maintain a critical stance and forsake all the pleasures of mass culture or, if he decides he would have a good time after all, he must allow himself to fall prey to ideology. Writing at a time when French intellectual life was inseparable from existentialism, he calls this "alienation": "The fact that we cannot manage to achieve more than an unstable grasp of reality doubtless gives the measure of our present alienation: we constantly drift between the object and its demystification, powerless to render its wholeness. For if we penetrate the object, we liberate it but we destroy it; and if we acknowledge its full weight, we respect it, but we restore it to a state which is still mystified."[61]

At the same time, however, the "tool" that Barthes uses to deal with this ancient problem of myth—the tool of semiotics—does not allow him to stop simply at the moralistic stance of "turning ideology on its head" that he took from Marx and Engels. Once it is understood that the sign is constituted in a *shifting* relationship between signifier and signified, the halting of signifiers at specific signifieds that leads to the formation of ideology is, far from being permanent, itself subject to further shifting. In other words, there is nothing in the makeup of the sign itself that is intrinsic to myth; accordingly, semiotics, when used radically, would render the "content" part of Barthes's analysis (the understanding of ideology as upside-down reality, as distortion, as deception) problematic. The "tool" that Barthes is using hence becomes no longer merely a tool but a fundamental challenge to his thesis about ideology: this tool shows that not only is signification ideology but ideology, too, is signification. And as signification, ideology also is constructed from a shifting relationship between signifier and signified, and thus subject to change.

Eventually, Barthes would realize the untenability of his position in *Mythologies* and fundamentally revise his thesis. As he writes in the 1970s:

> I believe . . . that even if the new semiology . . . has not applied itself further to the myths of our time since the last of the texts in *Mythologies* where I sketched out an initial semiotic approach to social language, it is at least conscious of its task: no longer simply to *upend* (or *right*) the mythical message, to stand it back on its feet, with denotation at the bottom and connotation at the top, nature on the surface and class interest deep down, but rather to change the object itself, to produce a new object, point of departure for a new science.[62]

My point in recapitulating the problems epitomized by Barthes's book—problems that are no doubt already familiar to many readers—is to underscore how persistent the habit of thinking about ideology as illusion remains. This is particularly so in academic circles, because the scholarly way of thinking specializes in analysis and penetration, and, therefore, in showing that things are not what they seem. As scholars, we tend to distrust what appears and to believe in what does not appear. We are, in other words, much closer to Chen Kaige than to Zhang Yimou in our ways of approaching the world. Consequently, when dealing with someone like Zhang, scholarly investigations continue to be mired in their own deep habits and to move farther and farther away from the obvious intervention—from the intervention that takes the form of the obvious—introduced by Zhang.[63] The result of such investigations is that the prejudices already built into ethnic paradigms of evaluation such as *xu* and *shi* are now reinforced *transculturally* by the equally strong anti-illusion compulsions that characterize many critiques of cross-cultural representation, and vice versa.

If, on the other hand, we give up our deep habits (positive or negative), we will see that the challenge offered by Zhang's films is so basic that it undermines the ways of seeing—to use John Berger's famous title—that are cherished in *both* Western and non-Western cultures. In the remainder of this chapter I will attempt to specify what this challenge is.

The Oriental's Orientalism; or, Exhibitionism Between Cultures

Surfaces are not simply another type of "production." The superficiality of Zhang's films does not arise simply from the fact that they constitute a spectacle of oppression and dehumanization in feudal China. Equally important is that such a spectacle seems familiar, conventional, at times even banal. In other words, if a certain force emanates from surfaces, it is not only because surfaces are glossy but also because they are hackneyed and clichéd. To explain this, I will take a key series of scenes from *Judou*.

Near the beginning of the film, Tianqing secretly watches his aunt wash herself every morning through a hole in the wall. As Judou discovers this to her shame, she first tries to cover up the hole but then changes her mind. One morning, after making certain that Tianqing is watching as usual, she slowly turns around and, while sobbing, uncovers her naked upper body. Jenny Kwok Wah Lau observes perceptively in regard to this scene:

> One finds that the explicit erotic content of the film—beginning when Judou deliberately turns around to expose her naked body to the peeping Tianqing—is not derived from a simple act of narcissism. Indeed, her tired, dirty, and bruised body, together with the melancholy accompanying music, offers no "visual pleasure" for Tianqing or the film audience. Judou's turning around repre-

sents a decisive move against the gerontocratic and patriarchal rule that operates against her. And I propose that it is her implicit attack on this rule that has aroused the Chinese authorities' antagonism and the Chinese audience's unease.[64]

Lau's comments point succinctly to the basic *defiant* mood of all three of Zhang's films. Similarly, writing about *Judou*, W. A. Callahan points out that "Ju Dou makes a political decision when she decides to let Tianqing peek at her through a hole in the wall as she bathes."[65] As Judou turns around, what begins as an episode of voyeuristic eroticism takes on entirely different implications. As she confronts Tianqing with her naked body, Judou is, we may say, taking into her own hands the "to-be-looked-at—ness" that conventionally constitutes femininity. If the female body in its "to-be-looked-at—ness" is a cultural cliché, Judou's move is that of *quoting the cliché*: she exhibits her female body for the male gaze literally, in the manner that one cites a well-used platitude. The effect of this gesture—of quoting the most-quoted, of displaying the most fetishized—is no longer simply voyeuristic pleasure but a heightened self-consciousness.

But even though this level of self-display-as-citation marks Zhang's film with a postmodernist sense of irony, the mood of defiance does not stop at the formalism of irony only. With her naked front in full view to Tianqing, what Judou exposes is not the beauty of her body but the way it has been abused. What is on display, what is being cited, is not simply the cliché of the female body but, crucially, the signs of violence it bears.[66] Judou's "turn" thus amounts to an exposition of what we might call the *brutality of the cliché and the brutality of convention* (brutality in the sense of both cruelty and bruteness/rawness): she turns the eroticism of the spectacle into a deliberate *demonstration* of and against the patriarchal order that crushes her. Her female body—that crude, banal surface that patriarchy raids and idealizes at will—becomes in this scene a literal means of confrontation.

At the same time, this brave self-display also changes the relationship between voyeur and fetishized woman. The erotic interest that initiates Tianqing's and Judou's exchange now takes on the additional significance of a sympathy and empathy between them as *fellow victims* of the same feudal order, in which those who are dependent on the master for their survival—be they a man or a woman, a horse or a pig—are fed, used, and exploited uniformly. If Judou's self-display gratifies Tianqing's fantasies, it also turns the classic masculinist greediness of those fantasies into an identification between them, an identification that would continue in the form of their lifelong *alliance* against the patriarchal order that sacrifices women and powerless men alike.[67]

Other examples from Zhang's films also indicate the force of defiance that he associates with surfaces and surface behavior. If such defiance is a sign of resistance against power, this resistance is consistently being externalized. We think of Jiuer's unfeminine gesture of assuming her dead husband's wine-making business and turning it from private proprietorship into a communally owned production, and her "unchaste" gesture of openly letting another man into her widowed life. We think of Songlian's deliberately uncooperative behavior and her blatant lie about being pregnant as well as of her spiteful way of picking fights with her rivals in the Chen household. Most of all, we think of the young maidservant Yaner's death in *Raise the Red Lantern*. On discovering that Yaner helped expose her fake pregnancy, thus robbing her of her esteemed status in the house, Songlian takes revenge on Yaner in a cruel way: she shows everyone Yaner's most treasured secret—a collection of old red lanterns that Yaner secretly lights in her servant's quarters in imitation of the family ritual so cherished by the ladies of the house. But it is not enough to put Yaner to shame in public: as her lanterns are set on fire in the courtyard, the first wife of the house also orders that Yaner be punished by kneeling in the cold until she apologizes. Yaner refuses to apologize and, in a debilitated state, dies. By demonstrating with her own life, Yaner's is the ultimate gesture of defiance. She does not harbor her resistance inside her; instead she uses her female body— that pathetic, insignificant piece of banality—to *face* the monstrosity of an order whose victims, such as Songlian and the other wives, can just as easily turn into victimizers.

In Zhang's films, all such behavior of defiance signifies a challenge in the literal sense of a fronting, facing, and daring of convention with the self-assurance of desperation. The power of surfaces is thus the power of confrontation, which ultimately makes us, the spectators, aware of the sensation of being stared at. Against the screen of vivid colors and images, we suddenly find ourselves the objects of the gaze emanating from the images on the screen. This gaze is intense and discomforting:

especially for those spectators whose identities are sutured with the culture-specific images on the screen—who think of themselves as "Chinese," in other words—the force of surfaces jolts them into a particular kind of *self*-consciousness, a consciousness of their "ethnicity" in none-too-flattering terms.

At this point, I would like to borrow from Thomas Elsaesser's study of Rainer Werner Fassbinder in order to contend that, like Fassbinder's, Zhang's cinema is about the affect of exhibitionism rather than (as is often assumed) that of voyeurism.[68] In his analysis, Elsaesser associates the exhibitionism in Fassbinder's films with specific historical happenings, such as the German security state during and after the Second World War. Elsaesser suggests, for instance, that the pleasure of fascism for the average German is perhaps "less the sadism and brutality of SS officers than the pleasure of being seen, of placing oneself in view of the all-seeing eye of the State."[69] Fassbinder's films, accordingly, capture the structure of identification that is inscribed in the fascistic specularization of public and private life and that may be sloganized as "to be is to be perceived."[70]

For Elsaesser, Fassbinder's films are interesting not simply because he represents this structure of "being seen" but also because Fassbinder takes the all-pervasive surveillance of a state machinery and its coercive formation of subjectivity as his starting point, and produces, *in parody*, a kind of self-estranged exhibitionism in his characters: "In the face of a bureaucratic surveillance system ever more ubiquitous, Fassbinder toys with . . . an act of terrorist exhibitionism which turns the machinery of surveillance—including the camera—into an occasion for self-display."[71] By arguing that exhibitionism is actually a way of problematizing the state's all-pervasive gaze, Elsaesser thus shows that exhibitionism does not have to be the frivolous gesture it is taken to be by moralistic critics but instead can be seen as a subversive way of engaging with political authoritarianism.

Even though the film contents of Fassbinder and Zhang are worlds apart, what they share is, I think, this understanding of exhibitionism. This understanding is part of a determination to respond to political authoritarianism aesthetically through popular rather than elitist (philosophical) means. These means include banal and at times sentimental cinematic elements that recur in both Fassbinder's and Zhang's films, such as melodrama,[72] pretty women, stereotyped characters, illicit sex, petty gossipy neighbors, collective memories of the oppressiveness of fascism, playacting, intense colors and color contrasts, and melodious music. But what makes a comparison between the German and Chinese filmmakers especially revealing is their mutual sensitivity to the immobility of conventional social boundaries, to the pernicious vigilance and hypocrisy engendered by such boundaries, and to the severe ostracization awaiting transgressors. This sensitivity leads, in different but equally remarkable ways, to Fassbinder's and Zhang's tactical deployments of stylized gestures of self-display in constructing the chief interests of their cinemas.

In Zhang, the machine of surveillance is not the German security state before or after the Second World War but *the double gaze of the Chinese security state*[73] *and the world's, especially the West's, orientalism.* The exhibitionism of his films hence moves beyond the male masochists that typically embody Fassbinder's use of exhibitionism to include the "primitives" that are women and the ethnographic details that signify "China." In other words, for Zhang, the problem of a predominantly visual culture-writing is how to look at this double gaze of the Chinese state and the West in such a way as to return to it the very cruelty that emanates from it. How, his films ask, do we make images so as to "render unto Caesar the things which are Caesar's"?

What Zhang's films display are therefore also double. We see, on the one hand, the sadness of powerless lives under Chinese rule. In films like *Judou* and *Raise the Red Lantern*, the melodramatic staging of ethnic practices—such as the naming ceremony for a newborn son, the ritual of *lan lu dang guan* ("blocking the road and coffin") required of survivors to show filial piety to the dead, the absurd family customs of raising red lanterns, giving massages to favored concubines, requiring wives and concubines to share meals, and so forth—amounts to an exhibitionism that returns the gaze that is the Chinese family and state's inhuman surveillance. On the other hand, as I already argued in part 2, chapter 1, the "ethnicity"—"Chineseness"—of Zhang's films is also the sign of a cross-cultural commodity fetishism, a production of value between cultures. Precisely because ethnic practices are theatricalized as arcane and archaic, Zhang is showing a "China" that is at once subalternized and exoticized by the West. The "ethnicity" of his films amounts to an exhibitionism that returns the gaze of orientalist surveillance, a gaze that demands of non-Western peoples mythical pictures and stories to which convenient labels of otherness such as "China," "India," "Africa," and so forth can be affixed.

It would hence be imprecise, though not erroneous, to say that directors such as Zhang are producing a new kind of orientalism. For if orientalism, understood in the sense Said uses it, is in part a form of voyeuristic aggression, then what Zhang is producing is rather an exhibitionist self-display that contains, in its very excessive modes, a critique of the voyeurism of orientalism itself. (Mis)construed by many as mere self-display (in the spirit of airing one's dirty laundry in public), this exhibitionism—what we may call the Oriental's orientalism—does not make its critique moralistically or resentfully. Instead, it turns the remnants of orientalism into elements of a new ethnography. Like a Judou turning around, citing herself as fetishized woman and displaying to her voyeur the scars and wounds she bears, this ethnography accepts the historical fact of orientalism and performs a critique (i.e., evaluation) of it by staging and parodying orientalism's politics of visuality. In its self-subalternizing, self-exoticizing visual gestures, the Oriental's orientalism is first and foremost a demonstration—the display of a tactic.

The result of all this, paradoxically, is that Zhang has won high international acclaim for all his films, including those for which he served as cinematographer and actor, such as *Yellow Earth* and *Old Well*. Perhaps in response to the no longer negligible worldwide renown that Zhang is enjoying, the Chinese government first banned *Judou* and *Raise the Red Lantern* and then, for reasons that are equally incomprehensible, lifted the ban in 1992. The Chinese Xinhua News Agency even applauded Zhang's more recent *The Story of Qiuju* (1992), claiming that it was, "after all, the work of a first-rate director."[74]

Elsaesser writes in regard to the West German Cinema:

The strategy of treating artefacts and cultural objects as commodities, in order to make them enter into but also create a market, is much clearer with the New German Cinema than in other cases. . . . It was a cinema created around the very contradictions of culture and commodity, of (self-)expression value and (self-)exhibition value, in a modern capitalist economy that depends on export to sustain internal growth . . .[75]

Some Contemporary Chinese Films

The Germans are beginning to love their own cinema because it has been endorsed, confirmed, and benevolently looked at by someone else: for the German cinema to exist, it first had to be seen by non-Germans. It enacts, as a national cinema, now in explicitly economic and cultural terms, yet another form of self-estranged exhibitionism.[76]

If we substitute the word *Chinese* for the word *German*, these passages could become precise descriptions of the fates of Zhang's films in mainland China as well. If their glossy surfaces are the "myths" that commodify and betray China, Zhang's films nonetheless achieve for modern Chinese culture the attention and status that many sophisticated others fail to bring. Most important, they do this with a force of defiance that challenges us to abandon our most deeply cultivated—and most deeply cherished—intellectual habits.

Part 3

Film as Ethnography; or, Translation Between Cultures in

the Postcolonial World

How can one write/think/talk the non-West in the academy
without in some sense anthropologising it?
Dipesh Chakrabarty, "Marx After Marxism"

Anthropological "scientific method" *is* the decay of dialogue, the
sustained, cultivated, and epistemologically enforced atrophy of
dialogue. . . . As psychiatry has been the modern West's
monologue about madness and unreason, so anthropology has
been the modern West's monologue about "alien cultures."
Bernard McGrane, *Beyond Anthropology*

Ethnography is still very much a one-way street.
James Clifford, introduction to *Writing Culture*

For if the sentence is the wall before the language of the
original, literalness is the arcade. (Denn der Satz ist die Mauer
vor der Sprache des Originals, Wörtlichkeit die Arkade.)
Walter Benjamin, "The Task of the Translator"

. . . a novel anthropology not of the Third and Other worlds,
but of the West itself as mirrored in the eyes and handiwork
of its Others.
Michael Taussig, *Mimesis and Alterity*

The Deadlock of the Anthropological Situation

Throughout this book I have been using the term *ethnography* to describe some of the outstanding features of contemporary Chinese cinema, but a more systematic theoretical articulation of what I mean by "ethnography" is still in order, in particular of how this new ethnography may be conceived through visuality. Already, in discussing Zhang Yimou, we see the surfacing of a major problem of cross-cultural politics—the problem of the "foreign devil." The critics who accuse the Chinese directors of pandering to a "foreign" audience rather than to a "Chinese" audience—are they not prioritizing some "original essence" of the Chinese culture? Some readers will object: But wait, do such "nativist" critics not in fact alert us to the ongoing reality of Western cultural imperialism? Is their distrust of the "foreign" (meaning the West) not after all a justifiable reaction to the long history of Western hegemony, in which "exchange" between East and West has always meant the demand on non-Western peoples to conform to Western standards and models but not vice versa? As Kwai-cheung Lo writes in a different context, "When the concept of modernity still implies 'progress' and 'westernization,' any translation or introduction of modern texts is by no means free from cultural imperialism."[1] The incensed reaction of nativist critics, the same readers might continue, only demonstrates the point Mary Louise Pratt makes about the artistic activities of "autoethnography" in metropolitan areas—that such activities are bound to be very differently received by metropolitan audiences and by the literate sectors of the artists' own social groups.[2] As Jane Ying Zha writes: "All my American friends love Zhang's movies, all my Chinese friends hate them. . . . Why? What offended the Chinese in these movies? . . . It could all be summed up in one thing: selling oriental exoticism to a Western audience."[3]

What these observations about cross-cultural "exchange" indicate is what may be called the deadlock of the anthropological situation as created by Western imperialism and colonialism of the past few centuries. We can describe this deadlock by going back to the most basic anthropological scenario—that of the Western anthropologist traveling abroad to study the "primitive" cultures around the world. In order to perform his task, the Western anthropologist must insert himself and his social practices (such as "scientific" observation and recording) into these "primitive" contexts. In spite of the grandiose salvational motives of his profession, the very presence of the Western anthropologist means, effectively, that these "other" cultures are changed and displaced forever from their "origins." Subsequently, in order to find out authoritatively about their cultures, members of such culture often have to look up Western source books. In many cases, the methods and practices of anthropology and ethnography have simply served to reinforce and empower colonial administration, and thus to bring about the systematic destruction of these "other" cultures.[4]

The deadlock of the anthropological situation in the postcolonial world is summarized in the epigraphs by Chakrabarty, McGrane, and Clifford that appear at the beginning of this section of the book:[5] we cannot write/think/talk the non-West in the academy without in some sense anthropologizing it, and yet anthropology and ethnography, atrophied in their epistemological foundations, remain "very much still a one-way street." By their remarks, Chakrabarty, McGrane, and Clifford refer to the inequality inherent to the binary structure of observer/observed that is classical anthropology's operating premise and that has become *the* way we approach the West's "others." For non-Western peoples, the most obvious consequence of this classical operating premise is the continual privileging of Western models of language, philosophy, and historiography as "standard knowledge," and the continual marginalization of the equivalents from the non-West.[6] Because of such fundamental disparity in the classical anthropological and ethnographic situation, any process of cultural translation between West and East will, as Talal Asad writes, likely continue to be marked by an asymmetry of privileges:

The process of "cultural translation" is inevitably enmeshed in conditions of power—professional, national, international. And among these conditions is the authority of ethnographers to uncover the implicit meanings of subordinate societies. Given that that is so, the interesting question for enquiry is . . . how power enters into the process of "cultural translation," seen both as a discursive and as a non-discursive practice.[7]

Film as Ethnography

Anthropology is . . . rooted in an unequal power encounter between the West and Third World which goes back to the emergence of bourgeois Europe, an encounter in which colonialism is merely one historical moment. It is this encounter that gives the West access to cultural and historical information about the societies it has progressively dominated, and thus not only generates a kind of universal understanding, but also re-enforces the inequalities in capacity between the European and the non-European worlds (and derivatively, between the Europeanized elites and the "traditional" masses in the Third World). We are today becoming increasingly aware of the fact that information and understanding produced by bourgeois disciplines like anthropology are acquired and used most readily by those with the greatest capacity for exploitation.[8]

To put it crudely: because the languages of Third World societies—including, of course, the societies that social anthropologists have traditionally studied—are "weaker" in relation to Western languages (and today, especially to English), they are more likely to submit to forcible transformation in the translation process than the other way around. The reason for this is, first, that in their political-economic relations with Third World countries, Western nations have the greater ability to manipulate the latter. And, second, Western languages produce and deploy *desired* knowledge more readily than Third World languages do.[9]

Understandably, therefore, it is in response to this fundamentally unequal and unfair situation of knowledge organization and distribution in the postcolonial world that criticisms of contemporary Chinese films' "betrayal" of "China" have been made. The moral question behind such criticisms is this: because the exoticizing of the East is part of the agenda of Western imperialism, how could we support directors such as Zhang, who make images that seemingly further this agenda? As I argued in the previous chapter, however, charges of "betrayal" or "infidelity" are themselves far from being innocent; they are part of a defensive nativism that, in the case of Chinese film, is itself deeply rooted in the hierarchical criteria of traditional aesthetics. What such zealous charges accomplish is not exactly the preservation of the ethnic culture as such but often an unwitting complicity in perpetuating the deadlock of the anthropological situation. The Euro-American homogenization of the world is then steadily polarized against an equally overwhelming attempt on the part of some "natives" and nativists to hold on to "tradition" even as tradition is disintegrating. Instead of enabling alternatives to the deadlock, nativist demands of cultural "fidelity" have great potential of becoming prohibitive deterrents *against* cultural translation altogether.

To intervene in this deadlock, I will in the following pages argue for a redefinition of ethnography by explicitly linking ethnography with translation. Before doing that, I will explain how a focus on visuality as such is really the first step toward a dismantling of the classic epistemological foundations of anthropology and ethnography.

The Primacy of To-Be-Looked-At–ness

In an essay on representation and anthropological knowledge, Kirsten Hastrup writes: "For the non-anthropologist, all films dealing with exotic cultures may look equally anthropological, while to professional anthropologists it is much more a question of method and theory than of subject-matter."[10]

Contrary to Hastrup's suggestion, the increasingly blurred distinction between "theory and method" on the one hand and "subject matter" on the other is, I think, precisely the new object of ethnographic work in the postcolonial world. Rethought rigorously, ethnography can no longer be the "science" that its practitioners once imagined it to be, nor is it simply a "documentation" of "other" ways of life. Despite its traditional claims to objectivity, ethnography is a kind of representation with subjective origins. But how do we come to terms with such subjective origins? *Whose* subjective origins should concern us? Instead of simply arguing for the necessity of discursive self-reflexivity on the part of *Western* practitioners, with the politically correct admonition that we must watch what we say more carefully,[11] I think it is by focusing on visuality that we can come to terms with the subjective origins of ethnography most productively. In other words, I do not think that an ethnography alternative to the one we have been criticizing can materialize simply through a call for "self-consciousness"—"let's look at ourselves, our language, and our assumptions more carefully"—since such a call only con-

firms, once again, what was long ago established by Hegel as the distinguishing trait of Western Man, his capacity for being aware of himself.
Rather, I believe that *a new ethnography is possible only when we turn our*
attention to the subjective origins of ethnography as it is practiced by those who
were previously ethnographized and who have, in the postcolonial age, taken up
the active task of ethnographizing their own cultures.

This, however, does not mean exploring subjectivity in the verbal
realm only. How are the "subjective origins" of the previously ethnographized communicated in *visual* terms? They are, I think, communicated
not so much through the act of looking as through what may be called
"to-be-looked-at–ness"—the visuality that once defined the "object"
status of the ethnographized culture and that now becomes a predominant aspect of that culture's self-representation. We remember that in
her famous article "Visual Pleasure and Narrative Cinema," Laura Mulvey alerts us to "to-be-looked-at–ness" as what constitutes not only the
spectacle but the very way vision is organized; the state of being looked
at, she argues, is built into the way we look. Because in our culture,
looking and being looked at are commonly assigned respectively to men
and women, vision bears the origins of gender inequality.[12] Supplementing Mulvey's argument with the anthropological situation, we may
argue, in parallel, that vision bears the origins of ethnographic inequality. But we must go one step further: the state of being looked at not
only is built into the way non-Western cultures are viewed by Western
ones; more significantly it is part of the *active* manner in which such cultures represent—ethnographize—themselves.

What this means is that in the vision of the formerly ethnographized,
the subjective origins of ethnography are displayed in amplified form
but at the same time significantly redefined: what are "subjective" origins now include a memory of past *objecthood*—the experience of being
looked at—which lives on in the subjective act of ethnographizing like
an other, an optical unconscious.[13] If ethnography is indeed autoethnography—ethnography of the self and the subject—then the perspective
of the formerly ethnographized supplements it irrevocably with the
understanding that being-looked-at–ness, rather than the act of looking,
constitutes the primary event in cross-cultural representation.

With visuality as its focus, this reformulation of ethnography
destroys the operational premises—of a world divided in the form of us
and them, of viewing subject and viewed object—of classical anthropology. "Us" and "them" are no longer safely distinguishable; "viewed

object" is now looking at "viewing subject" looking. Moreover, through the reading of films that are not documentary and hence not ethnographic in the conventional sense, this reformulated ethnography challenges as well the factualism that typifies anthropology's hold on representation. These lines from Dai Vaughan on the documentary may be used as a critique of such factualism—if we substitute the words *ethnographers* and *ethnography* for *documentarists* and *documentary*: "Documentarists . . . like to believe that documentary is the 'natural' form of cinema. But fiction film, like painting and literature, rests no special claims upon the provenance of its linguistic elements. It must surely be clear that it is documentary which is the paradoxical, even aberrant form."[14] In studying contemporary Chinese films as ethnography and autoethnography, I am thus advocating nothing less than a radical deprofessionalization of anthropology and ethnography as "intellectual disciplines." Once these disciplines are deprofessionalized—their boundaries between "us" and "them" destabilized; their claims to documentary objectivity deconstructed—how do we begin to reconceive the massive cultural information that has for so long been collected under their rubric? It is at this juncture that I think our discussion about ethnography must be supplemented by a theory of translation.

A similar observation is made by Thomas Elsaesser in his study of the New German cinema of the 1970s. Concluding that German cinema was the consequence of "a vast transcription process," Elsaesser introduces the notion of translation as a way to understand it:

[The New German cinema] was an attempt to gather, record and report the images, sounds and stories—including those that the cinema itself produced—which make up the memory of a generation, a nation and a culture, and *to translate them, from their many perishable supports in people's minds to the one medium that, after all, promises paradoxically to be the most permanent: the cinema*. Literature, popular culture, architecture, fashion, memorabilia and the contents of junk shops have all been enlisted in a vast effort to preserve the traces of lives lived for oblivion. This hastily accumulated visual wealth has not yet been tapped or even properly inspected for its meanings or uses. As *a source of understanding the changes from a culture living mainly by the written text to one dominated by the image*, the New German Cinema still awaits to be discovered.[15]

Contemporary Chinese cinema, insofar as it collects images not only of rural but of modern urban China, not only of ancient emperors and scholars but also of women, children, lower classes, and minority cultures, can, like the New German cinema, be thought of in the sense of a "vast transcription process." But of much greater relevance is Elsaesser's notion of translation. Elsaesser's rich passage suggests, crucially, that there are at least two types of translation at work in cinema. First, translation as inscription: a generation, a nation, and a culture are being translated or permuted into the medium of film; and second, translation as transformation of tradition and change between media: a culture oriented around the written text is in the process of transition and of being translated into one dominated by the image. Elsaesser's words are equally applicable to other "national" cinemas such as the Chinese, because these "national" cinemas are, in themselves, at the crossroads of different types and stages of cultural translation. The bulk of this book, then, has in effect been dealing with the filmic transcriptions of Chinese modernity as processes of cultural translation.

In accordance with the movement of the epigraphs at the beginning of this section of the book, what I will attempt in the remaining pages is a focused discussion of translation in the sense of translation between cultures. Although contemporary Chinese film will serve as a major point of reference, various theories of translation will also be introduced in order to highlight the problems of cross-cultural exchange—especially in regard to the commodified, technologized image—in the postcolonial, postmodern age.

Translation and the Problem of Origins

Etymologically, the word *translation* is linked, among other things, to "tradition" on the one hand and to "betrayal" on the other.[16] The Italian expression *Traduttore, traditore*—"Translator, traitor"—allows us to grasp the pejorative implication of infidelity that is often associated with the task of translating. Because faithfulness is such a crucial issue here, the analogy between translation and a human convention such as matrimony is, as Barbara Johnson writes, far-reaching: "It might seem . . . that the translator ought, despite or perhaps because of his or her oath of fidelity, to be considered not as a duteous spouse but as a faithful bigamist, with loyalties split between a native language and a foreign tongue."[17] To complicate things further, the matrimony that is translation is seldom established on the basis of the equality of the partners. In the classical thinking about translation, Johnson goes on, it is the signified, not the signifier, that is given priority: "Faithfulness to the text has meant faithfulness to the semantic tenor with as little interference as possible from the constraints of the vehicle. Translation, in other words, has always been the translation of *meaning*."[18]

Given these deeply entrenched assumptions about translation, it is hardly surprising that the rendering of "China" into film, even at a time when the literary bases of Chinese society are increasingly being transformed by the new media culture, is bedeviled by suspicion and replete with accusations of betrayal. While these suspicions and accusations may express themselves in myriad forms, they are always implicitly inscribed within the ideology of fidelity. For instance, to return to our main concern in the previous chapter, is not the distrust of "surfaces"—the criticism of Zhang Yimou's lack of depth—a way of saying that surfaces are "traitors" to the historical depth that is "traditional China"? And yet the word *tradition* itself, linked in its roots to translation and betrayal, has to do with handing over. Tradition itself is nothing if it is not a transmission. How is tradition to be transmitted, to be passed on, if not through translation?

The common assumption about translation is that it is a rendering of one language into another language. Even though what is involved is actually the traffic between two languages, we tend to suppress our awareness of this by prioritizing one language over the other, by pretending that the traffic goes in one direction only. How does this happen? Consider the terminology we use, which reveals the epistemological uncertainties involved and hence the ideological need to prioritize: we call one language the "original" and the other the "translation" (meaning "unoriginal" and "derivative"). This terminology suppresses the fact that the "unoriginal" language may well be the "native tongue"— that is, the original language—of the translator, whose translating may involve turning the "original" which is actually *not* her native/original language into her "native"/"original" language. (A simple explanation like this already suffices to illustrate the vertiginous nature of any attempt to theorize translation.)

Precisely because translation is an activity that immediately prob-lematizes the ontological hierarchy of languages—"which is primary and which is secondary?"—it is also the place where the oldest preju-dices about origins and derivations come into play most forcefully. For instance, what does it mean to make a translation sound "natural"? Must the translation sound more like the "original," which is not the language into which it is translated—meaning that it is by resemblance to the "original" that it becomes "natural"? Or, must it sound more like the lan-guage into which it is translated, in which case sounding "natural" would mean forgetting the "origin"? When we say, derogatorily, "This reads like a translation," what we mean is that even though we understand what the "original" meaning might be, we cannot but notice its translated-ness—and yet is that not precisely what a translation is supposed to be—*translated* rather than "original"? As in all bifurcated processes of signification, translation is a process in which the notion of the "origi-nal," the relationship between the "original" and its "derivations," and the demand for what is "natural" must be thoroughly reexamined.

Using contemporary Chinese cinema as a case in point, I think the criticism (by some Chinese audiences) that Zhang and his contempo-raries "pander to the tastes of the foreign devil" can itself be recast by way of our conventional assumptions about translation. The "original" here is not a language in the strict linguistic sense but rather "China"—"China" as the sum total of the history and culture of a people; "China" as a content, a core meaning that exists "prior to" film. When critics say that Zhang's films lack depth, what they mean is that the language/vehi-cle in which he renders "China" is a poor translation, a translation that does not give the truth about "China." For such critics, the film medi-um, precisely because it is so "superficial"—that is, organized around surfaces—mystifies and thus distorts China's authenticity. What is implicitly assumed in their judgment is not simply the untranslatability of the "original" but that translation is a unidirectional, one-way process. It is assumed that translation means a movement from the "original" to the language of "translation" but not vice versa; it is assumed that the value of translation is derived solely from the "original," which is the authenticator of itself and of its subsequent versions. Of the "transla-tion," a tyrannical demand is made: the translation must perform its task of conveying the "original" without leaving its own traces; the "original-ity of translation" must lie "in self-effacement, a vanishing act."[19]

Our discussion here can be facilitated by turning to the work of Walter Benjamin, not least because Benjamin himself was writing at the crossroads of cultural transformation. Though Benjamin's essay "The Work of Art in the Age of Mechanical Reproduction" may seem most immediately relevant to our topic in that it deals with the transformation of traditional art (which possesses "aura") to mass-produced images such as those of photography and film,[20] I find his essay "The Task of the Translator" to be more useful in helping me think through the problem of translation between cultures.[21] In this latter essay, Benjamin offers a theory of translation that is distinctively different from most theories.

It is often assumed, writes Benjamin, that the point of translation is to impart information or convey the meaning of the original; this is, however, not so. Instead, what needs to be translated is an "intention" ("intentio") in the "original" that Benjamin calls "the great longing for linguistic complementation" (p. 79). His mystical language notwithstanding, Benjamin is arguing for a materialist though elusive fact about translation—that translation is primarily a process of *putting together.* This process demonstrates that the "original," too, is something that has been put together. But this "putting together" is not, as I will go on to argue, simply a deconstructive production of differences.[22] It is *also* a process of "literalness" that *displays* the way the "original" itself was put together—that is, in its violence.

Before elaborating this last point, we need to examine closely the way Benjamin discusses the "putting together" that is linguistic translation. What needs to be translated from the original, he writes, is not a kind of truth or meaning but the way in which "the original" is put together *in the basic elements of human language*—words. Hence it is words—in their wordness, their literality—rather than sentences, that matter the most in translation. A real translation, Benjamin writes, "may be achieved, above all, by a literal rendering of the syntax which proves words rather than sentences to be the primary element of the translator. For if the sentence is the wall before the language of the original, literalness is the arcade" (p. 79).

The German "original" of this passage indicates that where Benjamin's English translator, Harry Zohn, uses the words *literal* and *literalness,* Benjamin has used the word *Wörtlichkeit.* But even though the English translation does not exactly reproduce Benjamin's word, a verbatim translation of which would be something like "word-by-word–ness," it nonetheless supplements Benjamin's text in an unexpected, perhaps fateful, manner. To be "literal" in the English language is to be "verbatim," to follow the word strictly. At the same time, "literal" can also connote a certain *lack*—in the sense of that which is matter-of-fact, without imagination, without metaphor, without depth; that which is superficial, crude, or naive. It is this second notion of literalness—this supplement that exists in the translation but not in the original—that brings out, I think, the precise sense of Benjamin's *Wörtlichkeit*: a real translation is not only that which translates word by word but also that which translates literally, depthlessly, naively.

It is obvious that here I depart significantly from the view of literalness held by deconstructionist critics. For Jacques Derrida and Paul de Man, for instance, *literal* is a problematic word that designates "proper," in a way that is opposed to (their preferred) "metaphoric" or "figural." De Man's reading of Rousseau, for instance, is that Rousseau's language tells the story of "the necessary degradation . . . of metaphor into literal meaning," and that a "literal world" is one "in which appearance and nature coincide" whereas a "figural world" is one "in which this correspondence is no longer a priori posited."[23] For me, however, literalness is not simply "proper," but it is not simply "figural"/"metaphorical," either. Rather, I use the term to refer to a third area that is defined by neither of the two categories—the area we may loosely describe as the obvious, the superficial, and what immediately presents itself in signification. This "literal" area is what lacks and/or exceeds the clear boundary implied by Derrida and de Man between the categories of the "proper" and the "figural"/"metaphorical."

Zohn's translation-cum-supplement, then, makes explicit something that was merely lurking in the original in the form of what Benjamin himself calls the original's "intention." Remarkably, the "original" intention is what can only be grasped as a supplement, as what is added (because translated): "In all language and linguistic creations there remains *in addition to* what can be conveyed something that cannot be communicated; depending on the context in which it appears, it is something that symbolizes or something symbolized" (p. 79; my emphasis). For Benjamin, the task of the translator consists in communicating this additional something that nonetheless could come across as a lack and a deprivation. (I will return to this point once again toward the end.)

The elusiveness of his approach to the "original" makes it seem that Benjamin is saying with "translation" what deconstructionists are saying with "language," namely, that the original is self-différance. Examples of the deconstructionist definition of language include statements such as these: "Language . . . can only exist in the space of its own foreignness to itself," "the original text is always already an impossible translation that renders translation impossible,"[24] and so forth. However, even though a deconstructionist reading of Benjamin is useful and necessary,[25] it is inadequate. In the preceding passage by Benjamin, if we take the word *symbol* to mean not a full and complete representation of something but a sign that stands for something else, then what Benjamin is saying would suggest that the "original" intention is not only a *self*-différance, but also a process of standing-for-something-*else*, something other than the "self." For Benjamin, the act of translation is less a confirmation of language's "own" impossibility than it is a *liberation*, in a second language, of the "intention" of standing-for-something-else that is already put together but imprisoned—"symbolized"—in the original; hence "it is the task of the translator to release in his own language that pure language which is under the spell of another, to liberate the language imprisoned in a work in his re-creation of that work" (p. 80).

Because Benjamin's notion of the "original" intention comprises *both* self-différance and the act of symbolizing (standing for an other), it is important to emphasize that his theory is not simply that translation is the original's deconstruction, which is the reading proposed, for instance, by de Man. De Man's reading is a persuasive one, but it does not do justice to Benjamin's theory. In his typical manner, de Man zeroes in on the inherent *negativity* of writing: hence he elaborates on the notion of "failure" inscribed in the German title of Benjamin's piece, proving thus that translation is ultimately a failure—a failure, moreover, that is already present in the "original." Comparing the activity of translation to those of critical philosophy, literary theory, and history, de Man writes that all such *intralingual* activities have in common a disarticulation of the original: "They reveal that their failure, which seems to be due to the fact that they are secondary in relation to the original, reveals an *essential* failure, an *essential* disarticulation which was already there in the original."[26]

Because its rigor is a negative one, de Man's deconstructive reading is eminently useful in desacralizing and decanonizing the original. But deconstruction as such nonetheless does *not* depart from the view that there *is* some original—even if that should prove to be an illusion—to begin with. By concentrating its efforts on the disarticulated and unstable "essence" of the "original," the deconstructive reading in fact makes it unnecessary for one to move outside or down from the realm of the original. Translation would thus remain one-way in the sense that it is intralingual, with all the differences/misreadings it produces moving back to (deconstruct the self that is) the original. This is demonstrated, best of all, by de Man's own reading, in which he repeatedly shows Benjamin's translators up for missing Benjamin's points. In spite of his sacrilegious intentions, therefore, de Man returns a kind of sacredness—now defined as intralingual instability—to the original that is Benjamin's text. De Man's deconstructive reading does not in the end deviate significantly from the conventional, dogmatic belief in the purity or untranslatability of any original. Were a "translation" of culture to be based on de Man's reading, it would be, as he says, a failure: such a translation would be little more than the vicious circle of a search for a complete freedom from the "origin" that is the past, which nonetheless would keep haunting us like the indelible memory of a nightmare.

For Benjamin, on the other hand, translation is not simply deconstructive but, even more important, a "liberation" that is mutual and reciprocal *between* the "original" and the "translation." In Benjamin's text, the nihilistic rigor of deconstruction is combined with a messianic utopianism, a sense of openness that is absent in de Man. For Benjamin, both "original" and "translation," as languages rendering each other, share the "longing for linguistic complementarity" and gesture together toward something larger: "A translation, instead of resembling the meaning of the original, must lovingly and in detail incorporate the original's mode of signification, thus making both the original and the translation recognizable as fragments of a greater language, just as fragments are part of a vessel" (p. 78).[27] The quotation that Benjamin takes from Rudolf Pannwitz illustrates a similar point of complementarity, mutuality, and letting the foreign affect the self:

Pannwitz writes: "Our translations, even the best ones, proceed into German instead of turning German into Hindi, Greek, English. Our translators have a far greater reverence for the usage of their own language than for the spirit of the foreign works. . . . The basic error of the translator is that he preserves the state in which his own language happens to be instead of allowing his language to be powerfully affected by the foreign tongue. Particularly when translating from a language very remote from his own he must go back to the primal elements of language itself and penetrate to the point where work, image, and tone converge. He must expand and deepen his language by means of the foreign language." (pp. 80–81)

In these preceding passages, the relationship between the "original" and the "translation" is problematized by the fact that the "original" does not only refer to the original language in which something is written but can also refer to the (different) native/original language of the native speaker/translator; similarly, "translation" can mean not only the language into which something is translated but also a language foreign to the translator's mother tongue. But the gist of Benjamin's argument remains the same: most work of translation is done in the wish to make the "foreign" sound more like the "native," with the assumption that the "native" is the "original" point of reference; whereas translation is a process in which the "native" should let the foreign affect, or infect, itself, and vice versa. This radical notion of translation is what leads Jean Laplanche to describe Benjamin's theory as an "anti-ethnocentric" one: "Benjamin participates in the great 'anti-ethnocentric' movement . . . or what I call the 'anti-auto- or self-centred' movement of translation (*le mouvement anti-autocentrique de la traduction*): a movement that doesn't want translation to be self-enclosed and reduce the other to the terms of that self, but rather a movement out towards the other."[28] The question then is, How is this "movement out towards the other" to be conceived and theorized?

Translation as "Cultural Resistance"

In a recent work, *Siting Translation*, Tejaswini Niranjana takes up the formidable task of rethinking translation in the context of postcolonial postmodernity. Basing her arguments on poststructuralist theories of language, signification, and representation, Niranjana deconstructs the humanistic, binary oppositional assumptions underlying traditional notions of translation. Moreover, she proposes that both the theory and the practice of translation must be seen in the context of Western imperialism and colonialism, in which the European/Europeanist notions of knowledge reproduce themselves in Europe's encounter with and "translation" of its "others."[29] Readers must turn to Niranjana's book to see for themselves the extensive implications of her thoughtful and well-researched arguments. If my critique of her book below is a strong one, it is also offered in full appreciation of the significance of her intervention in a context where "cultural translation" is still by and large dominated by Western discourse. This critique will, I hope, be read as an interaction in alliance with that intervention rather than as its opposition.

If, in the hands of deconstructionists such as de Man, translation is that originary intralingual self-différance, in Niranjana's analysis, translation is an *interlingual* practice—the exchange of ideas, beliefs, and information between different languages (and thus cultures). Because Niranjana's goal is to rescue the term *translation* for "cultural resistance" even while she criticizes its use by the culturally dominant, the status of "translation" in her analysis is an ambivalent, empty, and ultimately idealist one: translation is fundamentally a "philosopheme" (pp. 2, 31). The idealist status of the term is what allows Niranjana implicitly to think of translation by differentiating between the good and the bad.

The bad: this is the European translation of its "others" that is otherwise known as "orientalism." Situating translation in the postcolonial context, Niranjana criticizes such orientalist texts for being imperialist and ethnocentric, for simply reinscribing in the "others" the orientalists' own preferences and prejudices. *The good*: on the other hand, Niranjana also wants to turn translation into something that Europe's colonized peoples can use. Translation is here given many analogies, chief of which is that it is an "act of resistance" when practiced by "natives" doing their own ethnography (pp. 84–85). Translation is, alternately, a "problematic" and a "field" (p. 8), a "transactional reading" (p. 42), a "hybrid" act (p. 46), a kind of citation and rewriting (p. 172). Finally, translation is what must be "put under erasure" (p. 48, n. 4).

These multiple analogies demonstrate the moves typical of a certain kind of poststructuralist discourse, which may be paraphrased as follows: deconstruct the danger and pitfalls of a term in its conventional usage; rescue that term for its inherent "heterogeneity" and "difference"; affirm this "heterogeneity" and "difference" *when it is used by certain groups of people*. By implicitly distinguishing between an incorrect and a correct practice of translation, what this type of poststructuralist rendering accomplishes is a *rationalist* understanding of "translation." This rendering returns "translation" to an *idea* (hence translation is first and foremost a "philosopheme"), debunks the dirty practice of the West, and reinstates the cleaner practice of the West's "others" as the alternative. Apart from idealism, this poststructuralist discourse also tends to invest heavily in the form of attentiveness that is a vigilance to words. Reading the *verbal text* meticulously becomes the fundamental way to "resist" the pitfalls of corrupt translation. In this regard, Niranjana's argument about translation does not add anything to the complex, nuanced arguments of writing, supplementarity, and différance that we already find in Derrida's work. "History" is here rewritten as a careful reading, with the verbal text as its primary and predominant frame of reference.

The idealism and verbalism of her parameters mean that Niranjana must leave unasked the entire question of translation from verbal language into other sign systems and, more important, of *the translation of ethnic cultures from their previous literary and philosophical bases into the forms of contemporary mass culture*, a translation that is, arguably, European colonialism's foremost legacy in the non-European world. The privileging of verbal texts prevents the poststructuralist critic from coming to terms with significations whose value does not necessarily reside in their linguistic profundity and complexity—that is, their hermeneutic depth. Since "to make complicated" remains poststructuralist textualism's primary strategy of resisting domination, surfaces, simplicities, and transparencies can only be distrusted as false. If Niranjana's point is that we need to bring "history" into "legibility," it is a legibility in the sense of a dense text. The decoding of this dense text, however, could mean exactly a perpetuation of the existing institutional practice of scholarly close reading.

On the other hand, does cross-cultural "translation" not challenge precisely the scholarly mode of privileging the verbal text? If translation is "transactional reading," must the emphasis fall on "reading"? What if the emphasis is to fall on "transaction," and what if the transaction is one between the verbal text and the visual image? It would seem that no consideration of cultural translation can afford to ignore these questions, simply because the translation between cultures is never West translating East or East translating West in terms of verbal languages alone but rather a process that encompasses an entire range of activities, including the change from tradition to modernity, from literature to visuality, from elite scholastic culture to mass culture, from the native to the foreign and back, and so forth.

If de Man's notion of translation ultimately revalorizes the "original" that is the untranslatability of the (original) text, there is a way in which contemporary cultural studies, in the attempt to vindicate the cultures of the West's "others," end up revalorizing the "original" that is the authentic history, culture, and language of such "others." In spite of its politically astute intentions, what a work such as Niranjana's accomplishes in reversing are the asymmetrical, hierarchical power relations between West and East but *not* the asymmetrical, hierarchical power relations between "original" and "translation." In an attempt to do justice to the East, Niranjana, like many antiorientalist critics, deconstruct/ destabilize the West by turning the West into an *unfaithful translator/translation* that has, as it were, betrayed, corrupted, and contaminated the "original" that is the East. When this revalorization of the "original" is done through a concentration on the depths and nuances of verbal texts, what continues to be obliterated is the fact that such texts are traditionally the loci of literate and literary culture, the culture through which *class hierarchy is established not only in Western but also in Eastern societies.*

The "Third Term"

My concerns about cultural translation up to this point can be summarized as follows: First, can we theorize translation between cultures without somehow valorizing some "original"? And second, can we theorize translation between cultures in a manner that does not implicitly turn translation into an *interpretation* toward depth, toward "profound meaning"?

To answer such questions, we would need to move beyond the intralingual and interlingual dimensions of translation that we have seen in de Man and Niranjana, and include within "translation" the notion of intersemiotic practices, of translating from one sign system to another.[30] Specifically, translation would need to encompass the translation, as Elsaesser suggests, of a "culture" into a medium such as film. Such translation, however, is not to be confused with "expression," "articulation," or even "representation," simply because these terms would too easily mislead us back into the comfortable notion that some pure "original" was there to be expressed, articulated, or represented. Instead, the notion of translation highlights the fact that it is an activity, a transportation between two "media," two kinds of already-mediated data, and that the "translation" is often what we must work with because, for one reason or another, the "original" as such is unavailable—lost, cryptic, already heavily mediated, already heavily translated. On the other hand, as I clarify in my discussion of de Man, I do not think that intersemiotic translation is simply "deconstruction," either, because the negative momentum of deconstruction, while effectively demystifying the spontaneism and mimeticism of terms such as expression, articulation, and representation, remains incapable of conveying a sense of the new medium into which the "original" is being transported.

What is useful from deconstruction, as is always the case, is the lesson about the "original"—a lesson I am pushing to the extreme here by asking that even in translation, where it usually goes without saying (even for deconstructionists) that the "original" is valued over the translated, we take absolutely seriously the deconstructionist insistence that the "first" and "original" as such is always already différance—always already translated. There are two possible paths from this lesson: one leads, as in the case of de Man, back to the painstaking study of the "original" as an original failure; the other leads to the work of translations and the values arising from them without privileging the "original" simply because it was there first. The choice of either path constitutes a major political decision.

And it is here, rather than in the opposition between "language" and "history" as Niranjana argues, that Benjamin's essay on translation, together with Benjamin's interest in mass culture, is most useful for a theory of cultural translation.[31]

There are multiple reasons why a consideration of mass culture is crucial to cultural translation, but the predominant one, for me, is precisely that asymmetry of power relations between the "first" and the "third" worlds. Precisely because of the deadlock of the more or less complete Europeanization of the world, which has led not only to the technocratic homogenization of world cultures but also to an organization of these cultures by way of European languages, philosophies, and sciences, the recourse to the archaic, authentic *past* of other cultures, in the assumption that somehow such past is closer to the original essence of humanity than Western culture, is a futile one. Critiquing the great disparity between Europe and the rest of the world means not simply a deconstruction of Europe as origin or simply a restitution of the origin that is Europe's others but a thorough dismantling of *both* the notion of origin and the notion of alterity as we know them today. This dismantling would be possible only if we acknowledge what Johannes Fabian speaks of as the *coevalness* of cultures[32] and consider the intersemiotic transformations that have happened as much to non-Western societies as to Western ones. The mass culture of our media, into which even the most "primitive" societies have been thrown, makes this coevalness ineluctable. The "primitive" is not "of another time" but is our contemporary.

The necessity of accepting the coevalness of cultures is what Laplanche, speaking in the context of translation, refers to as the necessity of "the third term":

> The difference between two terms and three terms seems important to me. Two terms don't allow for an orientation. Two terms—the translated and the translator—are either surrendered to a centring on the translator which we've called somewhat narrowly "ethnocentrism"; or they are surrendered to a centring on what's to be translated, which can in the extreme lead to a refusal to translate. . . . There must be a third term so that translation (and interpretation) exit from [the first two terms'] subjectivity.

> Every interpretative trajectory which links two terms is doomed to be arbitrary if it doesn't relate to a third term, and if it doesn't postulate something which is unconscious.[33]

Besides acknowledging the co-temporality of cultures through our media, the "third term" would also mean acknowledging that the West's "primitive others" are equally caught up in the generalized atmosphere of unequal power distribution and are actively (re)producing *within themselves* the structures of domination and hierarchy that are as typical of non-European cultural histories as they are of European imperialism. As Dipesh Chakrabarty writes in regard to India, the project of "provincializing Europe"—a project that is essential to deconstructing European history's hegemony over other ethnic histories—"cannot be a nationalist, nativist, or atavistic project. . . . One cannot but problematize 'India' at the same time as one dismantles 'Europe.'"[34] In other words, genuine cultural translation is possible only when we move beyond the seemingly infinite but actually reductive permutations of the two terms—East and West, original and translation—and instead see both as full, materialist, and most likely equally corrupt, equally decadent participants in contemporary world culture. This would mean, ultimately, a thorough disassembling of the visualist epistemological bases of disciplines such as anthropology and ethnography as we know them to date.

Weakness, Fluidity, and the Fabling of the World

To elaborate my argument further, I will turn briefly to the work of Gianni Vattimo.[35] Basing his philosophy primarily on readings of Nietzsche and Heidegger, Vattimo's concern is that of figuring out possibilities of survival that are *practically* available in the deadlock of the European domination, homogenization, and standardization of the world. Among the most compelling ideas in Vattimo's writings is that of a weakening Western metaphysics, which he theorizes by drawing upon Nietzsche's idea of the death of God and Heidegger's notions of *Andenken* (recollection) and *Verwindung* (the overcoming that is not a transcendence but an acceptance and that carries with it the meaning of a cure, a convalescence).[36] For Vattimo, weakening—in the sense of a gradual decline, an ability to die—signals not a new, radical beginning but rather a turning and twisting of tradition away from its metaphysical foundations, a movement that makes way for the hybrid cultures of contemporary society.

Reading specifically for a tactics of translation between cultures, I find Vattimo's writings useful in several ways. First, he takes as his point of departure, realistically, the deadlock of the anthropological situation that has resulted from Western hegemony and that has led to the disappearance of alterity. Second, he refuses to think through this deadlock by constructing a brand-new beginning that is typical of the heroic radicalism of modernist narratives. Third, he attempts an alternative way of conceiving of the coevalness of cultures that is neither cynical and negative (in its criticism of the West) nor idealist and idealistic (by valorizing the East). Most important, Vattimo urges that we need to recognize the fact that these "other" cultures, rather than being lost or disappearing, are themselves transforming and translating into the present. He cites from Remo Guidieri:

> Those who have lamented the deaths of cultures have neither known how to see, nor wanted to see, that these same cultures— which are as obsessed as we are with the myth of abundance— have nevertheless produced their own specific way of entering into the Western universe. Although they may be paradoxical, irrational, or even caricatural, these modalities are just as authentic as the ancient ways, tributary as they are to the cultural forms from which they derive their condition of possibility. The non-Western contemporary world is an immense construction site of traces and residues, in conditions which have still to be analysed.[37]

This notion of the other—not as the idealized lost origin to be rediscovered or resurrected but as our contemporary—allows for a context of cultural translation in which these "other" cultures are equally engaged in the contradictions of modernity, such as the primitivization of the underprivileged, the quest for new foundations and new monuments, and so forth, that have been blatantly exhibited by Western nations. The coevalness of cultures, in other words, is not simply a peaceful co-existence among plural societies but the co-temporality of power structures—what Mary Louise Pratt calls the "contact zones"[38]—that mutually support and reinforce the exploitation of underprivileged social groups, nonhuman life forms, and ecological resources *throughout the world*.

Once the coevalness of cultures is acknowledged in this manner, cultural translation can no longer be thought of simply in linguistic terms, as the translation between Western and Eastern verbal languages alone. Instead, cultural translation needs to be rethought as the co-temporal exchange and contention between different social groups deploying different sign systems that may not be synthesizable to one particular model of language or representation. Considerations of the translation of or between cultures would thus have to move beyond verbal and literary languages to include events of the media such as radio, film, television, video, pop music, and so forth, without writing such events off as mere examples of mass indoctrination. Conversely, the media, as the loci of cultural translation, can now be seen as what helps to weaken the (literary, philosophical, and epistemological) foundations of Western domination and what makes the encounter between cultures a fluid and open-ended experience:

Contrary to what critical sociology has long believed (with good reason, unfortunately), standardization, uniformity, the manipulation of consensus and the errors of totalitarianism *are not* the only possible outcome of the advent of generalized communication, the mass media and reproduction. Alongside these possibilities—which are objects of political choice—there opens an alternative possible outcome. The advent of the media enhances the inconstancy and superficiality of experience. In so doing, it runs counter to the generalization of domination, insofar as it allows a kind of "weakening" of the very notion of reality, and thus a weakening of its persuasive force. The society of the spectacle spoken of by the situationists is not simply a society of appearance manipulated by power: it is also the society in which reality presents itself as softer and more fluid, and in which experience can again acquire the characteristics of oscillation, disorientation and play.[39]

What the fluidity of the co-presence of cultures signifies is not the harmony but—to use a word from Vattimo—the thorough "contamination" of the world, so thorough that it has made the world become "soft" and tender. If the Western domination of the world has been the result of rationalistic progress, a progress that moves the world toward the general transparency that is evidenced by our media, this transparency is also a recovery, a convalescence from rationalistic progress in that it shows the world to be, finally, a fable:

> Instead of moving toward self-transparency, the society of the human sciences and generalized communication has moved towards what could, in general, be called the "fabling of the world." The images of the world we receive from the media and the human sciences, albeit on different levels, are not simply different interpretations of a "reality" that is "given" regardless, but rather constitute the very objectivity of the world. "There are no facts, only interpretations," in the words of Nietzsche, who also wrote that "the true world has in the end become a fable."[40]

In the transcultural world market, contemporary Chinese films can be understood by way of this transparency becoming fable. In order to see this, we need to return once again to the problem of translation and to Walter Benjamin's essay.

The Light of the Arcade

We come to what is perhaps the most difficult point in Benjamin's discussion: besides the "longing for linguistic complementarity," what exactly is that "active force in life" (p. 79) that Benjamin describes as being imprisoned in the original and that the translation should liberate? How is this "active force" related to the "longing for linguistic complementarity"? Much as Benjamin's phrase carries with it a kind of organicist baggage, I propose that we think of it in terms other than organicism. By way of contemporary Chinese film, I would suggest that, *first*, the "active force of life" refers to the cultural violence that is made evident or apparent by the act of translation. In its rendering of the prohibitions, the oppressive customs, and the dehumanizing rituals of feudal China, for instance, the translation that is film enables us to see how a culture is "originally" put together, in all its *cruelty*. This putting together constitutes the violent active force to which the culture's members continue to be subjugated. For anyone whose identity is sutured with this culture, filmic representation thus makes it possible to see (with discomfort) one's "native origins" as foreign bodies.

Second, the "active force of life" refers also to the act of transmission. While the callousness and viciousness of "tradition" is clearly visible on the screen, what makes it possible for Chinese audiences to become not simply inheritors of but also foreigners to their "tradition" is the act of transmission—the fact that whatever they experience, they experience as a passing-on. Writing in another context, Benjamin has defined transmission as what distinguishes Franz Kafka's work from that of his contemporaries. A work's transmissibility, Benjamin writes, is in opposition to its "truth":

> The things that want to be caught as they rush by are not meant for anyone's ears. This implies a state of affairs which negatively characterizes Kafka's works with great precision. . . . Kafka's work presents a *sickness of tradition*. . . . [The haggadic] consistency of truth . . . has been lost. Kafka was far from being the first to face this situation. Many had accommodated themselves to it, clinging to truth or whatever they happened to regard as truth and, with a more or less heavy heart, [forsaking] its transmissibility. Kafka's real genius was that he tried something entirely new: he sacrificed truth for the sake of *clinging to its transmissibility*, its haggadic element.[41]

Following Benjamin, we may argue that transmissibility is what *intensifies* in direct proportion to the sickness, the weakening of tradition. Ironically, then, it is indeed "tradition" that is the condition of possibility for transmission, but it is tradition in a debilitated and exhausted state.

Furthermore, in the age of multimedia communication, transmissibility is that aspect of a work which, unlike the weight of philosophical depth and interiority, is literal, transparent, and thus capable of offering itself to a popular or naive *handling*. What is transmissible is that which, *in addition to* having meaning or "sense," is accessible. This last point, incidentally, is quite the opposite of the manner in which we usually think of accessibility, which is typically regarded as a *deprivation*, a *lack* of depth and meaning. For Benjamin, however, transmissibility and accessibility are not pejorative or negligible qualities; instead they are what enable movement—that is, translation—from language to language, from medium to medium. Transmissibility and accessibility are what give a work its afterlife.

Once we see these implications of transmission, the "literalness" or *Wörtlichkeit* in Benjamin's essay that I have already discussed can be further defined as a transmissibility oriented toward a here and now—that is, a simultaneity rather than an alterity in place and time. Rather than a properly anchored "truth," "literalness" signifies mobility, proximity, approximation. Thus "literalness" is, as Benjamin writes, an arcade, a passageway.

Juxtaposing "The Task of the Translator" with Benjamin's interest in mass culture, we can now say that the "literalness" of popular and mass culture is not "simplistic" or "lacking" as is commonly thought. Rather, in its naive, crude, and literal modes, popular and mass culture is a supplement to truth, a tactic of passing something on. In the language of visuality, what is "literal" is what acquires a light *in addition to* the original that is its content; it is this light, this transparency, that allows the original/content to be transmitted and translated: "A real translation is transparent; it does not cover the original, does not block its light, but allows the pure language, as though reinforced by its own medium, to shine upon the original all the more fully" (p. 79).

For most interpreters, Benjamin's notion of "light" and "transparency" in this passage corroborates that of "literalness" and "arcade" in the sense of "letting light through." Derrida, for instance, writes that "whereas the wall braces while concealing (it is *in front of* the original), the arcade supports while letting light pass and the original show."[42] John Fletcher, commenting on Laplanche's reading of Benjamin's text, defines "Benjamin's Wörtlichkeit" as "the arcade that gives access and circulation rather than blocks out."[43] According to these interpretations, the arcade casts a light on the original in such a way as to make the original shine more brilliantly. *But what about the arcade itself—the "word-for-word-ness," the translation?*

By putting the emphasis on the arcade as a letting-light-through, critics such as Derrida and Fletcher alert us correctly to the "passageway" that is the *conventional* meaning of the arcade. Insofar as it understands the relationship between "original" and "translation" in terms of clarity and obscurity, this is a familiar move, which Derrida himself has described and critiqued in the following terms: "The appeal to the criteria of clarity and obscurity would suffice to confirm . . . [that the] entire philosophical delimitation of metaphor already lends itself to being constructed and worked by 'metaphors.' How could a piece of knowledge or a language be properly clear or obscure?"[44]

We may borrow Derrida's passage to critique the way *translation* is often evaluated (even by himself) in terms of clarity and obscurity, light and blockage. "Light" in this common philosophical tradition is assumed to be transparent in the sense of a *nonexisting* medium—and the arcade, which is equated with light, implicitly becomes a *mere* passageway. Since the "arcade" also corresponds in this context to translation, we are back once again in the classical situation in which "translation" is a mere vehicle, disposable once it completes its task.

And yet, does light not have another kind of transparency, the transparency of our media and consumer society? Such transparency moves us, it seems to me, not back to the "original" but rather to the *fabulous constructedness* of the world as spoken of by Nietzsche and Vattimo. Rather than some original text, it is the brilliance of this "fabling of the world" to which Benjamin's "arcade" leads us.

What is forgotten, when critics think of translation only in terms of literary and philosophical texts, is that the arcade, especially in the work of Benjamin, is never simply a linguistic passageway; it is also a commercial passageway, a passageway with shop fronts for the display of merchandise.[45] I would therefore emphasize this *mass culture aspect of the arcade* in order to show that the light and transparency allowed by "translation" is also the light and transparency of commodification. This is a profane, rather than pure and sacred, light, to which non-Western cultures are subjected if they want a place in the contemporary world. In "literal," "superficial" ways, this arcade is furnished with exhibits of modernity's "primitives" such as the women in contemporary Chinese film, who stand like mannequins in the passageways between cultures. The fabulous, brilliant forms of these primitives are what we must go through in order to arrive—not at the new destination of the truth of an "other" culture but at the weakened foundations of Western metaphysics as well as the disintegrated bases of Eastern traditions. In the display windows of the world market, such "primitives" are the toys, the fabricated play forms with which the less powerful (cultures) negotiate the imposition of the agenda of the powerful.[46] They are the "fables" that cast light on the "original" that is our world's violence, and they mark the passages that head not toward the "original" that is the West or the East but toward survival in the postcolonial world.[47]

Contemporary Chinese films are cultural "translations" in these multiple senses of the term. By consciously exoticizing China and revealing China's "dirty secrets" to the outside world, contemporary Chinese directors are translators of the violence with which the Chinese culture is "originally" put together. In the dazzling colors of their screen, the primitive that is woman, who at once unveils the corrupt Chinese tradition and parodies the orientalism of the West, stands as the naive symbol, the brilliant arcade, through which "China" travels across cultures to unfamiliar audiences. Meanwhile, the "original" that is film, the canonically Western medium, becomes destabilized and permanently infected with the unforgettable "ethnic" (*and* foreign) images imprinted on it by the Chinese translators. To borrow Michael Taussig's words, contemporary Chinese films constitute that "novel anthropology" in which the "object" recorded is no longer simply the "third world" but "the West itself as mirrored in the eyes and handiwork of its others." This novel anthropology is, we may add, translation in the sense of the "interlinear version" and "plurality of languages" as described by Benjamin (p. 82).

Like Benjamin's collector, the Chinese filmmakers' relation to "China" is that of the heirs to a great collection of treasures, the most distinguished trait of which, writes Benjamin, "will always be its transmissibility."[48] If translation is a form of betrayal, then the translators pay their debt by bringing fame to the ethnic culture, a fame that is evident in recent years from the major awards won by Chinese films at international film festivals in Manila, Tokyo, Nantes, Locarno, London, Honolulu, Montréal, Berlin, Venice, and Cannes.[49] Another name for fame is afterlife. It is in translation's faithlessness that "China" survives and thrives. A faithlessness that gives the beloved life—is that not . . . faithfulness itself?

Notes

―――――

Preface

1. "Film studies," for instance, "are currently polarizing between those who work from within a strict disciplinary sense of the field and those . . . who bring an interdisciplinary perspective to it. Unfortunately, this polarization frequently leads each side to virtually dismiss or disparage the work of the other." Peter Lehman, *Film Quarterly* 47, no. 1 (Fall 1993): 55–56 (book review).

Part 1:Visuality, Modernity, and Primitive Passions

1. The quotation in the title of this section is taken from Jay Leyda, *Dianying: An Account of Films and the Film Audience in China* (Cambridge, Mass.: MIT Press, 1972), p. 13.

2. Lu Xun, "Preface to the First Collection of Short Stories, 'Call to Arms,' " *Selected Stories of Lu Hsun*, trans. Yang Hsien-yi and Gladys Yang (Beijing: Foreign Languages Press, 1960), pp. 2–3; translation modified. This episode is cited in Leyda, *Dianying*, pp. 13–14. Leyda includes a picture (p. 421, plate 3a) that is supposed to be "the newsreel that determined the career of Lu Hsun" and "helped to change modern Chinese history." In Leyda's picture, however, the execution has already taken place (with a severed human head on the ground), whereas in Lu Xun's account it is about to take place.

3. See, for instance, the allusions to this event in the following sources: Lin Niantong, *Zhongguo dianying meixue* [The aesthetics of Chinese film] (Taipei:

Part 1. Visuality, Modernity, and Primitive Passions

Yunchen wenhua shiye gufen youxian gongsi, 1991), pp. 18 and 113; Leyda, *Dianying*, pp. 1–2; Ma Qiang, "The Chinese Film in the 1980s: Art and Industry," *Cinema and Cultural Identity: Reflections on Films from Japan, India, and China*, ed. Wimal Dissanayake (New York: University Press of America, 1988), pp. 165–66; and Paul Clark, "The Sinification of Cinema: The Foreignness of Film in China," in *Film and Cultural Identity*, p. 176.

4. According to Lin, *Zhongguo dianying meixue* (p. 70), films began to be made in China in 1905, but these films no longer exist.

5. See *Lu Xun quanji*, vol. 1 (Beijing: Renmin chubanshe, 1987), pp. 416–17.

6. Martin Heidegger, "The Origin of the Work of Art," in *Poetry, Language, Thought*, trans. and with an intro. by Albert Hofstadter (New York: Harper Colophon Books, 1971), pp. 17–87; Walter Benjamin, "The Work of Art in the Age of Mechanical Reproduction," in *Illuminations*, ed. and with an intro. by Hannah Arendt, trans. Harry Zohn (New York: Schocken, 1969), pp. 217–51; and Gianni Vattimo, "Art and Oscillation," in *The Transparent Society*, trans. David Webb (Cambridge: Polity Press, 1992), pp. 45–61. For related interest, see also Benjamin's essay "On Some Motifs in Baudelaire," in *Illuminations*, pp. 155–200; as well as Benjamin, *Charles Baudelaire: A Lyric Poet in the Era of High Capitalism*, trans. Harry Zohn (London: New Left Books, 1973).

7. Jonathan Crary distinguishes the "observer" from the "spectator." The problem of the observer is "the field on which vision in history can be said to materialize, to become itself visible. Vision and its effects are always inseparable from the possibilities of an observing subject who is both the historical product and site of certain practices, techniques, institutions, and procedures of subjectification." Crary further defines the observer as "one who sees within a prescribed set of possibilities, one who is embedded in a system of conventions and limitations." See Crary, *Techniques of the Observer: On Vision and Modernity in the Nineteenth Century* (Cambridge, Mass.: MIT Press, 1990), pp. 5–6. Even though I use "observer" and "spectator" interchangeably in my study, Crary's definition of the observer as a subject within a continually shifting field of representational practices is a useful one.

8. The Chinese term used by Lu Xun is *shangjian*, which is usually translated as "appreciate." Etymologically, the character *jian* means "bronze mirror" and has since ancient times been used to refer to mirroring, reflection, examination, scrutiny, and warning. For a discussion of *jian* as a concept in Chinese filmmaking, see Lin, *Zhongguo dianying meixue*. Distinguishing between *jian* and *you* (traveling, roving) as different epistemological and aesthetic functions, Lin uses the terms *jingjian* (the camera lens's reflective/scrutinizing gaze) and *jingyou* (the camera lens's leisurely roving gaze) to formulate a theory of what is uniquely "Chinese" in Chinese cinema. See Lin, *Zhongguo dianying meixue*, especially chaps. 1–5.

9. See, for instance, Leo Ou-fan Lee, *The Romantic Generation of Modern Chinese Writers* (Cambridge, Mass.: Harvard University Press, 1973), p. 37; Lee, "Gene-

Part 1. Visuality, Modernity, and Primitive Passions

sis of a Writer: Notes on Lu Xun's Educational Experience, 1881–1909," *Modern Chinese Literature in the May Fourth Era*, ed. Merle Goldman (Cambridge, Mass.: Harvard University Press, 1977), pp. 177–79; Lee, *Voices from the Iron House: A Study of Lu Xun* (Bloomington: Indiana University Press, 1987), pp. 17–19; Wendy Larson, *Literary Authority and the Modern Chinese Writer: Ambivalence and Autobiography* (Durham, N.C.: Duke University Press, 1991), pp. 5 and 99; David Der-wei Wang, *Fictional Realism in Twentieth-Century China: Mao Dun, Lao She, Shen Congwen* (New York: Columbia University Press, 1992), pp. 2, 214–18. Other critics, while noting the significance of elements of visuality such as the camera eye, seeing, spectatorship, crowds, and exhibitions for Lu Xun's thinking about his Chinese nationality/ethnicity, nonetheless also remain concerned primarily with literature in their analyses. See, for instance, Marston Anderson's discussion in *The Limits of Realism: Chinese Fiction in the Revolutionary Period* (Berkeley and Los Angeles: University of California Press, 1990), pp. 77–79. Anderson's sensitivity to visuality, a sense perception he nonetheless distrusts, is indicated by the title of the section—"Lu Xun: The Violence of Observation"—of which his discussion of the event of the slide show is a part.

10. Larson, *Literary Authority and the Modern Chinese Writer*, p. 8. Larson's thesis is that modern Chinese literature of the early twentieth century was characterized by a perceptible change in the authority and referentiality that were used to justify literary or textual labor. The authority of textual reference was steadily giving way to the authority of the sociomaterial world. Because tradition was crumbling, writers increasingly came to view textual labor in negative terms but continued nonetheless to privilege textual work.

11. This is suggested by Leo Lee, *Voices from the Iron House*, p. 18: "Since no such news slide has been found, Lu Xun may again have engaged in fiction." For the question of the news slide, see n. 2.

12. As Norman Bryson writes, the terror that philosophers like Jacques Lacan portray as intrinsic to sight must be understood socially: "Terror comes from the way that sight is constructed in relation to power, and powerlessness. To think of a terror intrinsic to sight makes it harder to think what makes sight terroristic, or otherwise. . . . What should ensue from Lacan's portrayal of the terror of sight is analysis, analyses, many of them, of how power uses the social construct of vision, visuality." See Bryson, "The Gaze in the Expanded Field," in *Vision and Visuality*, ed. Hal Foster (Seattle: Bay Press, 1988), pp. 107–8. Although Bryson's argument is persuasive, Lacan is probably much closer to a biological understanding of human anxiety and the affinity between human and nonhuman fears. Substantiating this point is well beyond my capability, but I can point the interested reader to an article such as Ned H. Kalin, "The Neurobiology of Fear," *Scientific American*, May 1993, pp. 94–101. Kalin writes that, apart from monkeys and humans, "Animals as diverse as crabs, lizards and birds all perceive staring as a threat. Some fishes and insects have evolved protective spots that resemble eyes" (pp. 95–96).

Part 1. Visuality, Modernity, and Primitive Passions

13. In his reading, Anderson describes the impact of the slides on Lu Xun as a writer in terms of a "troublesome aesthetic dilemma." Anderson's words are interestingly precise for my point here, even though, reading primarily as a literary critic who disapproves of melodrama and visual spectacles, he intends by these words a very different kind of argument from the one I am making: "A troublesome aesthetic dilemma must be addressed: lest Lu Xun's own work be guilty of further disseminating the spectacle of the violence, the [literary] narration must, while faithfully rendering scenes of paradigmatic social significance such as that depicted in the slide, disallow the *unthinking transmission* of their original message" (Anderson, *The Limits of Realism*, pp. 78–79; my emphasis). Anderson goes on to describe Lu Xun's awareness of "the dangers of transmission" and "the violence of the communication" of the spectacle (p. 79).

14. "Zhufu," *Panghuang* [Hesitation], *Lu Xun quanji*, vol. 2, pp. 5–23; and "The New Year's Sacrifice," *Selected Stories*, pp. 125–43.

15. For a discussion of how the approach of May Fourth intellectuals to crisis and change was deeply rooted in the "monistic and intellectualistic mode of thinking" of Confucianism, see Lin Yusheng, *The Crisis of Chinese Consciousness: Radical Antitraditionalism in the May Fourth Era* (Madison: University of Wisconsin Press, 1979), p. 55 and passim.

16. I use the term *neurotic* in accordance with the distinction between neurosis and psychosis described by Sigmund Freud in "Neurosis and Psychosis" and "The Loss of Reality in Neurosis and Psychosis," in *The Standard Edition of the Complete Psychological Works of Sigmund Freud*, trans. James Strachey (London: Hogarth Press, 1961), vol. 19, pp. 149–53, 183–87. Put in a simplified manner, the distinction is as follows: in neurosis, reality is not disavowed but ignored, and the behavior of the neurotic continues to signify the presence of that reality; in psychosis, reality is replaced altogether by a new, imaginary world. Freud summarizes the distinction this way: "Whereas the new, imaginary external world of a psychosis attempts to put itself in the place of external reality, that of a neurosis, on the contrary, is apt, like the play of children, to attach itself to a piece of reality—a different piece from the one against which it has to defend itself—and to lend that piece a special importance and a secret meaning which we (not always quite appropriately) call a *symbolic* one" (p. 187; emphasis in the original).

17. Paul de Man, *Blindness and Insight: Essays in the Rhetoric of Contemporary Criticism*, 2d rev. ed., with an intro. by Wlad Godzich (Minneapolis: University of Minnesota Press, 1983), p. 111.

18. An interesting exception here, because it correctly understands the deconstructive, ambivalent significance of Lu Xun's story even though it still reads it only in terms of literary history, is David Der-wei Wang's discussion in *Xiaoshuo zhongguo: wan qing dao dangdai de zhongwen xiaoshuo* [Small talk (on) China: Chinese fiction from the late Qing to the contemporary period] (Taipei: Ryefield Publishing, 1993), pp. 15–29. Wang writes about the "beginning" of modern Chinese lit-

Part 1. Visuality, Modernity, and Primitive Passions

erature by suggestively bringing together the many associations of "the head" (*tou*) in the Chinese language, such as origin, decapitation, important figure, and so forth, and thus deconstructs the notion of "beginning" itself.

19. Martin Jay, "Scopic Regimes of Modernity," in *Vision and Visuality*, p. 3. By the "modern era," Jay means Western culture since the sixteenth century.

20. For an exemplary study of the history and politics of Western visualism, see Johannes Fabian, *Time and the Other: How Anthropology Makes Its Object* (New York: Columbia University Press, 1983). Fabian links the domination of anthropology as a discipline to Western visualism and to the denial of coevalness among different societies that exist contemporaneously. See also Bernard McGrane, *Beyond Anthropology: Society and the Other* (New York: Columbia University Press, 1989), for an erudite discussion of the history of Western conceptions and constructions of otherness, as well as of the philosophical and disciplinary foundations of anthropology.

21. Timothy Mitchell, "The World as Exhibition," *Comparative Studies in Society and History* 31, no. 2 (April 1989): 218, 222. This essay is taken from Mitchell's book *Colonising Egypt* (Cambridge: Cambridge University Press, 1988). Mitchell counterposes Derrida's notion of the labyrinth to exhibition. While the exhibition represents a fixed point of view, the labyrinth suggests an immersion in the text and the other, thus deconstructing the certainty of the exhibition.

22. Martin Heidegger, "The Turning"; "The Age of the World Picture," *The Question Concerning Technology and Other Essays*, trans. and with an intro. by William Lovitt (New York: Harper Colophon Books, 1977), pp. 36–49, 115–54. For a study of the experience of cinema that is based on Heidegger's philosophy, see Stanley Cavell, *The World Viewed: Reflections on the Ontology of Film*, enlarged ed. (Cambridge, Mass.: Harvard University Press, 1979). Cavell is interested in specifying the differences between the physical bases of the film medium and the artistic achievements made possible by them (p. 145); see in particular chaps. 11–19 of his book.

23. Mitchell, "The World as Exhibition," p. 229.

24. For other examples of readings of visuality, particularly film, that derive their logic from Said's *Orientalism*, see Martin Blythe, "The Romance of Maoriland: Ethnography and Tourism in New Zealand Films," *East-West Film Journal* 4, no. 2 (June 1990): 90–110; Ella Shohat, "Imaging Terra Incognita: The Disciplinary Gaze of Empire," *Public Culture* 3, no. 2 (1991): 41–70; and Yosefa Loshitzky, "The Tourist/Traveler Gaze: Bertolucci and Bowles's *The Sheltering Sky*," *East-West Film Journal* 7, no. 2 (July 1993): 111–37.

25. Guy Debord, *The Society of the Spectacle* (Detroit: Black and Red Press, 1970) and *Comments on the Society of the Spectacle*, trans. Malcolm Imrie (London: Verso, 1990); Friedrich Kittler, *Discourse Networks 1800/1900*, trans. Michael Metteer with Chris Cullens, with a foreword by David Wellbery (Stanford: Stanford University Press, 1990); Paul Virilio, *Speed and Politics: An Essay on Dromology*,

trans. Mark Polizzotti (New York: Semiotext(e), 1977); and Vattimo, *The Transparent Society*.

26. Paul G. Pickowicz, "Melodramatic Representation and the 'May Fourth' Tradition of Chinese Cinema," in *From May Fourth to June Fourth: Fiction and Film in Twentieth-Century China*, ed. Ellen Widmer and David Der-wei Wang (Cambridge, Mass.: Harvard University Press, 1993), p. 296. In this essay, Pickowicz argues for the close connections between the so-called May Fourth tradition of filmmaking and the popular melodrama films of the 1920s. He claims that we can indeed speak of a May Fourth tradition in Chinese cinema as long as "we carefully define it to mean the marriage between classical melodrama and elementary Marxism that took place in the 1932–1937 period and resurfaced in the 1946–1949 period" (p. 324). In spite of his interest in melodrama, however, Pickowicz's conclusion is, strangely, that it is "a genre that severely limits the imagination" (p. 326). Readers are asked to see my discussion of this last point in n. 72 of part 2, chap. 4.

27. Lu Xun, "Ben yue," in *Gushi xinpian* [Old tales retold], *Lu Xun quanji*, vol. 2, pp. 357–70; and "The Flight to the Moon," in *Selected Stories*, pp. 226–36.

28. See Anderson's discussion in *The Limits of Realism*, especially pp. 76–84.

29. This observation is Patrick Hanan's. The context here is Lu Xun's story "Shi zhong" ("Peking Street Scene," or "A Public Example"), in *Lu Xun quanji*, vol. 2, pp. 68–73. The story describes how a criminal is brought out on the street as a "public example." A crowd of observers gather with expectation. When they see that nothing is about to happen, they break away instead to look at a rickshaw accident. Hanan comments: "Lu Hsun's narrative is like a camera, moving here and there, picking up this detail and that action, reflecting the surface of things. It is the camera's detachment which constitutes irony. . . . (It was a scene of a similar kind, literally cinematic, which traumatically moved Lu Hsun and caused him to devote himself to literature.) All emotion is suppressed. . . . Like *voyeurs*, we watch the onlookers who, like *voyeurs*, watch the criminal, uncomprehending." See Hanan, "The Technique of Lu Hsun's Fiction," *Harvard Journal of Asiatic Studies* 34 (1974): 89.

30. Some scholars interpret such effectiveness as the effectiveness of dramatic action. See, for instance, the analogy that William A. Lyell, Jr., makes of "story theater" in "The Short Story Theater of Lu Hsun" (Ph.D. dissertation, University of Chicago, 1971).

31. See, for instance, Leo Lee, *Voices from the Iron House*, pp. 51–53.

32. Leyda, *Dianying*, p. 332. This is part of an interesting discussion about how cinema ideas are waiting at every turn for Chinese filmmakers who want to broaden and deepen their medium. See also p. 327: "Eisenstein wrote in 1929 about Japanese cinema, as 'the cinema of a country that has, in its culture, an infinite number of cinematographic traits, strewn everywhere with the sole exception of—its cinema'; as much, or more, cinema is waiting in Chinese art to be discovered by Chinese cinema."

Part 1. Visuality, Modernity, and Primitive Passions

33. The privileging of literature continues, for many, to be *the* way to understand film in China. "The early emphasis on the film script has continued to be strong and is a reflection of the primacy of literature in Chinese culture. Even the generation trained after 1949 not infrequently regarded film as a means to bring other arts (particularly fiction and stage performances) to the screen. Many regarded the reverential adaptation of the great works of May Fourth writers as their classic achievements." Clark, "The Sinification of Cinema," p. 182. Apart from literature, traditional theater also plays a dominant role in some critics' thinking. For debates among mainland Chinese film critics on the relations among literature, drama, and film, see the essays in *Chinese Film Theory: A Guide to the New Era*, ed. George S. Semsel, Xia Hong, and Hou Jianping, trans. Hou Jianping, Li Xiaohong, and Fan Yuan, and with a foreword by Luo Yijun (New York: Praeger, 1990).

34. See the chapter entitled " 'A Literature of Blood and Tears': May Fourth Theories of Literary Realism" in Anderson, *The Limits of Realism*, pp. 27–75.

35. For general discussions about the problems of literary language in May Fourth debates, readers are asked to consult, in addition to the works on modern Chinese literature that have already been cited, the following works in English: Chow Tse-tsung, *The May 4th Movement* (Cambridge, Mass.: Harvard University Press, 1960); Jaroslav Průšek, *The Lyrical and the Epic: Studies of Modern Chinese Literature*, ed. Leo Ou-fan Lee (Bloomington: Indiana University Press, 1980); Theodore Huters, intro. to *Reading the Modern Chinese Short Story*, ed. Theodore Huters (Armonk: M. E. Sharpe, 1990), pp. 3–21; and Rey Chow, *Woman and Chinese Modernity: The Politics of Reading between West and East* (Minneapolis: University of Minnesota Press, 1991).

36. See Huters's discussion of the dilemma posed by the May Fourth demand for a new language, intro. to *Reading the Modern Chinese Short Story*, especially pp. 6–9. Huters, however, associates the direct, unmediated voice demanded by May Fourth theorists and writers with "personal expression," whereas my argument here is that the demand for such a voice must be seen in relation to the global trend toward creating a medium that has to do with transparency, speed, efficiency, etc. For a related discussion, see Chow, *Writing Diaspora: Tactics of Intervention in Contemporary Cultural Studies* (Bloomington: Indiana University Press, 1993), chap. 8.

37. Michel Foucault, *Discipline and Punish: The Birth of the Prison*, trans. Alan Sheridan (New York: Vintage Books, 1979), p. 110. It has often been pointed out that the English translation of Foucault's original title, *Surveiller et Punir: Naissance de la prison*, fails to convey the significance of surveillance—a visual concept—as intended by Foucault.

38. Foucault, *Discipline and Punish*, p. 110.

39. Lu Xun, *A Brief History of Chinese Fiction*, trans. Yang Hsien-yi and Gladys Yang (Peking: Foreign Languages Press, 1959). See Leo Lee's discussion of this ambitious work in *Voices from the Iron House*, pp. 28–32.

40. Roman Jakobson, "On Linguistic Aspects of Translation," in *On Transla-tion*, ed. Reuben A. Brower (Cambridge, Mass.: Harvard University Press, 1959), p. 232.

41. For discussions of nonelite culture in China around the turn of the twenti-eth century, see some of the essays in *Popular Culture in Late Imperial China*, ed. David Johnson, Andrew J. Nathan, and Evelyn S. Rawski (Berkeley and Los Ange-les: University of California Press, 1985), in particular Leo Ou-fan Lee and Andrew J. Nathan, "The Beginnings of Mass Culture: Journalism and Fiction in the Late Ch'ing and Beyond," pp. 360–95. However, although Lee and Nathan allude to film, radio, and other media forms, their discussion remains centered on verbal texts.

42. Sally Price, *Primitive Art in Civilized Places* (Chicago: University of Chicago Press, 1989); Marianna Torgovnick, *Gone Primitive: Savage Intellects, Modern Lives* (Chicago: University of Chicago Press, 1990); and *Modernist Anthropology: From Fieldwork to Text*, ed. and with an intro. by Marc Manganaro (Princeton: Princeton University Press, 1990).

43. For a related discussion, see Ivan Karp, "Other Cultures in Museum Per-spectives," in *Exhibiting Cultures: The Poetics and Politics of Museum Display*, ed. Ivan Karp and Steven D. Lavine (Washington: Smithsonian Institution Press, 1991), pp. 373–85; this essay contains a critique of William Rubin's introductory essay, "Modernist Primitivism," in *"Primitivism" in Twentieth-Century Art: Affinity of the Tribal and the Modern* (New York: Museum of Modern Art, 1984). For an account of modernism's rootedness in orientalism (especially modernism's use of the "Ori-ent," including the former Soviet Union, as a subversive force), see some of the chapters in Peter Wollen, *Raiding the Icebox: Reflections on Twentieth-Century Culture* (Bloomington: Indiana University Press, 1993). It should be pointed out, howev-er, that Wollen's interest is in writing an intellectual history of the political-artis-tic events in the West rather than in criticizing orientalism as exploitation of peo-ples of the non-West.

44. Sterling Seagrave, with the collaboration of Peggy Seagrave, *Dragon Lady: The Life and Legend of the Last Empress of China* (New York: Knopf, 1992). It should be pointed out that there have been historical accounts of Cixi in the Chinese language that argue against the "dragon lady" image. Seagrave's book is unique, however, in that it shows how Cixi is part of the discourse of primitivism in modernity, and how even the "Chinese" understanding of her—in part due to the secrecy accorded to imperial matters and in part because many Chinese doc-uments were mindlessly destroyed by Western soldiers in the course of raiding Chinese imperial grounds—has been derived from Backhouse's scandal-mon-gering.

45. Yue Ming-Bao has analyzed this phenomenon in terms of the "case study" approach favored by Chinese male writers writing about lower-class women. See Yue, "Gendering the Origins of Modern Chinese Fiction," in *Gender and Sexuality*

Part 1. Visuality, Modernity, and Primitive Passions

in *Twentieth-Century Chinese Literature and Society*, ed. Tonglin Lu (Albany: State University of New York Press, 1993), pp. 47–65.

46. See the volume *Cinema and Cultural Identity*. See also the discussions of culture, national identity, and film in Roy Armes, *Third World Film Making and the West* (Berkeley and Los Angeles: University of California Press, 1987).

47. My thinking on "primitive passions" owes much to the following works: Jacques Derrida, *Of Grammatology*, trans. Gayatri Chakravorty Spivak (Baltimore: Johns Hopkins University Press, 1976); Benedict Anderson, *Imagined Communities: Reflections on the Origin and Spread of Nationalism* (London: Verso, 1983); Fabian, *Time and the Other*; James Clifford, *The Predicament of Culture: Twentieth-Century Ethnography, Literature, and Art* (Cambridge, Mass.: Harvard University Press, 1988); E. J. Hobsbawm, *Nations and Nationalism since 1780: Programme, Myth, Reality* (Cambridge: Cambridge University Press, 1990); Nancy Armstrong and Leonard Tennenhouse, *The Imaginary Puritan: Literature, Intellectual Labor, and the Origins of Personal Life* (Berkeley and Los Angeles: University of California Press, 1992). The thoughtful discussion of the discourse of nationality in chap. 3 of John Tomlinson's *Cultural Imperialism: A Critical Introduction* (London: Pinter Publishers, 1991) has also been generally if not directly helpful.

48. C. T. Hsia, "Obsession with China: The Moral Burden of Modern Chinese Fiction," in his *A History of Modern Chinese Fiction*, 2d ed. (New Haven: Yale University Press, 1971), pp. 533–34. This obsession is what accounts for the "native soil" (*xiangtu*) literature initiated by May Fourth writers in the 1920s and the "search for roots" (*xungen*) movements in the literature of the 1980s. For a brief discussion of this general "native soil discourse," see David Der-wei Wang, intro. to *From May Fourth to June Fourth*, pp. 1–15. See also Wang's chapter "Imaginary Nostalgia: Shen Congwen and Native Soil Fiction," in his *Fictional Realism in Twentieth-Century China*, pp. 247–89.

49. I borrow this phrase from Raymond Williams, *Marxism and Literature* (Oxford: Oxford University Press, 1977), pp. 128–35.

50. Clark, "Chinese Cinema Enters the 1990s," in *China Briefing, 1992*, ed. William A. Joseph (Boulder: Westview Press, 1993), p. 126.

51. Leyda writes of Ruan: "Any one of her films, even one of her worst, will support my opinion that here was one of the great actresses of film history, as perfectly and peculiarly adapted to the film as we recognize Greta Garbo to be" (Leyda, *Dianying*, p. 87). The life of Ruan was recently made into a film, *Ruan Lingyu* (*Center Stage*, 1992) by the Hong Kong director Stanley Kwan.

52. See Karl Marx, *Capital: A Critique of Political Economy*, ed. Frederick Engels, trans. Samuel Moore and Edward Aveling, rev. and amplified by Ernest Untermann (New York: Modern Library, 1906), book 1, part 1, chap. 1, "Commodities," pp. 41–96; Freud, "Fetishism" and "Splitting of the Ego in the Defensive Process," in *The Standard Edition*, vol. 21, pp. 152–57, and vol. 23, pp. 275–78; and also the section "Unsuitable Substitutes for the Sexual Object—Fetishism," in

Part 1. Visuality, Modernity, and Primitive Passions

"Three Essays on the Theory of Sexuality," in *The Standard Edition*, vol. 7, pp. 153–55.

53. I am thinking of, for instance, *Xiao wanyi* [Small toys, 1933], *Tiyu huanghou* [The queen of sports, 1934], and *Dalu* [The big road, 1934], all directed by Sun Yu; and *Xin nüxing* [New women, 1935], directed by Cai Chusheng.

54. Pier Paolo Pasolini: "It is not true that the smallest unit in cinema is the image, when by image we mean that 'view' which is the shot, or, in other words, what one sees looking through the lens . . . *the various real objects that compose a shot are the smallest unit of film language*." "The Written Language of Reality," in *Heretical Empiricism*, ed. Louise K. Barnett, trans. Ben Lawton and Louise K. Barnett (Bloomington: Indiana University Press, 1988), p. 200; emphasis in the original. By analogy with "phonemes," Pasolini goes on to name such objects in the film image "kinemes." The quotation from Pasolini at the beginning of part 1 is taken from p. 232 of the same book.

55. Pasolini, "The Cinema of Poetry," in ibid., p. 168.

56. For a discussion of the changing metaphors or analogies used to describe the film experience, see Charles F. Altman, "Psychoanalysis and Cinema: The Imaginary Discourse," in *Movies and Methods*, vol. 2, ed. Bill Nichols (Berkeley and Los Angeles: University of California Press, 1985), pp. 517–31. This essay was originally published in *Quarterly Review of Film Studies* 2, no. 3 (August 1977).

57. Works in the English language include Leyda, *Dianying*; Clark, *Chinese Cinema, Culture, and Politics since 1949* (Cambridge: Cambridge University Press, 1987); *Chinese Film: The State of Art in the People's Republic*, ed. George Stephen Semsel (New York: Praeger, 1987); *Perspectives on Chinese Cinema*, ed. Chris Berry (London: British Film Institute, 1991); and *New Chinese Cinemas: Forms, Identities, Politics*, ed. Nick Browne et al. (New York: Cambridge University Press, 1994). All these works contain useful glossaries, chronologies, and bibliographies. For an overview of works on Chinese film in English, see H. C. Li, "Chinese Electric Shadows: A Selected Bibliography of Materials in English," *Modern Chinese Literature* 7, no. 2 (Fall 1993; a special issue on filming modern Chinese literature): 117–53. See also Régis Bergeron, *Le cinéma chinois: 1905–1983* (Paris: Editions l'Harmattan, 1983–84), 4 vols.; and *Le cinéma chinois*, ed. Marie-Claire Quiquemelle and Jean-Loup Passek (Paris: Centre Georges Pompidou, 1985). Special book series, journal issues, and individual essays on Chinese cinema are cited in the many discussions to follow.

58. See, for instance, the many essays in *Writing Culture: The Poetics and Politics of Ethnography*, ed. James Clifford and George E. Marcus (Berkeley and Los Angeles: University of California Press, 1986); George E. Marcus and Michael M. J. Fischer, *Anthropology as Cultural Critique: An Experimental Moment in the Human Sciences* (Chicago: University of Chicago Press, 1986); *Modernist Anthropology*; and *Exhibiting Cultures* (in particular part 5).

Part 1. Visuality, Modernity, and Primitive Passions

59. A general discussion of this point can be found in Graeme Turner, *Film as Social Practice* (London: Routledge, 1988).

60. Japanese cinema is perhaps the best case in point here, simply because some of its reviewers have been honest enough to admit their ignorance of the Japanese language. See for instance Noël Burch, *To the Distant Observer: Form and Meaning in the Japanese Cinema*, rev. and ed. Annette Michelson (Berkeley and Los Angeles: University of California Press, 1979), p. 14. My point is not that a mastery of the language is absolutely essential to the study of a national cinema but rather that the inequality between "East" and "West" in situations of cultural "exchange" is still persistent. For a discussion of how the problematic division of labor (into "theory" vs. "history") in national cinema studies repeats and mirrors the geopolitical configuration and division of the postcolonial world, see Mitsuhiro Yoshimoto, "The Difficulty of Being Radical: The Discipline of Film Studies and the Postcolonial World Order," *boundary 2* 18, no. 3 (Fall 1991): 242–57. Yoshimoto's article contains an informed analysis of the problems of Western scholarship on Japanese cinema.

61. In *Ethnographic Film* (Austin: University of Texas Press, 1976), Karl G. Heider maintains this divide and sees film primarily as a tool for ethnography (p. 4). Because of this, even though Heider allows that films about other cultures may be ethnographically significant, such films can only be considered, he writes, "naive ethnography" (p. 5). For an argument similar to Heider's in its rejection of specifically filmic or aesthetic/representational considerations, see Peter Fuchs, "Ethnographic Film in Germany," *Visual Anthropology* 1 (1988): 217–33. See also the essays in the collection *Film as Ethnography*, ed. Peter Ian Crawford and David Turton (Manchester: Manchester University Press, 1992). Unlike Heider and Fuchs, many of the authors in this collection are highly conscious of the material complexities of photography, film, and vision in general. But ethnography remains for them a science and a discipline whose rationale is still unproblematically assumed to be the study of "other" peoples: "These essays make up the most comprehensive appraisal yet published of the relationship between filmed and written representations of *other ways of life*" (from the page facing the title page; my emphasis). I will draw on this collection in a more extended manner in part 3.

62. Speaking primarily of film studies, Judith Mayne has argued that the search for an alternative cinema is always closely related to the emphasis on classical Hollywood cinema as the norm: "Frequently, the very notion of an 'alternative' is posed in the narrow terms of an either-or: either one is within classical discourse and therefore complicit, or one is critical of and/or resistant to it and therefore outside of it." *Kino and the Woman Question* (Columbus: Ohio State University Press, 1989), p. 3. For a discussion of how "avant-garde" film practice is not necessarily a guarantee against the pitfalls of mainstream orientalism or cultural rela-

tivism, see Jane Desmond, "Ethnography, Orientalism, and the Avant-Garde Film," *Visual Anthropology* 4, no. 2 (1991): 147–60.

63. Clark, *Chinese Cinema*, p. 125. The chronology of Clark's book runs from 1949 to 1984. See chaps. 4 and 5 for the historical background to films during the Cultural Revolution period.

64. Maurice Meisner, *Mao's China and After: A History of the People's Republic* (a revised and expanded ed. of *Mao's China*) (New York: Free Press, 1986), p. 336.

65. Andrew Solomon, "The Howl that Could Free China," *New York Times Magazine*, December 19, 1993, p. 70.

66. Wu Wenguang, quoted in program notes on *1966: My Time in the Red Guards*, Seventeenth Hong Kong International Film Festival (1993).

67. In China Mao's popularity as a picture was preceded by the immense popularity of comic books. Of absolute relevance to our discussion here is an interesting account by Leyda: "The clearest lessons taught by films to another medium (and vice versa!) appeared in the picture–story books—a child of ancient illustrated literature and the comic books introduced to China by American soldiers. Chinese picture–story books of the 1960s still show stylistic traces of Harold Foster's Tarzan and Prince Valiant and (even!) Milton Caniff's Terry and the Pirates. Since their introduction in 1935, they had moved beyond the children for whom they were first intended. By the 1960s it was not unusual to see adults depending on the pictorial supports of this dubious literature that seemed to increase the dangers of simplification. And children read little else. Filmgoing in China is very inexpensive—comic books are even cheaper and have the added powers of possession and personal circulation: much like the dream of everyone owning his own film library. Roughly half the comic books to be found (before *Quotations from Chairman Mao Tse-tung* took over most printing facilities) were reproductions of popular and required films." Leyda, *Dianying*, p. 334.

68. André Bazin, "The Stalin Myth in Soviet Cinema" (with an intro. by Dudley Andrew), trans. Georgia Gurrieri, in *Movies and Methods*, vol. 2, pp. 29–40. The essay was first published in *L'Esprit* (July–August 1950) and then in English in *Film Criticism* 3, no. 1 (Fall 1978).

69. On this point see also Bazin, "The Ontology of the Photographic Image," in his *What is Cinema?* (essays selected and translated by Hugh Gray), vol. 1, with a foreword by Jean Renoir (Berkeley and Los Angeles: University of California Press, 1967), pp. 9–16. Pointing to its precise resemblance to the thing it copies, Bazin argues that the photographic image embalms time and prevents it from corruption, the way Egyptian mummy wrappings preserve bodies.

70. Pasolini, "Observations on the Sequence Shot," in *Heretical Empiricism*, pp. 236–37; emphases in the original.

71. Alice Yaeger Kaplan, *Reproductions of Banality: Fascism, Literature, and French Intellectual Life* (Minneapolis: University of Minnesota Press, 1986), p. 155.

Part 1. Visuality, Modernity, and Primitive Passions

72. Louis Althusser, "Ideology and Ideology State Apparatuses (Notes towards an Investigation)," in *Lenin and Philosophy and Other Essays*, trans. Ben Brewster (London: Monthly Review Press, 1971), pp. 127–86; see pp. 174–77 for his formulation of "interpellation."

73. Bazin, "The Stalin Myth," p. 35.

74. That the Mao-worship of the Cultural Revolution days is far from being over is evident from the kind of nostalgia and idealism attached to it today. Li Xianting, a leader of avant-garde art in contemporary Beijing, is quoted as saying: "Even those of us who were opposed were believers, at least part way. Mao was a very convincing man, and we intellectuals felt we were sad figures. In the Cultural Revolution, the people thought only of building a pure and perfect society. I disagreed with their particular idealism and fought against it, and would fight against it again, but I can say without hesitation that there is nothing in our commercialist society today that is equal to it. A misguided idealism is better than no idealism at all." See Solomon, "The Howl that Could Free China," p. 66. Geremie Barmé comments on the leader cults continually promoted by the party propaganda machine in the 1980s and 1990s in the following terms: "While the Party promoted the great revolutionaries of the past to confirm its present authority, the masses often responded to them as revived deities, bereft of immediate political and historical significance, embodying rather traditional charismatic elements: Mao Zedong, the laconic and brilliant thinker and strategist, Zhou Enlai the loyal minister who works himself to death, Jiang Qing the fickle and crazed woman, Lin Biao an evil genius and a host of other revolutionaries who made history. Compared to the grey bureaucrats of today—Jiang Zemin, Li Peng, Zhu Rongji, et al.—who rose to power through murky bureaucratic infighting—these are real saints (or devils)." Barmé, "The Greying of Chinese Culture," *China Review 1992*, ed. Kuan Hsin-chi and Maurice Brosseau (Hong Kong: Chinese University Press, 1992), sec. 13, p. 20.

75. Paul Virilio, *War and Cinema: The Logistics of Perception*, trans. Patrick Camiller (London: Verso, 1989), p. 71; emphases in the original.

76. Quoted in ibid., p. 53.

77. Ibid., p. 81.

78. For a more extensive discussion of the arguments I am making about technology and fascism, see Rey Chow, "The Fascist Longings in Our Midst," forthcoming in *Ariel*.

79. It should be emphasized that not only mainland Chinese films exhibit these symptoms of primitivist longing. If we think of the popular genre of Kung Fu film—a genre that is mass-produced in Hong Kong and Taiwan—from this perspective, it would be possible to say that Kung Fu films are inscriptions of the cathexes of primitivism situated between the past as nature and the present as technology. Nature here is none other than the human body, which inscribes itself like a hieroglyph in space, while the kinetic possibilities of this ancient,

Part 1. Visuality, Modernity, and Primitive Passions

primitive body are magnified and multiplied a thousandfold by dazzling cinematic techniques to create a distinct form of modern visual culture that is marked "Chinese." For an interesting discussion of the Kung Fu genre that uses the philosophy of Heidegger, See Kwai-cheung Lo, "Once Upon a Time: Technology Comes to Presence in China," *Modern Chinese Literature* 7, no. 2 (Fall 1993): 79–96.

80. For discussions of the politics of museum culture, see the essays in the collection *Exhibiting Cultures*.

81. Mary Louise Pratt, *Imperial Eyes: Travel Writing and Transculturation* (New York: Routledge, 1992), pp. 7–9; emphasis in the original. Pratt writes that autoethnographic texts are "typically heterogeneous on the reception end as well, usually addressed both to metropolitan readers and to literate sectors of the speaker's own social group, and bound to be received very differently by each." As my analyses of contemporary Chinese films will go on to indicate, Pratt's point is especially true in the case of films that are popular with "foreign" audiences.

82. Geoffrey O'Brien, "Blazing Passions," *New York Review of Books*, September 24, 1992, p. 38. See also general discussions of the Fifth Generation in Clark, "Reinventing China: The Fifth Generation Filmmakers," *Modern Chinese Literature* 5, no. 1 (Spring 1989): 121–36; Ma Ning, "Notes on the New Filmmakers," in *Chinese Film: The State of the Art in the People's Republic*, pp. 63–93; Tony Rayns, "Chinese Vocabulary: An Introduction to *King of the Children* and the New Chinese Cinema," in *"King of the Children" and the New Chinese Cinema* (London: Faber and Faber, 1989), pp. 1–58; and Zhang Jiaxuan, "New Development of Chinese Films in the 1980s," *Jintian (Today)* 2 (1992): 12–19.

83. Chen, in an interview quoted in Ma Qiang, "The Chinese Film in the 1980s," p. 173.

84. See Li Tuo, "Huangtudi gei women dailaile shenmo?" [What has *Yellow Earth* brought us?], in *Huangtudi* (Dianying: Zhongguo mingzuo xuan, no. 2), ed. Jiao Xiongping (Taipei: Wanxiang tushu gufen youxian gognsi, 1990), pp. 132–46.

85. "To an extent not seen since the War of Resistance to Japan, the Cultural Revolution was an upheaval of national dimensions. Large numbers of people, particularly the educated young, had an opportunity to travel, rare under a regime usually offering its citizens about as much geographical mobility as a medieval or peasant society. This experience on such a scale meant that the Cultural Revolution had a profound impact on the perceptions of both the educated, political public and the wider population." Clark, *Chinese Cinema*, p. 183.

86. For a discussion of China's ecological problems, see He Bochuan, *China on the Edge: The Crisis of Ecology and Development* (San Francisco: China Books and Periodicals, 1991). Originally written in Chinese, this book was first published in China in 1988.

Part 1. Visuality, Modernity, and Primitive Passions

87. "Report from Dachau," *New Yorker*, August 3, 1992, pp. 43–61. The quoted passage (on p. 55) is preceded by a description of how, for some, the memory of the concentration camp has made landscape painting almost a kind of moral crime in present-day Dachau. Adorno subsequently revised his earlier pronouncement (which had been made in his *Critique of Culture and Society*) by saying that "it may have been wrong to say that after Auschwitz you can no longer write poems." See *Negative Dialectics*, trans. E. B. Ashton (New York: Continuum, 1973), pp. 362–63.

88. Pasolini, "Is Being Natural?" in *Heretical Empiricism*, p. 243.

89. Pasolini, "Living Signs and Dead Poets," in ibid., p. 250.

90. Cavell describes this as "that specific simultaneity of presence and absence" unique to cinema; *The World Viewed*, p. 42. See also pp. 209–15 for an extended discussion of the same point.

91. Hobsbawm, "Introduction: Inventing Traditions," in *The Invention of Tradition*, ed. Eric Hobsbawm and Terrence Ranger (Cambridge: Cambridge University Press, 1983), p.4.

92. Clark: "*Yellow Earth* is as international as the older Shanghai film and artistic tradition, and yet its message and setting derive from Yan'an" (*Chinese Cinema*, p. 181). For related interest, see Jonathan D. Spence, "Film and Politics: Bai Hua's *Bitter Love*," in *Chinese Roundabout: Essays in History and Culture* (New York: Norton, 1992), pp. 277–92, for a discussion of how a contemporary film that is extremely critical of the communist regime is at the same time deeply rooted in the symbolisms of historical Chinese culture.

93. For a discussion of this point, see the section "Film as Cross-Cultural Discourse" in Ma Ning, "Notes on the New Filmmakers," pp. 82–92.

94. Clark, "Reinventing China," p. 134.

95. Clark refers to the film *One and Eight* as "directly masculine in its harshness of landscape, bluntness of characters, and directness of visual form." "Reinventing China," p. 123.

96. Chen, interview with Liu Xiaobo, *Lianhe bao* (Taipei), May 8, 1993; my translation and emphases. The book he mentions is probably *Shaonian Kaige* [Young Kaige] (Taipei: Yuanliu chuban shiye gufen youxian gongsi, 1991).

97. Meisner, *Mao's China and After*, pp. 316–17. In literary narrative terms, this iconoclasm is what Theodore Huters calls the "monological confrontation" with "tradition's monolithic weight." See Huters, "Lives in Profile: On the Authorial Voice in Modern and Contemporary Chinese Literature," in *From May Fourth to June Fourth*, p. 272.

98. David Wang: "Perhaps the patriarchal system in modern Chinese society is itself a signifier, not an essentialized signified, as some feminists would have it." Intro. to *From May Fourth to June Fourth*, p. 8.

99. See Clark, "Chinese Cinema Enters the 1990s." Zhang Yuan, a young director in his early thirties, says of the difference between his generation and the Fifth Generation: "Most of the Fifth Generation directors are intellectual youths

who've spent time in the country, while we're urbanites. . . . [Tian] Zhuangzhuang and his peers all went through the Cultural Revolution, and they remained kind of romantic. We didn't. . . . I don't like being subjective, and I want my films to be objective. It's objectivity that'll empower me." Quoted from *Yingxiang (Imagekeeper Monthly)* 32 (September 1992), in program notes on *Mama*, Seventeenth Hong Kong International Film Festival (1993).

100. Xie Fei's *Xiang hun nü (Oilmakers' Family*, 1992) is an exception to this. It is a film about how women in rural areas, regardless of generational difference, are still bound by oppressive feudal practices.

101. See Zhang Yimou's remarks in Mayfair Yang, "Of Gender, State Censorship, and Overseas Capital: An Interview with Director Zhang Yimou," *Public Culture* 5, no. 2 (Winter 1993): 306–7. See also Ma Qiang, "The Chinese Film in the 1980s," for a summary of the conditions under which Chinese films are usually made and moved through the various levels of bureaucracy.

102. Much like Bazin's discussion of the Stalin films in the Soviet Union of the 1940s, films about the foreign invasion of China in the nineteenth century, about the revolutionary history and military achievements of the communist government, and about monumental figures such as Mao Zedong and Zhou Enlai are used, in the 1990s, in an attempt to erase the crimes committed by the Chinese government with carefully (re)constructed stories and images. See the section "More Mao than Ever" in Chris Berry, "A Nation T(w/o)o: Chinese Cinema(s) and Nationhood(s)," *East-West Film Journal* 7, no. 1 (January 1993): 24–51.

103. For a discussion of the ways mainland Chinese intellectuals feel alienated from their government, see Merle Goldman, Perry Link, and Su Wei, "China's Intellectuals in the Deng Era: Loss of Identity with the State," in *China's Quest for National Identity*, ed. Lowell Dittmer and Samuel S. Kim (Ithaca, N.Y.: Cornell University Press, 1993), pp. 125–53. See also Fang Lizhi, *Bringing Down the Great Wall: Writings on Science, Culture, and Democracy in China*, ed. James H. Williams, trans. James H. Williams et al., with an intro. by Orville Schell (New York: Knopf, 1991).

104. Chen, interview with Liu Xiaobo.

105. Zhang, interview with Liu Xiaobo, *Lianhe bao* (Hong Kong), May 1, 1993.

106. Geremie Barmé, "The Chinese Velvet Prison: Culture in the 'New Age,' 1976–89," *Issues and Studies* 25–27 (1989–91): 54–79; the quoted statement is on p. 61.

107. Ibid., pp. 62–63. For a companion piece of criticism of contemporary Chinese culture, see also Barmé's "The Greying of Chinese Culture": "What does it mean to be grey in China these days? . . . It is a syndrome, rather, combining hopelessness, uncertainty and ennui with irony, sarcasm and a large dose of fatalism. It is a mood that both envelopes the individual and an ambience suffusing the society; it is a *Zeitgeist* that is particularly prevalent in youth culture. It is the temper, in particular, of the capital Beijing" (sec. 13, p. 2).

Part 2: Some Contemporary Chinese Films

1. Digging an Old Well: The Labor of Social Fantasy

1. The Jameson epigraph at the opening of this section is from "Third-World Literature in the Era of Multinational Capital," *Social Text* 15 (Fall 1986): 69. For the most widely cited piece of criticism of Fredric Jameson's position, see Aijaz Ahmad, "Jameson's Rhetoric of Otherness and the 'National Allegory,' " *Social Text* 17 (Fall 1987): 3–25; and Jameson, "A Brief Response," *Social Text* 17 (Fall 1987): 26–27. (See also the relevant pages in Ahmad, *In Theory: Classes, Nations, Literatures* [London: Verso, 1992].) For a criticism of Jameson's "A Brief Response," see Kwai-cheung Lo, "Crossing Boundaries: A Study of Modern Hong Kong Fiction from the Fifties to the Eighties" (M.Phil. thesis, University of Hong Kong, 1990), pp. 165–73. For Jameson's recent reinstatement of the concept of national allegory, see his "Foreword: In the Mirror of Alternate Modernities," Karatani Kōjin, *Origins of Modern Japanese Literature*, a collective translation edited by Brett de Bary (Durham, N.C.: Duke University Press, 1993), pp. vii–xx; see in particular pp. xix–xx, on which he issues the call for a moral rectification of "our" (i.e., the United States') "national" character. The epigraphs from Benjamin and Hobsbawm are taken respectively from *The Origin of German Tragic Drama*, trans. John Osborne (London: New Left Books, 1977), p. 233, and from *Nations and Nationalism since 1780: Programme, Myth, Reality* (New York: Cambridge University Press, 1990), p. 152.

2. Ashish Rajadhyaksha, "Debating the Third Cinema," in *Questions of Third Cinema*, ed. Jim Pines and Paul Willemen (London: British Film Institute, 1989), p. 170.

3. For instance, see Paul Willemen, "The Third Cinema Question: Notes and Reflections," in *Questions of Third Cinema*, pp. 1–29.

4. "[The] dominant *radical* reader in the Anglo-U.S. reactively homogenizes the Third World and sees it only in the context of nationalism and ethnicity." Gayatri Chakravorty Spivak, *In Other Worlds: Essays in Cultural Politics* (New York: Methuen, 1987), p. 246; emphasis in the original.

5. Ibid., p. 254.

6. "I shall argue, as a basic issue of the Third Cinema, that almost always the reference [to the 'outside,' to class struggle/imperialism/that which is documented] is used to *shore up* the discourse, and that the problem begins here—in the way the reference is submerged into the discourse, and then the discourse is submerged into the political act, and the act itself into the 'choices' set before it." Rajadhyaksha, "Debating the Third Cinema," pp. 174–75; emphasis in the original.

7. Among those who have used the concept of "national allegory" in relation to Chinese film, see, for instance, Yingjin Zhang, "Ideology of the Body in *Red Sorghum*: National Allegory, National Roots, and Third Cinema," *East-West Film*

Part 2. Some Contemporary Chinese Films

Journal 4, no. 2 (June 1990): 38–53; E. Ann Kaplan, "Melodrama/ Subjectivity/Ideology: The Relevance of Western Melodrama Theories to Recent Chinese Cinema," ibid., vol. 5, no. 1 (January 1991): 6–27; Chen Ruxiu, "*Da hong denglong gao gao gua* yu tongsu lilun" [*Raise the Red Lantern* and theories of the melodramatic], *Dangdai (Con-Temporary Monthly)*, April 1, 1992, a special issue on Chinese film, pp. 52–61. The editors of this issue of *Dangdai* also echo Chen Ruxiu: "As Jameson says, all third world literature, including Chinese literature, is, to put it in a nutshell, political allegory, a product of the political unconscious. *Judou*, *Yellow Earth*, *Hibiscus Town*, and *Raise the Red Lantern* are all footnotes." *Dangdai*, p. 150; my translation.

8. Jameson, "Third-World Literature in the Era of Multinational Capital," p. 66.

9. Ibid.

10. Liu Heng, "Fuxi Fuxi," *Zhongguo xiaoshuo yi jiu ba ba* [Chinese fiction 1988], ed. Wang Ziping and Li Tuo (Hong Kong: Sanlian shudian, 1989), pp. 80–171. For an informative analysis of the story, see Marie-Claire Huot, "Liu Heng's *Fuxi Fuxi*: What about Nüwa?" in *Gender and Sexuality in Twentieth-Century Chinese Literature and Society*, ed. Tonglin Lu (Albany: State University of New York Press, 1993), pp. 85–105.

11. This phrase is Chandra Talpade Mohanty's. See "Under Western Eyes: Feminist Scholarship and Colonial Discourses," in *Third World Women and the Politics of Feminism*, ed. Chandra Talpade Mohanty, Ann Russo, and Lourdes Torres (Bloomington: Indiana University Press, 1991), p. 53. An earlier version of this essay was published in *boundary 2* 12, no. 3–13 (Spring–Fall 1984) and reprinted in *Feminist Review* 30 (Autumn 1988).

12. Teshome H. Gabriel, "Towards a Critical Theory of Third World Films," in *Questions of Third Cinema*, pp. 48–49. For a discussion of why pictorial aesthetics and "third world" ethnic identity/agency cannot be mapped onto each other in this manner, see the following chapter.

13. Jean Baudrillard, *For a Critique of the Political Economy of the Sign*, trans. and with an intro. by Charles Levin (St. Louis, Mo.: Telos Press, 1981), p. 93.

14. *Judou*, for instance, was nominated for "best foreign language film" at the Oscars in 1991 while being banned in China until the spring of 1992. Since June 1989, the Chinese authorities have been tightening control over "culture" by a conscious return to leftist educational strategies. The "nationalistic" view of Ai Zhisheng, the minister for radio, film, and television, that only Chinese people are eligible to praise Chinese films, is an example of this ridiculously reactionary turn in mainland Chinese cultural politics. For a relevant discussion, see Tony Rayns, "The Tunnel Vision of Minister Ai." This essay appears as "L'étroitesse d'esprit du ministre Ai," trans. Corinne Durin, in the program notes, *Festival international du cinéma chinois, 4e édition, du 23 mai au 2 juin 1991* (Montréal), pp. 65–67.

15. Baudrillard, *For a Critique*, p. 94; emphasis in the original.

1. Digging an Old Well

16. The recent films by Chen Kaige and Zhang Yimou obtained financial support from Hong Kong, Taiwan, Japan, England, Germany, and Holland. As Jean-Paul Aubert writes about Chen's 1991 film *Life on a String* (a philosophical treatment of contemporary Chinese culture): "Le plus étonnant sera d'apprendre que ce film si profondément chinois est en fait une production anglo-allemande . . . le gouvernement chinois n'a pas mis un seul yuan dans la production. C'est peut-être même la première fois qu'un film chinois . . . est entièrement financé par des producteurs occidentaux." See "Le retour des enfants prodiges," *Cahiers du cinéma*, no. 442 (1991): 85. Zhang Yimou, for his part, apparently had no problem accepting exclusively Japanese financial backing (from a company called the Tokuma Group) for *Judou* even though in *Red Sorghum* he expressed "nationalistic" sentiments by portraying Japanese violence against Chinese villagers during the period around the Second World War.

17. In an interview with Chinese and non-Chinese reporters in early 1991, the Chinese premier Li Peng responded to questions about the Tiananmen massacre with the following kind of "rationality": "It has already been two years since the June Fourth incident; there is no need to discuss it any more. . . . Under the urgent circumstances of the time, had the Chinese government not acted decisively, we would not be able to have the stability and economic prosperity we see in China today." "Zhong wai jizhe zhaodaihui shang Li Peng huida wenti" [Li Peng's responses to questions at the press conference for Chinese and foreign reporters], *Ming Pao Daily News* (Vancouver ed.), April 11, 1991; my translation.

18. I am grateful to Teresa de Lauretis for telling me that I needed to clarify my point about "coloniality."

19. Gayatri Chakravorty Spivak, "Scattered Speculations on the Question of Value," in *In Other Worlds*, p. 158. This essay was originally published in *diacritics* in 1985. See also Spivak, "Speculations on Reading Marx: After Reading Derrida," in *Poststructuralism and the Question of History*, ed. Derek Attridge, Geoff Bennington, and Robert Young (New York: Cambridge University Press, 1987), pp. 30–62.

20. For a discussion of how the (re)invention of native and national origins functions *within Western discourses* as a way to mask the realities of Western imperialism, see Nancy Armstrong and Leonard Tennenhouse, *The Imaginary Puritan: Literature, Intellectual Labor, and the Origins of Personal Life* (Berkeley and Los Angeles: University of California Press, 1992).

21. Zheng Yi, *Lao jing* (Taipei: Haifeng chubanshe, 1988). The novel was first published in a literary magazine in China in February 1985. It is also available in English. See Zheng Yi, *Old Well*, trans. David Kwan, with an intro. by Anthony P. Kane (San Francisco: China Books and Periodicals, 1989).

22. Such a reading informs, for instance, the discussions collected in *Lao jing* (*Dianying/Zhongguo mingzuo xuan*, no. 1), ed. Jiao Xiongping (Taipei: Wanxiang tushu gufen youxian gongsi, 1990).

23. "Hence, as we can now see in melancholy retrospect, it was the great achievement of the communist regimes in multinational countries to limit the disastrous effects of nationalism within them. . . . Indeed, it may be argued that the current wave of ethnic or mini-ethnic agitations is a response to the overwhelmingly non-national and non-nationalist principles of state formation in the greater part of the twentieth-century world." E. J. Hobsbawm, *Nations and Nationalism since 1780*, p. 173.

24. For a discussion of the construction of the "Chinese" ethnic identity, see David Yen-ho Wu, "The Construction of Chinese and Non-Chinese Identities," *Daedalus: Journal of the American Academy of Arts and Sciences* 120, no. 2 (Spring 1991): 159–79. For a discussion, of related interest, of the traditional ethnic conflict between the Hans (who make up 94 percent of the Chinese population) and the Huis (Chinese-speaking Muslims), see Jonathan N. Lipman, "Ethnic Violence in Modern China: Hans and Huis in Gansu, 1781–1929," in *Violence in China: Essays in Culture and Counterculture*, ed. Jonathan N. Lipman and Stevan Harrell (Albany: State University of New York Press, 1990), pp. 65–86.

25. The common view among some feminist China scholars is that issues of female sexuality have been subsumed under either the traditional kinship family or the modernist discourse of the nation. In the early twentieth century, when nationalism was replacing familial pieties as the valid self-strengthening discourse in the "third world," the family and the nation could indeed be looked upon as equally "major" historical forces that dwarf and erase women in different but comparable ways. However, the major shortcoming of this view lies in that, after pointing out the masculinism of nationalism, it cannot explain why nationalism has such a great appeal to women as well as men. The analysis of the relation between "woman" and "the nation" I offer here is quite different from this common view.

26. The story ends with these lines: "Below, on the flowery banks of the Qinglong River, in the little village half hidden by the morning smoke, lie his dry land, his small son, his virtuous wife, his dearest elders and brothers, and memories of the love that he will never forget." Zheng, *Lao Jing*, p. 224; my translation.

27. For a recent discussion of how the Chinese extracted brine for making salt by drilling the deepest well (one kilometer) in the world over a century and a half ago, see Hans Ulrich Vogel, "The Great Well of China," *Scientific American*, June 1993, pp. 116–21. According to Vogel, the Xinhai well, which is located in Sichuan Province, "was the culmination of an 800-year-old technology." The epigraphs by Hobsbawm and Chatterjee at the beginning of the present section are taken respectively from *Nations and Nationalism since 1780*, p. 169 (emphasis in the original), and from *Nationalist Thought and the Colonial World—A Derivative Discourse?* (United Nations University, Tokyo: Zed Books, 1986), p. 11.

28. The "technological" interest is evident even in films that are not explicitly about technology. For instance, in Zheng Dongtian's *Yuanyang lou* (*Young Couples*, 1987), we find the stories of six couples living in the same apartment complex that

2. Silent Is the Ancient Plain

are cinematically narrated against a background of new common household objects, from the vacuum cleaner to the cassette tape player. Even as mere silent background, technology in the home effectively demonstrates the changes in cultural value.

29. The films that are set in big cities are, by contrast, always about the loss of such humanistic values. Recent examples include Zhou Xiaowen's *Fengkuang de daijia* (*Obsession*, 1989), and Xie Fei's *Ben ming nian* (*Black Snow*, 1990).

30. Slavoj Žižek, "Eastern Europe's Republics of Gilead," *New Left Review* 183 (September–October 1990): 53; emphases in the original. As he argues in another context, social fantasy is "precisely the way the antagonistic fissure is masked. . . . Fantasy is a means for an ideology to take its own failure into account in advance." See Žižek, *The Sublime Object of Ideology* (London: Verso, 1989), p. 126.

31. If we substitute the word *communal* for *national*, the following quotation would apply well to our present discussion: "Where national memories are concerned, griefs are of more value than triumphs, for they impose duties, and require a common effort." Ernest Renan, "What Is a Nation?" trans. and annotated by Martin Thom, in *Nation and Narration*, ed. Homi K. Bhabha (New York: Routledge, 1990), p. 19.

32. *Old Well* won four of the thirteen awards given by the festival, including the "special affirmation award by international film critics."

2. Silent Is the Ancient Plain: Music, Filmmaking, and the Concept of Social Change in the New Chinese Cinema

1. *Playboy* (Chinese ed.), no. 22 (May 1988): 44. Hereafter page references are given in the text. All translations are mine.

2. Yuejin Wang, "The Cinematic Other and the Cultural Self? Decentering the Cultural Identity on Cinema," *Wide Angle* 11, no. 2 (1989): 35. For another example of a discussion of the "othering" of China, see Esther C. M. Yau, "Is China the End of Hermeneutics? Or, Political and Cultural Usage of Non-Han Women in Mainland Chinese Films," *Discourse* 11, no. 2 (Spring–Summer 1989): 115–36.

3. Fredric Jameson, "Third-World Literature in the Era of Multinational Capital," *Social Text* 15 (Fall 1986): 69.

4. Ann Kaplan, "Problematizing Cross-Cultural Analysis: The Case of Women in the Recent Chinese Cinema," *Wide Angle* 11, no. 2 (1989): 47. Kaplan's piece can also be found in *Perspectives on Chinese Cinema*, ed. Chris Berry (London: British Film Institute, 1991), pp. 141–54.

5. Ibid., p. 45.

6. Mitsuhiro Yoshimoto has criticized the notion of "cross-cultural" exchange/ analysis adopted by many Western critics in the following manner: "By designating only one direction of subject-object relation, this popular notion elides the issue of power/knowledge. While Western critics as subject can analyze a non-

Part 2. Some Contemporary Chinese Films

Western text as object, non-Western critics are not allowed to occupy the position of subject to analyze a Western text as object. When non-Western critics study English literature or French cinema, it is not called cross-cultural analysis. Whatever they say is interpreted and judged only within the context of Western discourses. The cross-cultural analysis, which is predicted on the masking of power relations in the production of knowledge, is a newer version of legitimating cultural colonization of the non-West by the West." See Yoshimoto, "The Difficulty of Being Radical: The Discipline of Film Studies and the Postcolonial World Order," *boundary 2* 18, no. 3 (Fall 1991): 250.

7. For discussions of *Yellow Earth* in Chinese, see the debates collected in *Huashuo huangtudi* [On *Yellow Earth*] (Beijing: Zhongguo dianying chubanshe, 1986). For an account in English of *Yellow Earth*'s plot, filming, release, and receptions, see Bonnie S. McDougall, *"The Yellow Earth": A Film by Chen Kaige with a Complete Translation of the Film Script* (Hong Kong: Chinese University Press, 1991).

8. In *Seeds of Fire: Chinese Voices of Conscience*, ed. Geremie Barmé and John Minford (New York: Hill and Wang, 1988), p. 268. See also the interview with Chen entitled "Huaizhe shenzhi de chizi zhi ai" [With the deep and sincere love of a newborn babe] in *Huangtudi* (*Dianying/Zhongguo mingzuo xuan*, no. 2), ed. Jiao Xiongping (Taipei: Wanxiang tushu gufen youxian gongsi, 1990), pp. 147–73, in which Chen talks about his strong feelings for the land, the people, and their lives in the Shaanbei area.

9. Paul Clark, *Chinese Cinema: Culture and Politics since 1949* (Cambridge: Cambridge University Press, 1987), p. 180.

10. *Film Quarterly* 41, no. 2 (Winter 1987–88): 22–33. Hereafter page references are given in the text. Yau's piece can also be found in *Perspectives on Chinese Cinema*, pp. 62–79.

11. For related interest, see the essays by Li Suyuan, Huang Shixian, and Zhao Yuan in *Huangtudi* (pp. 89–131), which all discuss the film in terms of a new kind of poetry about the Chinese people. Zhao's discussion also explores the significance of Chen's use of blank space.

12. For another example of this untenable logic, see Jenny Kwok Wah Lau, "*Judou*: A Hermeneutic Reading of Cross-Cultural Cinema," *Film Quarterly* 45, no. 2 (Winter 1991–92): 2–10.

13. For instance, Yau says with regard to the Yellow River: "In an inconspicuous way, the Yellow River's meaning is . . . contemplated: the peasants are nourished by it and are sometimes destroyed by it. A *narrative function* is attached: this is a place in dire need of reform, and it is also stubbornly resistant" (Yau, "*Yellow Earth*: Western Analysis and a Non-Western Text," p. 26). With regard to Cuiqiao: "When Cuiqiao is alive, the sour tunes she sings fills the film's sound track—musical signifiers *narrating* the sadness and the beauty of 'yin' " (ibid., p. 29). Emphases are mine.

14. Yau, "Cultural and Economic Dislocations: Filmic Phantasies of Chinese Women in the 1980s," *Wide Angle* 11, no. 2 (1989): 15.

15. For debates on the question of the nationalization of film in China, see *Chinese Film: The State of Art in the People's Republic*, ed. George Stephen Semsel (New York: Praeger, 1987), pp. 52–58; *Chinese Film Theory: A Guide to the New Era*, ed. George S. Semsel, Xia Hong, and Hou Jianping (New York: Praeger, 1990), part 4 (pp. 97–140).

16. Xiao Hong, *Hulan he zhuan* (Hong Kong: Lianhe wen cong 008, 1987), chap. 4, p. 101; my translation.

17. Speaking against the tendency of literature and art toward the "exposure" of wrongs, Mao says: "The masses too have shortcomings, which should be overcome by criticism and self-criticism within the people's own ranks, and such criticism and self-criticism is also one of the most important tasks of literature and art. But this should not be regarded as any sort of 'exposure of the people.' As for the people, the question is basically one of education and of raising their level." See "Talks at the Yenan Forum on Literature and Art," in *Mao Tse-tung on Literature and Art* (Beijing: Foreign Languages Press, 1967), p. 33.

18. Jacques Attali, *Noise: The Political Economy of Music*, trans. Brian Massumi, with a foreword by Fredric Jameson and an afterword by Susan McClary (Minneapolis: University of Minnesota Press, 1985). Hereafter page references are given in the text.

19. I have discussed the media-related ideological implications of the "China crisis" of 1989 in "Violence in the Other Country: China as Crisis, Spectacle, and Woman," in *Third World Women and the Politics of Feminism*, ed. Chandra Talpade Mohanty et al. (Bloomington: Indiana University Press, 1991), pp. 81–100.

20. In *Illuminations*, trans. Harry Zohn, ed. and with an intro. by Hannah Arendt (New York: Schocken, 1969), pp. 217–51.

21. Jean-Louis Comolli, "Machines of the Visible," in *The Cinematic Apparatus*, ed. Teresa de Lauretis and Stephen Heath (London: MacMillan, 1978), p. 123; emphasis in the original.

22. "When Chen Kaige disavows any 'political' intentions behind *Yellow Earth* (as he has done in countless interviews), he is merely stressing the distance that separates his work from the didactic, propaganda cinema of earlier years. *Yellow Earth* is, in fact, profoundly 'political' in its own, questioning way. The film's narrative deconstructs one of the Communist Party's most cherished myths, which holds that Communist ideology spread like wildfire through China's peasant communities in the 1930s—as celebrated in countless propaganda movies of the 1950s and 1960s." Tony Rayns, "Chinese Vocabulary: An Introduction to *King of the Children* and the New Chinese Cinema," in *"King of the Children" and the New Chinese Cinema* (London: Faber and Faber, 1989), p. 28.

23. For samples of derogatory criticisms of the film, see *Seeds of Fire*, pp. 259–67.

24. Ibid., p. 260.

25. Ibid., p. 255.

26. Carol Flinn, "The 'Problem' of Femininity in Theories of Film Music," *Screen* 27, no. 6 (November–December 1986): 57.

27. Ibid., p. 63.

28. Silverman, *The Acoustic Mirror: The Female Voice in Psychoanalysis and Cinema* (Bloomington: Indiana University Press, 1988), p. 57.

29. Ibid., p. 45.

30. In contrast, the scene in which Hanhan sings his broad piece about the Dragon King presents the singing in ways that are vocally, verbally, and geographically specific; Hanhan is clearly seen to be performing, and Gu Qing and Cuiqiao listening.

31. Flinn, "The 'Problem' of Femininity," pp. 67–68. Flinn argues this interplay in relation to music's ties with melodrama.

32. Flinn suggests this way of understanding music on p. 58.

33. Jacques Lacan, "Seminar of 21 January 1975," in *Feminine Sexuality*, ed. Juliet Mitchell and Jacqueline Rose (New York: Norton, 1983), p. 164.

34. Lacan, *The Four Fundamental Concepts of Psycho-Analysis*, trans. Alan Sheridan (New York, Norton, 1978), p. 103.

35. See Freud, "Some Psychological Consequences of the Anatomical Distinction between the Sexes," "Fetishism," and "Splitting of the Ego in the Defensive Process," in *Sexuality and the Psychology of Love*, ed. and with an intro. by Philip Rieff (New York: Collier Books, 1963), pp. 183–93, 214–19, 220–23. These essays can also be found in *The Standard Edition of the Complete Psychological Works of Sigmund Freud*, trans. James Strachey (London: Hogarth Press, 1959), vols. 19, 21, 23.

36. See Silverman's criticism of Derrida along similar lines on p. 45 of *The Acoustic Mirror*. Paul de Man's reading of Rousseau's discussion of music in the *Essai sur l'origine des langues* is an interesting intertext here, if only because it points to Derrida's blindness to Rousseau's nonsensory, semiotic understanding of musical signification. De Man's point is that music as it appears in Rousseau's text is, contrary to Derrida's assumption about the voice/sound, not about plenitude but about emptiness, not about representation as presence but about representation as void. See de Man, *Blindness and Insight: Essays in the Rhetoric of Contemporary Criticism*, 2d rev. ed., with an intro. by Wlad Godzich (Minneapolis: University of Minnesota Press, 1983), pp. 123–36.

37. See Chen's interesting discussion of this point in "Huaizhe shenzhi de chizi zhi ai," p. 172. Chen considers the orchestral backing to Cuiqiao's singing a technical mistake.

38. I take this phrase from Noël and Patrick Caroll, "Notes on Movie Music," *Studies in the Literary Imagination* 19, no. 1 (Spring 1986): 77.

39. Chen, "Huaizhe shenzhi de chizi zhi ai," p. 151.

2. Silent Is the Ancient Plain

40. Silverman, *The Acoustic Mirror*, p. 1.

41. Sergei Eisenstein, "Synchronization of Senses," in *The Film Sense*, ed. and trans. Jay Leyda (Cleveland and New York: Meridian Books, 1957), p. 101.

42. See, for instance, Catherine Yi-Yu Cho Woo, "The Chinese Montage: From Poetry and Painting to the Silver Screen," in *Perspectives on Chinese Cinema*, pp. 21–29.

43. Leo Ou-fan Lee, "The Tradition of Modern Chinese Cinema: Some Preliminary Explorations and Hypotheses," in ibid., p. 17.

44. Clark, *Chinese Cinema*, p. 179.

45. In *Haizi wang* (*King of the Children*), which he adapted from A Cheng's novella of the same title, Chen once again focuses attention on the problem of repetition against a subdued background of the Cultural Revolution. See my discussion in the following chapter.

46. Clark, *Chinese Cinema*, p. 181.

47. Martin Heidegger, "The Age of the World Picture," in *The Question Concerning Technology and Other Essays*, trans. and with an intro. by William Lovitt (New York: Harper Colophon Books, 1977), pp. 115–54.

48. Ma Ning, "The Textual and Critical Difference of Being Radical: Reconstructing Chinese Leftist Films of the 1930s," *Wide Angle* 11, no. 2 (1989): 28. The distinction between what he calls "construction" and deconstruction is part of Ma's discussion of mainland Chinese films of the 1930s, but I find it useful in understanding Chen Kaige's films as well.

49. Susan McClary, "The Politics of Silence and Sound," afterword to Attali, *Noise*, p. 156.

50. In *Seeds of Fire*, p. 259.

51. According to Chen Kaige, the story of *Yellow Earth* was based on a prose article called "Echo in the Deep Valley" ("Shengu huisheng"), which he (Chen) never saw. This prose article was written by Ke Lan. The first time Chen saw the script was in 1983, when it had been adapted from Ke Lan's article by Zhang Ziliang and renamed "Silent is the Ancient Plain" ("Guyuan wusheng"). However, Chen and his crew had reservations about Zhang's script and revised it substantially in the process of making the film. See the interview with Chen in *Chinese Film: The State of the Art in the People's Republic*, p. 136. See also H. C. Li, "Color, Character, and Culture: On *Yellow Earth*, *Black Cannon Incident*, and *Red Sorghum*," *Modern Chinese Literature*, vol. 5, no. 1 (Spring 1989): 97, which offers a more accurate account of the origins of the script of *Yellow Earth*.

52. See the interview with Zhang Yimou, who was the cinematographer for *Yellow Earth*, in "Wopai *Huangtudi*" [I filmed *Yellow Earth*], *Huangtudi*, p. 7.

53. Eisenstein, "Color and Meaning," in *The Film Sense*, pp. 113–53.

54. Many thanks to Susan McClary and Chris Cullens for their helpful comments on an early version of this chapter.

Part 2. Some Contemporary Chinese Films

3. Male Narcissism and National Culture:
Subjectivity in Chen Kaige's *King of the Children*

1. *The Complete Stories of Lu Xun*, trans. Yang Xianyi and Gladys Yang (Beijing: Foreign Languages Press, 1981), p. 65. The epigraphs by Althusser and Benjamin at the beginning of this chapter are taken respectively from *Lenin and Philosophy and Other Essays* (New York: Monthly Review Press, 1971), p. 157, and from *Moscow Diary*, ed. Gary Smith, trans. Richard Sieburth (Cambridge, Mass.: Harvard University Press, 1986), p. 29.

2. *The Complete Stories of Lu Xun*, p. 65.

3. In an essay called "Xiwang," Lu Xun follows the Hungarian poet and revolutionary Petöfi Sándor to say that the unfoundedness of hopelessness is similar to that of hope itself. In a poem called "Hope," Sándor compares hope to a prostitute, implying by that traditional "metaphor" its faithlessness and mystery to men. See "Xiwang," *Yecao, Lu Xun chuanji*, vol. 2 (Beijing: Renmin wenxue chubanshe, 1981).

4. Marston Anderson, "The Morality of Form: Lu Xun and the Modern Chinese Short Story," in *Lu Xun and His Legacy*, ed. and with an intro. by Leo Ou-fan Lee (Berkeley and Los Angeles: University of California Press, 1985), pp. 32–53. Anderson's arguments are further elaborated in his *The Limits of Realism: Chinese Fiction in the Revolutionary Period* (Berkeley and Los Angeles: University of California Press, 1990).

5. Anderson, "The Morality of Form," p. 52.

6. Terry Eagleton, "Ideology, Fiction, Narrative," *Social Text* 2 (Summer 1979): 71; emphasis in the original.

7. A good example of this tension in the pre-1949 period is found in Mao Dun's essay "From Guling to Tokyo" (1928), in which he scrutinizes the question of what constitutes "proletarian literature." See "From Guling to Tokyo," trans. Yu-shih Chen, *Bulletin of Concerned Asian Scholars* (January–March 1976): 38–44.

8. "Talks at the Yenan Forum on Literature and Art," *Mao Tse-tung on Literature and Art* (Beijing: Foreign Languages Press, 1960; reprint, 1977), pp. 39–40. The couplet is from Lu Xun's "Zizhao" ("Self-mockery"), *Ji wai ji, Lu Xun chuanji*, vol. 7 (Beijing: Renmin wenxue chubanshe, 1981).

9. For a helpful discussion of how to interpret this image, I am grateful to the students who took my course, "Introduction to Literary Theory for Students of Modern Chinese Literature," Winter 1990, at the University of Minnesota.

10. See *A Cheng xiaoshuo: qi wang, shu wang, haizi wang* (Taipei: Haifeng chubanshe, 1988), pp. 163–213. For an English version of the film script of *King of the Children* (by Chen Kaige and Wan Zhi), see Bonnie S. McDougall's translation in *"King of the Children" and the New Chinese Cinema*, with an intro. by Tony Rayns (London: Faber and Faber, 1989), pp. 61–121.

11. See Louis Althusser, "Ideology and Ideological State Apparatuses."

12. Since I have already analyzed A Cheng's story at length elsewhere, my discussion of it here is brief. Interested readers are asked to see the chapter entitled "Pedagogy, Trust, Chinese Intellectuals in the 1990s—Fragments of a Post-Catastrophic Discourse," in Rey Chow, *Writing Diaspora: Tactics of Intervention in Contemporary Cultural Studies* (Bloomington: Indiana University Press, 1993). This chapter was originally published in *Dialectical Anthropology* 16 (1991): 191–207.

13. Boris Eikhenbaum, "Literature and Cinema (1926)," in *Russian Formalism: A Collection of Articles and Texts in Translation*, ed. Stephen Bann and John E. Bowlt (New York: Harper and Row, 1973), p. 123. For an extended version of Eikhenbaum's views on cinema, see his "Problems of Cinema Stylistics," in Herbert Eagle, ed., *Russian Formalist Film Theory* (Ann Arbor: University of Michigan Slavic Publications, 1981), pp. 55–80.

14. See for instance Mikhail Bakhtin, *Problems of Dostoevsky's Poetics*, ed. and trans. Caryl Emerson, with an intro. by Wayne C. Booth (Minneapolis: University of Minnesota Press, 1984); V. N. Vološinov, *Marxism and the Philosophy of Language*, trans. Ladislav Matejka and I. R. Titunik (Cambridge, Mass.: Harvard University Press, 1986).

15. In her work on the German director Rainer Werner Fassbinder, Kaja Silverman distinguishes the look, which is individualized and has a human bearer, from the gaze, which is external and collective. She argues that in Hollywood cinema, the male look is always exchangeable with the gaze because it is disburdened of lack: "The male look both transfers its own lack to the female subject, and attempts to pass itself off as the gaze." See "Fassbinder and Lacan: A Reconsideration of Gaze, Look, and Image," *camera obscura* 19 (January 1989): 54–84; the quotation is on pp. 71–72. Silverman's essay is also found, with slight modifications, in her *Male Subjectivity at the Margins* (New York: Routledge, 1992), 125–56. While making use of similar terms of contemporary film theory, I want to emphasize that the distribution of "male" and "female" characteristics in *King of the Children* reverses the Hollywood paradigm. The male look in Chen's film is the bearer of a lack; it is the male who occupies the passive (classically "feminine") position. The question is, Why? As I would argue in the second half of my chapter, this is a question of symbolic castration, or cultural violence, which is particularly germane to the understanding of the contemporary Chinese situation.

16. See my account of the humanistic and patriarchal meanings of Wang Fu's "success" in "Pedagogy, Trust, Chinese Intellectuals in the 1990s."

17. Althusser, "Ideology and Ideology State Apparatuses," p. 132.

18. Chen, interview with *Playboy* (Chinese ed.), no. 22 (May 1988): 48.

19. Chen, "Director's Notes," trans. Bonnie S. McDougall, "*King of the Children" and the Chinese New Cinema*, pp. 61–62.

20. See Martin Heidegger, "The Origin of the Work of Art," in *Poetry, Language, Thought*, trans. Albert Hofstadter (New York: Harper Colophon Books, 1971), pp. 15–87; "The Question Concerning Technology," in *The Question Con-*

cerning *Technology and Other Essays*, trans. and with an intro. by William Lovitt (New York: Harper Colophon Books, 1977), pp. 3–35.

21. "The Question Concerning Technology," p. 22.

22. See also the brief discussion of *The Big Parade* in Paul Clark, "Reinventing China: The Fifth-Generation Filmmakers," *Modern Chinese Literature* 5, no. 1 (Spring 1989): 129–31. For interesting brief discussions about the indeterminacy or ambiguity of the film's "message," see Yu Gang, "Da yue bing yao shuo de shi shenmo" [What does *The Big Parade* want to say], *Jintian* (Today) 2 (1992): 69–75; and Geoffrey O'Brien, "Blazing Passions," *New York Review of Books*, September 24, 1992, p. 38.

23. Chen's fascination with the inarticulate or verbally clumsy child is evident in his other films as well—for instance, Han Han in *Yellow Earth* and Hou, the young soldier who stutters, in *The Big Parade*.

24. Rubin, "The Traffic in Women: Notes on the 'Political Economy' of Sex," in Rayna Reiter, ed., *Toward an Anthropology of Women* (New York: Monthly Review Press, 1975), p. 168. The epigraph by Rubin at the beginning of the present section is taken from p. 200 of the same essay. The epigraph from Deleuze and Guattari is from *Anti-Oedipus: Capitalism and Schizophrenia*, trans. Robert Hurley et al., with a preface by Michel Foucault (Minneapolis: University of Minnesota Press, 1983), p. 48.

25. Freud, "On Narcissism: An Introduction" (1914), in *A General Selection from the Works of Sigmund Freud*, ed. John Rickman, M.D., with an appendix by Charles Brenner, M.D. (New York: Doubleday,1957), p. 113; my emphases. The epigraphs by Freud at the beginning of the present section are on pp. 112 and 115 of the same essay. This essay can also be found in *The Standard Edition of the Complete Psychological Works of Sigmund Freud*, trans. James Strachey (London: Hogarth Press, 1959), volume 14.

26. Ibid., p. 115 (my emphasis).

27. Ibid., p. 116. A perfect example of the massive destructiveness that results from the idealization of children, who are used to enact otherwise unrealizable fantasies, was Mao's mobilization of the Red Guards during the Cultural Revolution.

28. Ibid., p. 123.

4. The Force of Surfaces: Defiance in Zhang Yimou's Films

1. In an interview with Liu Xiaobo, Zhang himself described these three films as forming one continuity [*yi mai xiangcheng*] and mentioned that he regarded *Raise the Red Lantern* as the completion of a certain style of his. See "Zhang Yimou: Dianying chenggong tuo bu kai da huanjing" [Zhang Yimou: The success of films cannot be divorced from the greater social environment], *Xianggang lianhe bao*, May 1, 1993. The epigraph by Gramsci at the beginning of this chapter is taken from *Selections from Prison Notebooks*, ed. and trans. Quintin Hoare and Geoffrey Nowell Smith (London: Lawrence and Wishart, 1971), p. 185.

4. The Force of Surfaces

2. See Mo Yan, *Hong gaoliang jiazu* [The red sorghum family] (Beijing: Jiefangjun wenyi chubanshe, 1987); Zhang's film is based on the first two chapters of this novel. See also Liu Heng, "Fuxi Fuxi," in *Zhongguo xiaoshuo yijiubaba* [Chinese fiction 1988], ed. Wang Ziping and Li Tuo (Hong Kong: Sanlian shudian, 1989), pp. 80–171; and Su Tong, "Qiqie chengqun," in *Qiqie chengqun* [Wives and concubines] (Taipei: Yuanliu, 1990). In *Judou*, Zhang moves the time of the story (set in the 1940s in Liu Heng's novella) to the 1920s. The story of *Raise the Red Lantern* is set in the 1940s.

3. For instance, according to Zhang, the carriers' jolly jolting of the wedding sedan in the opening scenes of *Red Sorghum* was an invention rather than something based on ethnic custom. See Zhang Yimou, "Gaoliangdi de chuanshuo—yi zhi shengming de zange" [Legend from the land of sorghum—a eulogy to life], *Hong gaoliang* (Dianying/Zhongguo mingzuo xuan, no. 10), ed. Jiao Xiongping (Taipei: Wanxiang tushu gufen youxian gongsi, 1992), p. 93. One can probably say the same thing about the rituals of lighting lanterns and foot massage in *Raise the Red Lantern*.

4. For a severe indictment of the "inauthenticity" of details in *Raise the Red Lantern*, see Dai Qing, "Raised Eyebrows for *Raise the Red Lantern*," trans. Jeanne Tai, *Public Culture* 5, no. 2 (1993): 333–37.

5. Roland Barthes, *Mythologies*, selected and trans. from the French by Annette Lavers (Frogmore, St. Albans: Paladin, 1973), pp. 115–16; emphases in the original.

6. Ibid., p. 115; emphases in the original.

7. For a discussion of Zhang's films as melodramas, see Chen Ruxiu, "Da hong denglong gao gao gua yu tongsu lilun" [*Raise the Red Lantern* and theories of the melodramatic], *Dangdai* (Con-Temporary Monthly), April 1, 1992, pp. 52–61.

8. I discuss modernist collecting more extensively in the chapter entitled "Where Have All the Natives Gone?" in *Writing Diaspora: Tactics of Intervention in Contemporary Cultural Studies* (Bloomington: Indiana University Press, 1993).

9. Paul Virilio, *War and Cinema: The Logistics of Perception*, trans. Patrick Camiller (London: Verso, 1989), p. 39; my emphasis.

10. See Rey Chow, *Woman and Chinese Modernity: The Politics of Reading between West and East* (Minneapolis: University of Minnesota Press, 1991), pp. 34–83. See also Liu Xiaobo's comments in the interview "Zhang Yimou: Dianying chenggong." Liu uses the terms *tongsu* and *dazonghua* [popular, common] to describe Zhang's films, comparing them to the popular sentimental novels of the Taiwan authoress Qiong Yao.

11. In Su Tong's novella, Feipu is shown to have homosexual leanings. See Tonglin Lu's discussion in the chapter entitled "Femininity, Masculinity, and Male Bonding," in *Misogyny, Cultural Nihilism, and Oppositional Politics: Contemporary Chinese Experimental Fiction* (Stanford: Stanford University Press, forthcoming). Zhang, however, removes all traces of this homosexuality in *Raise the Red Lantern*. Obviously, a traditional heterosexuality with its twin Oedipal obses-

sions of killing the father and fetishizing the mother suits his filmic purposes much better.

12. For a lucid exploration of Oedipus as a narrative ideology and its relation to cinematic as well as other types of representation of women, see Teresa de Lauretis, *Alice Doesn't: Feminism, Semiotics, Cinema* (Bloomington: Indiana University Press, 1984).

13. Zhang is always clear about the specificity of the film medium. Even his seemingly casual remarks reveal this. For instance, this is the way he spoke retrospectively about the difficulty of adapting Mo Yan's *Red Sorghum Family*: "Mo Yan's fiction is marvelously expressive. Pebbles are icy; the air smells bloody; my grandma's voice reverberates in the land of the sorghum—but how was I supposed to shoot all this? I couldn't very well make blank shots in the midst of the sorghum, could I?" Jiao Xiongping, "Ti 'wo yeye' zheng kouqi—xianggang zhuan fang Zhang Yimou" [A vindication of "my grandpa"—a special interview with Zhang Yimou in Hong Kong], *Hong gaoliang*, p. 104; my translation.

14. See Tonglin Lu's discussion in "Femininity, Masculinity, and Male Bonding."

15. Jean Baudrillard, *Seduction*, trans. Brian Singer (New York: St. Martin's Press, 1990), p. 69.

16. "And it is because the sign has been turned away from its meaning or 'seduced,' that the story itself is seductive. It is when signs are seduced that they become seductive." "To be seduced is to be turned from one's truth. To seduce is to lead the other from his/her truth. This truth then becomes a secret that escapes him/her." Ibid., pp. 74, 81.

17. Ibid., p. 13.

18. My thanks to Jane Gallop for this important point.

19. Barthes, *Mythologies*, p. 109.

20. Baudrillard, *Seduction*, p. 2.

21. Zhang, "Gaoliangdi," pp. 94–96.

22. David Edelstein, "The Corn is Red," *Village Voice*, October 11, 1988, p. 64.

23. H. C. Li, "Color, Character, and Culture: On *Yellow Earth*, *Black Cannon Incident*, and *Red Sorghum*," *Modern Chinese Literature* 5, no. 1 (Spring 1989): 113.

24. Wu Ruozeng, "Luanshuo *Hong gaoliang*" [Random talk about *Red Sorghum*], *Hong gaoliang*, p. 85. "Objectively speaking," Wu says, "Zhang may not have any deep thought, but his feeling is very good, very artistic, very human. In this regard, he can even be called a genius."

25. Yang Zhao, "Yuanchu, huangliang de shifu chongdong—ping dalu dianying *Judou*" [Primitive, desolate patricidal impulse—a commentary on the mainland film *Judou*], *Judou* (*Dianying/Zhongguo mingzuo xuan*, no. 11), ed. Jiao Xiongping (Taipei: Wanxiang tushu gufen youxian gongsi, 1992), pp. 98–103.

26. Dai, "Raised Eyebrows for *Raise the Red Lantern*," p. 336.

27. Paul Clark, "Reinventing China: The Fifth-Generation Filmmakers," *Modern Chinese Literature* 5, no. 1 (Spring 1989): 121.

28. "One Chinese director at the Xian Film Studio contends that Zhang 'feeds his Western audience's image of exotic, primitive, timeless China. In fact, I'm going to take a leaf out of his book and set my next film in the boondocks, too. Why not? It's a formula that works.' " Lynn Pan, "A Chinese Master," *New York Times Magazine*, March 1, 1992, p. 38.

29. A mainland Chinese writer writes: "All my American friends love Zhang's movies, all my Chinese friends hate them. . . . Why? What offended the Chinese in these movies? . . . It could all be summed up in one thing: selling oriental exoticism to a Western audience." See Jane Ying Zha, "Excerpts from 'Lore Segal, Red Lantern, and Exoticism," *Public Culture* 5, no. 2 (1993): 329. I will cite these lines again in my discussion at the beginning of part 3.

30. Esther C. M. Yau, "Cultural and Economic Dislocations: Filmic Phantasies of Chinese Women in the 1980s," *Wide Angle* 11, no. 2 (1989): 19.

31. Peter Hitchcock, "The Aesthetics of Alienation, or China's 'Fifth Generation," *Cultural Studies* 6, no. 1 (January 1992): 116–41.

32. Laura Mulvey, "Visual Pleasure and Narrative Cinema," originally published in *Screen* 16, no. 3 (Autumn 1975); reprinted in *Movies and Methods*, ed. Bill Nichols (Berkeley and Los Angeles: University of California Press, 1985), vol. 2, pp. 303–15.

33. When *Red Sorghum* was shown in China, security teams were summoned in various cities for the screenings. "The film caused a few officials to raise their eyebrows, and outraged viewers accused the director of insulting the Chinese in order to please Westerners." Jenny Kwok Wah Lau, "*Judou*—A Hermeneutical Reading of Cross-Cultural Cinema," *Film Quarterly* 45, no. 2 (Winter 1991–92): 2.

34. As Lau points out, "films that emphasize the oppressive nature of feudal institutions, including marriage, such as *A Good Woman* (1985) and *Widow Village* (1989), are favored by the socialist officials and welcomed by the public." Ibid., p. 3.

35. Zhang, "Gaoliangdi," p. 94; my emphasis.

36. Even Zhang is not exempt from this way of thinking. Referring to the fact that *Red Sorghum* received considerable praise, Zhang writes, "Actually it does not deserve any higher praise [than what it has already received]. A film must offer especially deep inner meaning [*tebie shen de neihan*] and be able to let people perceive it closely, before it can be called great." "Gaoliangdi," p. 96.

37. I am thinking of expressions such as *qianxu* (modest, self-effacing) and *xuhuai ruo gu* (having a mind as open as a valley).

38. It is interesting that for Zhang himself, the foreigner is not a particular problem. In an interview in which he laments that he does not have a lot of opportunities to watch films from abroad, he says, "I don't understand a Western audience's taste." See Mayfair Yang, "Of Gender, State Censorship, and Overseas Capital: An Interview with Chinese Director Zhang Yimou," *Public Culture* 5, no. 2 (1993): 305.

39. Li, "Color," p. 110.

40. Yan Xianglin, "*Hong gaoliang* meixue xingge lun" [A discussion of the aesthetic character of *Red Sorghum*], *Hong gaoliang*, pp. 83–84.

41. Wu, "Luanshuo Hong gaoliang," p. 87.

42. For a reading of Zhang using Bakhtin, see Yingjin Zhang, "Ideology of the Body in *Red Sorghum*: National Allegory, National Roots, and Third Cinema," *East-West Film Journal* 4, no. 2 (June 1990): 38–53. For a comparison of Zhang to Racine, see the discussion of *Raise the Red Lantern* in Pan, "A Chinese Master": "Artistically, says Anthony Tatlow, a professor of comparative literature who runs a course on film at the University of Hong Kong, the movie 'is successful from beginning to end.' That Zhang 'is able to tell his story and at the same time find the visual esthetic means to externalize the very powerful and partly repressed emotions that the story's about is the mark of a great artist.' The film, he adds, has the kind of intensity, 'the quality of concentration that I associate with somebody like Racine' " (pp. 36, 38).

43. Yuejin Wang, "*Red Sorghum*: Mixing Memory and Desire," in *Perspectives on Chinese Cinema*, ed. Chris Berry (London: British Film Institute, 1991), pp. 80–103.

44. Yau, "Cultural and Economic Dislocations," p. 20.

45. It is perhaps not an accident, therefore, that several feminist critics turn to the original literary texts, rather than to Zhang's films, for their criticism of the sexism inherent in these stories. By doing so, what they astutely avoid is the problem of having to accuse the film medium itself as being *xu* and thus inevitably lending support to the sexist prejudices already built into the *xu/shi* structure. See Zhu Ling, "A Brave New World? On the Construction of 'Masculinity' and 'Femininity' in *The Red Sorghum Family*," in *Gender and Sexuality in Twentieth-Century Chinese Literature and Society*, ed. Tonglin Lu (Albany: State University of New York Press, 1993), pp. 121–34; Tonglin Lu, " 'Red Sorghum': Limits of Transgression," in *Politics, Ideology, and Literary Discourse in Modern China: Theoretical Interventions and Cultural Critique*, ed. Liu Kang and Xiaobing Tang, with a foreword by Fredric Jameson (Durham, N.C.: Duke University Press, 1993), pp. 188–208; Marie-Claire Huot, "Liu Heng's *Fuxi Fuxi*: What about Nüwa?" in *Gender and Sexuality in Twentieth-Century Chinese Literature and Society*, pp. 85–105; Tonglin Lu, "Femininity, Masculinity, and Male Bonding."

46. Michel Foucault, *The History of Sexuality*, vol. 1: *An Introduction*, trans. Robert Hurley (New York: Vintage Books, 1980), pp. 34–35; emphasis in the original.

47. For instance, Baudrillard gives the rather ingenious argument that Freudian analysis had to bypass the disorders caused by seduction (a fact well known to students of Freud, whose dismissal of his female patients' complaints about male seduction marked the turning point of his career as a psychoanalyst) in order to produce a machinery of interpretation that seeks to dis-cover the truth of

repressed desires. According to Baudrillard, what psychoanalysis bypasses is the "superficial abyss," the infinitely referentless, reciprocal, and reversible play among signifiers that is characteristic of seduction.

48. For a brief exposure of the kinds of factual errors Baudrillard makes in his self-serving romanticizing of "primitive" peoples, see E. San Juan, *Racial Formations/Critical Transformations: Articulations of Power in Ethnic and Racial Studies in the United States* (New Jersey: Humanities Press, 1992), pp. 84–85.

49. Zhang, in Jiao, "Ti 'wo yeye' zheng kouqi," p. 106; my translation. Zhang's almost militaristic grasp of the meaning of time in cinema compares well with Paul Virilio's theory in *War and Cinema*.

50. Of course, Zhang is making a strict distinction between cinema and television here. His notion of the audience is the audiences who watch films in movie theaters, not those equipped with time-manipulation machinery such as VCRs and remote controls.

51. Marie-Claire Huot uses the term *hanxu*—contained, implicit, indirect, veiled—to describe Chen in her talk "Persistent Bonds in Chinese Culture: Food and Writing," given at the conference "The Subject of China," University of California at Santa Cruz, January 1993; see also her "Deux pôles *yang* du nouveau cinéma chinois: Chen Kaige et Zhang Yimou," *Cinémas: Revue d'études cinématographiques/Journal of Film Studies* 3, nos. 2–3 (Spring 1993): 103–25. Ma Ning writes of *Yellow Earth*: "What Chen Kaige achieves in this film . . . is conceptual art rather than realism or naturalism. Most important are ideas, not appearances." Ma, "Notes on the New Filmmakers," in *Chinese Film: The State of the Art in the People's Republic*, ed. George Stephen Semsel (New York: Praeger, 1987), p. 82.

52. Huot: "Chen's favorite part of the body is the eye, the private inward eye and Zhang's is the mouth (or orifice)"("Persistent Bonds in Chinese Culture"). Ma: "By turning our attention inward, the film [*Yellow Earth*] sheds light on the root cause of our resistance to change" ("Notes on the New Filmmakers," p. 82).

53. In an interview with Liu Xiaobo, Chen said: "I like doing what other people don't like to do. And I will never say anything like 'I too am a common person' [*su ren*], because I think I am fundamentally not common." See "Chen Kaige: Jue bu shuo wo ye shi ge su ren" [Chen Kaige: I definitely don't say I too am a common person"], *Lianhe bao* (Taipei), May 8, 1993.

54. "One must always address an audience, but one must also not capitulate to them, or totally give them what they want. . . . It's best to go along with them, so as to get them to accept what you have to say." Zhang, in Mayfair Yang, "Of Gender, State Censorship, and Overseas Capital," pp. 305–6.

55. In the interview with Liu Xiaobo, Zhang describes himself this way: "The greatest merit about me as a person is that I don't indulge in the things that I am best at. Whatever I do, I never do it in such a way as to be unable to dig myself out of it." See "Zhang Yimou, Dianying chenggong."

Part 2. Some Contemporary Chinese Films

56. This incident is mentioned in the following places: Luo Xueying, "Chao zhe xin zhong de yishu shengdi—ji daoyan Zhang Yimou" [Toward the aesthetic holy land in the heart—remembering director Zhang Yimou], *Hong gaoliang*, p. 115; Chen Kaige, "Qinguo ren—ji Zhang Yimou" [The man from the kingdom of Qin—remembering Zhang Yimou], ibid., p. 124; and Zeng Chiliao, "Bei yabianliao de Judou—kan Beijing jinzhi Zhang Yimou chuxi ausika dianli de manheng yuxing" [The Judou that has been crushed—on Beijing's unreasonable stupid move of forbidding Zhang Yimou from attending the Oscar ceremony], ibid., p. 117. Pan describes it this way: "His first camera, a Seagull from Shanghai, cost 186 yuan (roughly $62 then), more than four times his monthly salary. He remembers the occasion exactly: it was on Dec. 14, 1974, and cameras were in such short supply that just to buy one he had to get his mother—who is a physician and 'the family's financial and social prop,' Zhang says—to pull strings. Back in his dormitory, he would develop his pictures crouched under a table wrapped around with black cloth from the factory." Pan, "A Chinese Master," p. 34.

57. Zhang: "I understand peasants pretty well; I was one for three years during the Cultural Revolution." Mayfair Yang, "Of Gender, State Censorship, and Overseas Capital," p. 305. "For Zhang, emigration is not an option. The mainspring of his art, he declares, is China: 'My identification with its people, particularly its peasants.' " Pan, "A Chinese Master," p. 36.

58. "Yishu si yu ziyou, huo yu yayi"—"Art dies in freedom, lives in oppression," Zhang, in Jiao, "Ti 'wo yeye' zheng kouqi," p. 113.

59. Huot notes in "Persistent Bonds" that in the films of Chen and Zhang, "the physical body is not given full-fledged. Even in Zhang's films which often contain scenes where Gong Li's face fills the screen: her open mouth is the center of attention. Her body is forever ungraspable because it is forever seen as if through a keyhole, fragmented: here a breast, or a nipple, there a nape, a back, and often enough, a foot."

60. See Barthes, *Mythologies*, p. 141: "The bourgeois ideology . . . transforms the reality of the world into an image of the world, History into Nature. And this image has a remarkable feature: it is upside down." This statement is supplemented by a footnote (n. 20) pointing the reader to *The German Ideology*.

61. Barthes, *Mythologies*, p. 159.

62. Barthes, "Change the Object Itself: Mythology Today," in *Image-Music-Text*, essays selected and trans. by Stephen Heath (Glasgow: Fontana/Collins, 1977), p. 169; emphases in the original.

63. It is in this light that we may understand Zhang's statement, "The deepest truth in the world may be the simplest—it may be what can be expressed in one sentence. . . . I like the kind of work which is thoroughly infiltrated by reflection and philosophy but which is still a good film—the kind that tells a very simple, not complex, story. It is tiresome to watch a film whose meaning is unclear." Jiao, "Ti 'wo yeye' zheng kouqi," p. 106; my translation.

64. Lau, "*Judou*," p. 3. Also: "It was *Red Sorghum*'s flouting of traditional sexual norms that elicited these responses [from the Chinese audience]" (ibid., p. 2). Unfortunately, after these interesting observations, Lau goes on to argue, in a manner that exemplifies an untenable scholarly nativism, that a film like *Judou* can be understood only within its "Chinese quality" and "logic."

65. W. A. Callahan, "Gender, Ideology, Nation: *Ju Dou* in the Cultural Politics of China," *East-West Film Journal* 7, no. 1 (January 1993): 55. Callahan's argument is that Judou is thus asserting control of her body. I share his observations even though my reading is a different one.

66. "Ju Dou adds meaning to her body by pointing to the bruises on her chest, rather than just the nipples on her breast." Ibid., p. 57.

67. See Callahan also for a very persuasive discussion of how Confucian patriarchy relies on the process of naming to establish its order. Thus, even though Tianqing is the biological father of his son, Jingshan's symbolic power as "father" is firmly reestablished once the little boy addresses him by that name; ibid., pp. 60–67. Mary Ann Farquhar makes a similar argument in her reading of *Red Sorghum* and *Judou*. Stressing that oedipality is not really desire for the biological mother but desire for the power and possessions of the father, and that the process of "rectification by names" is crucial to Chinese patriarchy, she argues that the meaning of patricide in Zhang's films is a symbolic one. See Farquhar, "Oedipality in *Red Sorghum* and *Judou*," *Cinémas* 3, nos. 2–3 (Spring 1993): 61–86.

68. See Thomas Elsaesser, "Primary Identification and the Historical Subject: Fassbinder and Germany," in *Narrative, Apparatus, Ideology: A Film Theory Reader*, ed. Philip Rosen (New York: Columbia University Press, 1986), pp. 535–49. This essay was first published in *Ciné-Tracts* (Fall 1980), no. 11, pp. 43–52. I am grateful to Patrice Petro for suggesting the essay as a possible comparative reference for the kinds of issues I am raising in the context of Chinese cinema. For related interest, see also Kaja Silverman's discussion of Fassbinder in *Male Subjectivity at the Margins* (New York: Routledge, 1992), pp. 125–56 and throughout. For my purposes in this chapter, Elsaesser's work is more directly useful because he is writing about Fassbinder from the perspective of cinema's relation to a national culture.

69. Elsaesser, "Primary Identification," p. 545.

70. Ibid.

71. Ibid.

72. Paul G. Pickowicz has argued that melodrama is a main strength of Chinese cinema from the 1920s to the 1980s; see his "Melodramatic Representation and the 'May Fourth' Tradition of Chinese Cinema," in *From May Fourth to June Fourth: Fiction and Film in Twentieth-Century China*, ed. Ellen Widmer and David Der-wei Wang (Cambridge, Mass.: Harvard University Press, 1993), pp. 295–326. Pickowicz's understanding of melodrama, which is based on Peter Brooks's *The Melodramatic Imagination: Balzac, Henry James, Melodrama, and the Mode of Excess* (New

Part 2. Some Contemporary Chinese Films

York: Columbia University Press, 1985), is that melodrama draws upon moral polarities and "teaches a morally confused audience how to recognize the difference between goodness and evil" (p. 303). This understanding leads Pickowicz to associate melodrama with clear language and popularity but also with the lack of subtlety, complexity, and sophistication (see, for instance, pp. 304, 326). My use of "melodrama," especially as it relates to Fassbinder and Zhang, is very different from Pickowicz's; the gist of this difference is that I see in the melodramatic a (possibly political) function of mockery and parody. The commonly recognized melodramatic "modes of excesses" do not, I think, have to mean simply the thematic polarization between good and evil (even though this is the way melodrama is typically read). Rather, such excesses can be seen to indicate a machinic amplification and exaggeration of gestures, expressions, and emotions that correspond to modern technologies of representation such as film. For a related discussion of this point, see my reading of Charles Chaplin's *Modern Times* in the chapter "Postmodern Automatons," in *Writing Diaspora*, pp. 60–63. For a related discussion of melodrama in Chinese cinema, see also Stephanie Alison Hoare, "Melodrama and Innovation: Literary Adaptation in Contemporary Chinese Film" (Ph.D. dissertation, Cornell University, 1989).

73. Coming from a family whose members were branded rightist by the Chinese communist government, Zhang is known to have said about his youth: "I grew up under the surveillance of people who kept an eye on me through the cracks of the door." See Luo, "Chao zhe xin zhong," p. 114.

74. *Xin bao* (*The Overseas Hong Kong Economic Journal*), July 17, 1992.

75. Elsaesser, *New German Cinema: A History* (New Brunswick: Rutgers University Press, 1989), p. 302.

76. Elsaesser, "Primary Identification," p. 549.

Part 3: Film as Ethnography; or, Translation between Cultures in the Postcolonial World

1. Kwai-cheung Lo, "Crossing Boundaries: A Study of Modern Hong Kong Fiction from the Fifties to the Eighties" (M.Phil. thesis, University of Hong Kong, 1990), p. 162.

2. Mary Louise Pratt, *Imperial Eyes: Travel Writing and Transculturation* (New York: Routledge, 1992), pp. 7–8.

3. Jane Ying Zha, "Excerpts from 'Lore Segal, Red Lantern, and Exoticism,'" *Public Culture* 5, no. 2 (Winter 1993): 329. See my extended discussion of these views in the previous chapter.

4. For a discussion of this point, see Talal Asad, "Two European Images of Non-European Rule," in *Anthropology and the Colonial Encounter*, ed. Talal Asad (New York: Humanities Press, 1973), pp. 103–18.

5. These epigraphs are taken from Dipesh Chakrabarty, "Marx after Marxism: Subaltern Histories and the Question of Difference," *Polygraph* 6, no. 7 (1993):

Part 3. Film as Ethnography

12; Bernard McGrane, *Beyond Anthropology: Society and the Other* (New York: Columbia University Press, 1989), p. 127 (emphasis in the original); James Clifford, introduction to *Writing Culture: The Poetics and Politics of Ethnography*, ed. James Clifford and George E. Marcus (Berkeley and Los Angeles: University of California Press, 1986), p. 22; Walter Benjamin, "The Task of the Translator," in *Illuminations*, ed. and with an intro. by Hannah Arendt, trans. Harry Zohn (New York: Schocken, 1969), p. 79 ("Die Aufgabe des Übersetzers," in *Illuminationen* [Frankfurt: Suhrkamp Taschenbuch 345, 1977], p. 59; hereafter, page references to the English version will be given in parentheses in the text); and Michael Taussig, *Mimesis and Alterity: A Particular History of the Senses* (New York: Routledge, 1993), p. 236.

6. Writing about the discipline of history, for instance, Dipesh Chakrabarty argues that while the names and works of Western historians are often taken as universal knowledge and cited as "musts" in studies of non-Western as well as Western histories, non-Western historians, no matter how astute and erudite they are, are often mentioned only in the context of their "specific" cultures. See Chakrabarty, "Postcoloniality and the Artifice of History: Who Speaks for 'Indian' Pasts?" *Representations* 37 (Winter 1992): 1–26.

7. Talal Asad, "The Concept of Cultural Translation in British Social Anthropology," in *Writing Culture*, p. 163. See also Asad's introduction to *Anthropology and the Colonial Encounter*.

8. Asad, intro. to *Anthropology and the Colonial Encounter*, p. 16.

9. Asad, "The Concept of Cultural Translation," pp. 157–58; emphasis in the original.

10. Kirsten Hastrup, "Anthropological Visions: Some Notes on Visual and Textual Authority," in *Film as Ethnography*, ed. Peter Ian Crawford and David Turton (Manchester: Manchester University Press, 1992), p. 17.

11. For such admonition, see Wilton Martinez, "Who Constructs Anthropological Knowledge? Toward a Theory of Ethnographic Film Spectatorship," in ibid., pp. 131–61. Martinez's conclusion is that the crisis in anthropological representation "requires that we enhance our self-reflexive and self-critical practices in order to identify the limits of our knowledge claims as well as their potential impact on the social construction of anthropological knowledge" (p. 156). See also Frances E. Mascia-Lees, Patricia Sharpe, and Colleen B. Cohen, "The Postmodernist Turn in Anthropology: Cautions from a Feminist Perspective," *Signs* 15, no. 1 (1989): pp. 7–33. According to these authors, the goal of a new ethnography is to "apprehend and inscribe 'others' in such a way as not to deny or diffuse their claims to subjecthood" (p. 12).

12. See Laura Mulvey, "Visual Pleasure and Narrative Cinema," in *Movies and Methods*, ed. Bill Nichols (Berkeley and Los Angeles: University of California Press, 1985), vol. 2, pp. 303–15; this is a reprint of the article originally published in *Screen* 16, no. 3 (Autumn 1975).

13. Walter Benjamin first used the term *optical unconscious* in the essay "A Small

Part 3. Film as Ethnography

History of Photography" (1931), in *One-Way Street*, trans. Edmund Jephcott and Kingsley Shorter (London: New Left Books, 1979), pp. 240–57; he again refers to "unconscious optics" in "The Work of Art in the Age of Mechanical Reproduction," in *Illuminations*, pp. 217–51.

14. Dai Vaughan, "The Aesthetics of Ambiguity," in *Film as Ethnography*, p. 102. Vaughan's entire essay, with its careful exposition of the documentary's representational ambiguities and its emphasis on the viewer's role in constructing meaning, can be read as a deconstruction of ethnography's fundamental claim to being simply a "record" rather than a language.

15. Thomas Elsaesser, *New German Cinema: A History* (New Brunswick: Rutgers University Press, 1989), pp. 322–23; my emphases.

16. See the comments under the root *do* in Joseph T. Shipley, *The Origins of English Words: A Discursive Dictionary of Indo-European Roots* (Baltimore: Johns Hopkins University Press, 1984), p. 73; also the comments under the root *do* in the "Indo-European Roots Appendix," in *The American Heritage Dictionary of the English Language*, 3d ed. (New York: Houghton Mifflin, 1992), p. 2101.

17. Barbara Johnson, "Taking Fidelity Philosophically," in *Difference in Translation*, ed. Joseph F. Graham (Ithaca, N.Y.: Cornell University Press, 1985), p. 143.

18. Ibid., p. 145; emphasis in the original.

19. See the pertinent discussion by Lawrence Venuti in his intro. to *Rethinking Translation: Discourse, Subjectivity, Ideology* (New York: Routledge, 1992), p. 4.

20. Walter Benjamin, "The Work of Art in the Age of Mechanical Reproduction," in *Illuminations*, pp. 217–51; see my references to this essay in part 2, chap. 2. I have also offered discussions at greater length elsewhere: see, for instance, my "Walter Benjamin's Love Affair with Death," *New German Critique* 48 (Fall 1989): 63–86; and the chapter entitled "Where Have All the Natives Gone?" in *Writing Diaspora: Tactics of Intervention in Contemporary Cultural Studies* (Bloomington: Indiana University Press, 1993).

21. Walter Benjamin, "The Task of the Translator," in *Illuminations*, pp. 69–82.

22. Cf. my discussion of *Yellow Earth* in part 2, chap. 2, in which "composition" or "putting together" can indeed be seen as a deconstructive production of differences.

23. Paul de Man, *Blindness and Insight: Essays in the Rhetoric of Contemporary Criticism* (Minneapolis: University of Minnesota Press, 1983), p. 136, and *Allegories of Reading: Figural Language in Rousseau, Nietzsche, Rilke, and Proust* (New Haven: Yale University Press, 1979), p. 151. For Derrida's discussion, see, e.g., Jacques Derrida, "White Mythology: Metaphor in the Text of Philosophy," in *Margins of Philosophy*, trans. and with additional notes by Alan Bass (Chicago: University of Chicago Press, 1992), pp. 207–71.

24. Johnson, "Taking Fidelity Philosophically," p. 146.

25. For a discussion of such readings, as well as of deconstruction's and post-

Part 3. Film as Ethnography

structuralism's contributions to the reconsideration of translation theory, see Venuti, intro. to *Rethinking Translation: Discourse, Subjectivity, Ideology*, pp. 6–17.

26. Paul de Man, " 'Conclusions': Walter Benjamin's 'The Task of the Translator,' " in *The Resistance to Theory*, with a foreword by Wlad Godzich (Minneapolis: University of Minnesota Press, 1986), p. 84; my emphases. De Man is insistent on the disarticulation of the original throughout his essay. For instance, "One of the reasons why [Benjamin] takes the translator rather than the poet [as the exemplary figure] is that the translator, per definition, fails" (p. 80); "The process of translation . . . reveals the death of the original" (p. 85); "This movement of the original is a wandering, an *errance*, a kind of permanent exile if you wish, but it is not really an exile, for there is no homeland, nothing from which one has been exiled" (p. 92; emphasis in the original); and "The translation is a way of reading the original which will reveal those inherent weaknesses in the original . . . in a . . . fundamental way: that the original is not canonical, that the original is a piece of ordinary language" (p. 98).

27. De Man would argue, instead, that "the translation is the fragment of a fragment. . . . There was no vessel in the first place" (ibid., p. 91). He relies for his argument on a firm notion of one correct translation—his own—of Benjamin's text.

28. Jean Laplanche, "The Wall and the Arcade," in *Seduction, Translation, Drives*, a dossier compiled by John Fletcher and Martin Stanton, with trans. by Martin Stanton (London: Institute of Contemporary Arts, 1992), p. 201.

29. Tejaswini Niranjana, *Siting Translation: History, Post-Structuralism, and the Post-Colonial Context* (Berkeley and Los Angeles: University of California Press, 1992). See in particular chap. 2 for an erudite account of the traditions and theories of translation. Hereafter page references to this book will be given in parentheses in the text.

30. Roman Jakobson calls intersemiotic translation *transmutation*, which he differentiates from both intralingual translation (which he terms *rewording*) and interlingual translation (which he terms *translation proper*). See Jakobson, "On Linguistic Aspects of Translation," in *On Translation*, ed. Reuben A. Brower (Cambridge, Mass.: Harvard University Press, 1959), p. 233.

31. The sidestepping of mass culture in Niranjana's reconsideration of translation can be glimpsed in the way she rewrites Benjamin's word *image*. Where Benjamin intends by *image* a concrete means—a constellation—for understanding the activity called reading, Niranjana elides such implications and rewrites *image* purely as *reading* in the deconstructive sense. In other words, where Benjamin's emphasis is on *image*, Niranjana's is on *reading*. See Niranjana, *Siting Translation*, pp. 171–72.

32. Johannes Fabian, *Time and the Other: How Anthropology Makes Its Object* (New York: Columbia University Press, 1983). For a critique of the repression of coevalness in European anthropological discourse, a repression that is accom-

plished through notions of "the primitive," which are mapped onto "other" societies, see, e.g., Bernard McGrane, *Beyond Anthropology*, in particular chap. 3 and the conclusion, pp. 77–112, 113–29. McGrane's book also contains interesting discussions of the changing nature of the work of anthropology and ethnography in the context of a heightened awareness of cultural difference.

33. Laplanche, "The Wall and the Arcade," pp. 207, 211. In a discussion of Caribbean cinema that is fully resonant with my discussion of Chinese cinema, Stuart Hall also uses the notion of "the third term" to refer to the cultural space of the New World, where creolizations, assimilations, and syncretisms are negotiated: "The New World is the third term—the primal scene—where the fateful/fatal encounter was staged between Africa and the West." See Hall, "Cultural Identity and Diaspora," in *Colonial Discourse and Post-Colonial Theory: A Reader*, ed. and with an intro. by Patrick Williams and Laura Chrisman (New York: Columbia University Press, 1994), pp. 392–403. This essay was originally published in *Identity: Community, Culture, Difference*, ed. J. Rutherford (London: Lawrence and Wishart, 1990), pp. 222–37.

34. Chakrabarty, "Postcoloniality and the Artifice of History," p. 21.

35. My reading here is based on Gianni Vattimo, *The End of Modernity: Nihilism and Hermeneutics in Post-Modern Culture*, trans. and with an intro. by Jon R. Snyder (Cambridge: Polity Press, 1988), and *The Transparent Society*, trans. David Webb (Cambridge: Polity Press, 1992).

36. See Snyder's lucid and helpful introduction in *The End of Modernity*.

37. This quote is from p. 60 in Remo Guidieri, "Les sociétés primitives aujourd'hui," in *Philosopher: les interrogations contemporaines*, ed. Ch. Delacampagne and R. Maggiori (Paris: Fayard, 1980), pp. 51–64. See Vattimo, "Hermeneutics and Anthropology," in *The End of Modernity*, p. 158.

38. " 'Contact zone' in my discussion is often synonymous with 'colonial frontier.' . . . A 'contact' perspective . . . treats the relations among colonizers and colonized . . . not in terms of separateness or apartheid, but in terms of copresence, interaction, interlocking understandings and practices, often within radically asymmetrical relations of power." Pratt, *Imperial Eyes*, pp. 6–7.

39. Vattimo, "Art and Oscillation," in *The Transparent Society*, p. 59, emphasis in the original.

40. Vattimo, "The Human Sciences and the Society of Communication," in ibid., pp. 24–25. "How the 'Real World' at Last Became a Myth [Fable]" is a chapter in Nietzsche's *Twilight of the Idols* (1889). See Friedrich Nietzsche, *Twilight of the Idols/The Anti-Christ*, trans. R. J. Hollingdale (Harmondsworth: Penguin Books, 1968), pp. 40–41.

41. Benjamin, "Franz Kafka: On the Tenth Anniversary of His Death," in *Illuminations*, pp. 143–44; my emphases.

42. Jacques Derrida, "Des Tours de Babel," in *Difference in Translation*, pp. 187–88; emphasis in the original. Derrida's discussions of Benjamin's essay on

translation, which are centered largely on verbal language, can also be found in *The Ear of the Other: Otobiography Transference Translation*, trans. Peggy Kamuf (Lincoln: University of Nebraska Press, 1988), pp. 93–161.

43. John Fletcher, "The Letter in the Unconscious," The Enigmatic Signifier in the Work of Jean Laplanche," in Laplanche, *Seduction, Translation, Drives*, p. 116.

44. Derrida, "White Mythology," p. 252.

45. I can merely refer to Benjamin's arcades project here. For an authoritative study in English, see Susan Buck-Morss, *The Dialectics of Seeing: Walter Benjamin and the Arcades Project* (Cambridge, Mass.: MIT Press, 1989).

46. I borrow this observation from Jeffrey Mehlman, *Walter Benjamin for Children: An Essay on His Radio Years* (Chicago: University of Chicago Press, 1993). Commenting on one of Benjamin's writings on toys, Mehlman writes: "The toy is thus above all that wherein the child negotiates the imposition of an adult agenda. A precarious coming to terms that is marked by a tearing apart (*Auseinandersetzung*), it is shot through with the unmastered 'traces' of the other" (p. 4; emphasis as in Mehlman's text).

47. In the 1990s, even the communist state has to adopt market strategies to promote its ideas. For an informed discussion, see Geremie Barmé, "The Greying of Chinese Culture," in *China Review 1992*, ed. Kuan Hsin-chi and Maurice Brosseau (Hong Kong: Chinese University Press, 1992), sec. 13, pp. 1–52.

48. Benjamin, "Unpacking My Library: A Talk about Book Collecting," *Illuminations*, p. 66.

49. These include Chinese films from Taiwan and Hong Kong as well. In 1992 and 1993 alone, major awards were won by Stanley Kwan's *Ruan Lingyu* (*Center Stage*), Xie Fei's *Xianghun nü* (*Oilmakers' Family*), and Ang Lee's *Xiyan* (*The Wedding Banquet*) at the Berlin Film Festival; Zhang Yimou's *The Story of Qiuju* at the Venice Film Festival; and Chen Kaige's *Bawang bie ji* (*Farewell to My Concubine*) at the Cannes Film Festival. Films by Ang Lee, Zhang Yimou, and Chen Kaige have also been nominated for the award of "Best Foreign Language Film" in various years at the Oscars.

Index

Index

Designer: Linda Secondari
Text: 11.5/13.5 Perpetua
Compositor: Columbia University Press
Printer: Maple Vail
Binder: Maple Vail